SPIRITUAL MEANINGS OF THE ḤAJJ RITUALS

SPIRITUAL MEANINGS OF THE ḤAJJ RITUALS

A Philological Approach
by Abdulla Galadari

FONS VITAE

First published in 2021 by
Fons Vitae
49 Mockingbird Valley Drive
Louisville, KY 40207
http://www.fonsvitae.com
Email: fonsvitaeky@aol.com

Library of Congress Control Number: 2021936635
ISBN 978-1941610-541

Printed in USA

To Truth

بِسْمِ اللَّهِ الرَّحْمَٰنِ الرَّحِيمِ

CONTENTS

PREFACE **11**
ACKNOWLEDGEMENTS **12**
NOTES ON ARABIC TRANSLITERATION **14**

FROM THE UNITY OF GOD
TO THE UNITY OF HUMANITY **15**
Outline 17
Why Are Ḥajj Rituals Prescribed as They Are? 18
Islam's Conclusive Message 20
The Rituals of the Ḥajj 22
Views of Ḥajj 24
The Meaning of the Word Ḥajj 29
Ḥajj and *Rĕgālîm* 30
Passover 30
Shavuot 35
Sukkot 36
Research Methodology 36

THE APPOINTED TIME (*MĪQĀT*) **41**
Definition from the Qur'an 44
The *Mīqāt* of the Sorcerers with Moses 48
The *Mīqāt* of Moses and the Seventy 50
The *Mīqāt* of Jesus 54
The *Mīqāt* of Prayer 56
Reflections on *Waqt* and *Mīqāt* 57

MECCA AND KAᶜBAH: *ṬAWĀF* DURING *IḤRĀM* **59**
Talbiyah 59
Mecca 61
Mother of Cities 61
Mecca 62
Sacred Mosque and Kaᶜbah 64
Circumambulation *(Ṭawāf)* 67
Ṭawāf in the Water of Life 67
Coming from Deep Mountain Highways 70
The Corners of the Kaᶜbah 74
The *Ṭawāf* of the Dead Pilgrim 87

MAQĀM IBRĀHĪM **89**
Abraham 90
Al-Maqām 93
Garment of God 96

JACOB'S LADDER (*SA*ᶜ*Ī*) **102**
The Desert Drama 102
Barren Desert 102
Ṣafā, Marwah, and Zamzam 108
Saᶜī 110
Heavenly Ladder 110
Soaring or Floating up the Ladder 115
Jacob's Ladder 118
Passing between Ṣafā and Marwah 122
Meaning of *Sa*ᶜ*ī* 122
*Sa*ᶜ*ī* of the Snakes with Moses 123
*Sa*ᶜ*ī* from Death to Life 127
*Sa*ᶜ*ī* of Friday 129
Emigration to God and Abandoning the World 130

HAIR: SHAVING OR CUTTING **132**
A Qur'anically Ordained Ritual 133
The Significance of Hair (*sha*ᶜ*r*) 133
Shaving (*ḥalq*) 135

THE ḤAJJ IS ᶜARAFAH: *WUQŪF* **138**
Meaning of ᶜArafah 138
Wuqūf on Mt. ᶜArafah 140
Seeking God 140
The Great Dispute (*al-Ḥajj*) 143
The Pilgrim at ᶜArafah 146

MUZDALIFAH **148**
What Is in the Name? 148
Meaning of *Muzdalifah* 148
Al-Mashᶜar al-Ḥarām 152
The Will of God 152
Pouring Down to *al-Mash*ᶜ*ar al-Ḥarām* 155

THE FINAL RITUALS **156**
Stoning the Pillar 157
Meaning of *Minā* and ᶜ*Aqabah* 157
Jamrah 160
Throwing (*ramī*) and Stoning (*rajm*) 161
Stones (*ḥaṣā* or *ḥajar*) 162
Stoning and Sacrifice 162
The Pillar and Sacrifice 162
The Bread and Wine of Sacrifice 166
The Ultimate Sacrifice 168
Ṭawāf al-Ifāḍah 169
The *Sa*ᶜ*ī* of the Ḥajj 170
The Days of Minā 171

The Nights of Minā 171
The Sign of Jonah 173
*Ṭawāf al-Wadā*ᶜ 175

CONCLUSION:
ESOTERIC EXEGESIS OF THE ḤAJJ RITUALS **176**

ABOUT THE AUTHOR **179**

BIBLIOGRAPHY **180**

PREFACE

This book is the product of a personal search for understanding (*ijtihād*) that seeks to delve into the mysteries of the Ḥajj, whose rituals convey meanings on numerous spiritual levels. Since performing the Ḥajj myself, I have spent a great deal of time pondering its meanings.

My first spiritual explorations began during the years I spent as a child living with my grandparents, Zainab and Abdulla, who were both especially close to me. Since I did not enjoy being around people my age, I always looked forward to my grandfather taking me to visit his friends. I loved joining him for daily prayers at the mosque, and I have happy memories of attending a *mawlid*, which is a Sufi commemoration of the Prophet's ﷺ birth, with my grandfather at a neighbor's house.

From a young age, I began reading religious books of all kinds, starting with Islamic books in the Sunnī tradition, which is the tradition that my family follows. However, I soon realized that my best friend at school espoused the Shīʿī tradition. Our friendship led me to visit Shīʿī mosques, and I often borrowed his father's books on the Shīʿī tradition. This sparked my interest in comparing different traditions within Islam.

Nonetheless, my spiritual journey as a child went beyond reading books and visiting mosques. It was more personal. My curiosity was so deep that I sought ways to connect to and understand the unknown. I was as fascinated with the sciences, particularly astronomy and astrophysics, as I was with religion. In fact, my scientific interests became such a passion that I would sometimes neglect my schoolwork to do my own astronomical observations and calculations.

While working on my bachelor's degree, I began to undergo a spiritual struggle. My curiosity for truth was being pushed to its limits. Hungry for answers to my questions, I read books from many religious traditions. Bookstores were heaven for me, and thanks to the many online outlets, almost any book was just a few clicks away. I made regular visits to Hindu and Buddhist temples, churches of various denominations, and synagogues. Over time I was able to see why Hindus, Buddhists, Jews, Christians, Muslims, Sikhs, and many others believed in what they did. Yet, despite all these lovely experiences and discoveries, I was still thirsty for answers.

After returning to Dubai and working in various fields, my spiritual journey continued to be quite intense. Eventually, I decided to perform the Ḥajj, an experience that was indescribably powerful and overwhelmingly personal. However, observing other pilgrims on the Ḥajj, it saddened me that so many of them appeared more interested in the *how* of the rituals' performance than they were in understanding the spiritual meanings underlying them. For many pilgrims, their sole emphasis seemed to be the correct performance of each step of the rituals. After that first pilgrimage, I felt the urge to write about the Ḥajj rituals in a way that would place less stress on their outer performance and more on their inner significance, which is what led me to the present exploration.[1]

I cannot say with certainty that all my interpretations are on the mark, of course. As the age-old Muslim adage says, "God knows best." Therefore, errors in this volume are mine alone, and for them, I ask the readers' forgiveness.

ACKNOWLEDGEMENTS

First, I would like to thank the truth: the fuel for my curiosity and the reason behind my spiritual journey. For the truth, I am forever grateful.

I would also like to thank my late grandparents, Zainab and Abdulla, who first taught me about life and death, the physical and the spiritual; my parents, Afaf and Ibrahim, who, though they never understood my spiritual quest, were attentive to all my

1. For a presentation of the methodology and framework employed in this volume, see my earlier study entitled, *Qur'anic Hermeneutics: Between Science, History, and the Bible* (Bloomsbury Publishing, 2018).

material needs; my siblings Hassan, Sarah, and Hind, who made sure I felt at home; and my wife and partner, Fatma, who shares my travels down this spiritual path wherever it takes us.

I am likewise indebted to the many mentors, friends, and colleagues who have steered and supported the mental exploration without which this work would not have been possible: Alhagi Manta Drammeh, Luqman Zakariyah, Martin O'Kane, Masoumeh Velayati, Francis X. Clooney, David Burrell, Hossein Godazgar, Gray Henry, Bruce Janson, Hue Nguyen, Kathy Jackson, Lynn Schreyer (Bennethum), Ramalingam Shanmugam, Judith Stalnaker, Anatolii Puhalski, Ahmad al-Khuraibet, Mansour al-Khouri, Kurt Anders Richardson, Ben and Diane Blackwell, and many others who have shared their wisdom and illumination over the years. I am also very grateful to Nancy N. Roberts who brought words to life.

Lastly, I thank the stars in the sky and the city lights. I thank the horizon for helping me see how the lights in the sky and the lights on the earth touch and unite. I thank the rivers and seas that run with living water; the living creatures that fly, swim, dig deep into the earth, or walk over its surface; plants and trees; the microbes that make us both healthy and ill; extraterrestrial life; the protons, electrons, and neutrons that sing and perform the cosmic dance (of Shiva); the dark energy and dark matter in the universe that we have yet to understand and appreciate; singularity and its inner essence; the Tao that makes opposites disappear; and the Supreme Being beyond which nothing exists.

NOTES ON ARABIC TRANSLITERATION

ء	ʾ	ر	r	ف	f
ا	a, ā	ز	z	ق	q
ب	b	س	s	ك	k
ت	t	ش	sh	ل	l
ث	th	ص	ṣ	م	m
ج	j	ض	ḍ	ن	n
ح	ḥ	ط	ṭ	ة, ه	h
خ	kh	ظ	ẓ	و	w, ū
د	d	ع	ᶜ	ي	y, i, ī
ذ	dh	غ	gh		

The short vowelization at the end of a word is typically, but not always, omitted.

Unless otherwise noted, I am using *The Study Qur'an* (henceforth *TSQ*) (Seyyed Hossein Nasr, ed., New York, NY: HarperOne, 2015) for all Qur'anic quotations.

For Hebrew and Aramaic, the transliteration follows *The SBL Handbook of Style*, 2nd Edition.

1

FROM THE UNITY OF GOD TO THE UNITY OF HUMANITY

The fourth Shīʿī Imām Zayn al-ʿĀbidīn ʿAlī b. al-Ḥusayn (d. 95/713), his son Imām Muḥammad al-Bāqir (d. 114/733), and his son Imām Jaʿfar al-Ṣādiq (d. 148/765) are said to have remarked, when they were told about the great number of pilgrims in Mecca for the Ḥajj, "How loud the ruckus, and how few the pilgrims (*mā akthar al-ḍajīj wa-aqall al-ḥajīj*)."[1] If this anecdote is true, then the inner meaning of the Ḥajj rituals was already being forgotten by the first and second centuries of Islam.

In broad cultural terms, a pilgrimage is a symbolic transformation intended to mediate the contradictions between the worlds of the human and the divine.[2] In Mexico, Huichol Indians go on an annual pilgrimage to their sacred site of Wirikuta to be reborn and return with the psychoactive plant, peyote, which is needed

1. Al-Majlisī (d. 1111/1698) (1983), *Biḥār al-anwār*, Beirut: al-Wafāʾ – Iḥyāʾ al-Turāth al-ʿArabī, 24: 124 (42/1), 27: 30 (13/2), 27: 181 (7/30), 46: 261 (4/62), 99: 258 (47/36).

2. R. Werbner, *Ritual Passage, Sacred Journey: The Process and Organization of Religious Movement* (Washington, DC: Smithsonian Institution Press, 1989).

to revitalize their world.[3] The Islamic Ḥajj is likewise intended to be a process of rebirth.[4]

Ritual is a human expression and there can be little doubt that the outward forms of the Ḥajj rituals possess an inner meaning—that within the rituals lies a deeper spiritual message. Speaking of the evolution of marriage ceremonies, Joseph Campbell states, "But the rituals that once conveyed an inner reality are now merely form."[5] This statement may be an appropriate description of the Ḥajj as well.

Of the five pillars of Islamic faith given to the Prophet Muḥammad ﷺ, the first declares the unity of God, and the last is the Ḥajj,[6] which is the last of the five pillars[7] performed by the Prophet Muḥammad ﷺ. Because so many people from various ethnicities and various occupations perform the Ḥajj rituals, one might say that, at least outwardly, Islam starts with the unity of God, and ends with the unity of humanity.

This study attempts to help answer the question of *why* the rituals of the Ḥajj are the way they are, and not *how* to perform them. A great many jurists and scholars have attempted to answer the question of *how*,[8] while few have attempted to answer the question of *why*.

---

3. Barbara Myerhoff, *Peyote Hunt: The Sacred Journey of the Huichol Indians* (Ithaca, NY: Cornell University Press, 1974).

4. Majed S. al-Lehaibi, "The Islamic Ritual of Hajj: Ancient Cosmology and Spirituality," *Journal of Inter-Religious Dialogue* (2012), 10: 31–32.

5. Joseph Campbell and Bill Moyers, *The Power of Myth,* ed. Betty Sue Flowers (New York, NY: Anchor Books, 1991), 106.

6. The five pillars are: i) witnessing that there is no god but God and that Muḥammad is His Messenger, ii) ritual prayer, iii) giving alms, iv) fasting Ramadan, and v) performing the Ḥajj for those who are able. See *Ṣaḥīḥ Muslim*, ed. Muḥammad Fuʾād ʿAbdul-Bāqī, (Beirut: Iḥyāʾ al-Turāth al-ʿArabī), 1: 45.

7. Some consider the Ḥajj to be the fourth pillar. See *Ṣaḥīḥ Muslim*, 1: 45 (#16). See also *Ṣaḥīḥ al-Bukhārī*, ed. Muḥammad Zuhayr bin Nāṣir al-Nāṣir (Beirut: Ṭawq al-Najāh, 2002), 1: 11 (#8).

8. For example, al-Nawawī (d. 676/1277), *al-Īḍāḥ fī manāsik al-ḥajj wal-ʿumrah* (Beirut: al-Bashāʾir al-Islāmiyyah), 1994.

OUTLINE

My main purpose in this book is to clarify the inner meaning of Ḥajj rituals using the method of intertextual polysemy.[9] Polysemy is defined as the existence of multivalent and related meanings for a single word or phrase, while intertextuality looks at how terms are used both intratextually within the Qur'an, and intertextually with the Bible.

After introducing the Ḥajj, this chapter compares the Ḥajj to the Jewish ritual of pilgrimage to Jerusalem according to the Hebrew Bible and presents the methodology and the reasoning behind its validity. Chapters 2 through 6 discuss the rituals common to the Ḥajj and the ᶜUmrah, while Chapters 7, 8, and 9 explore the specific rituals of the Ḥajj according to the chronological arrangement of their performance.

Chapter 2 discusses the inner meaning of the *mīqāt*, the location where a pilgrim enters into the state of ritual consecration, or *iḥrām*. Chapter 3 discusses the inner meaning of Mecca, the Kaᶜbah, and the circumambulation (*ṭawāf*) around it. Chapter 4 introduces the significance of Abraham, with whom the rituals are associated, while discussing the inner meaning of praying behind his station. Chapter 5 discusses the inner meaning of traversing the space between the hills of Ṣafā and Marwah, known as *saᶜī*. Chapter 6 discusses the inner meaning of the ritual of shaving or cutting the hair before leaving the state of ritual consecration (*iḥrām*). With this, the rituals of ᶜUmrah are concluded.

Chapter 7 looks at ᶜArafah, the most significant day and ritual of the Ḥajj. Chapter 8 discusses Muzdalifah, the place into which pilgrims pour on the eve of sacrifice. Chapter 9 discusses the remainder of the rituals, which are the days of sacrifice and the nights of Minā. After stoning the pillar, the sacrifice, and shaving or cutting the hair, the pilgrim leaves the state of ritual

9. For more about intertextual polysemy in the Qur'an, see Abdulla Galadari, *Qur'anic Hermeneutics: Between Science, History, and the Bible* (London: Bloomsbury Academic, 2018); "The Role of Intertextual Polysemy in Qur'anic Exegesis," *Quranica: International Journal on Quranic Research* (2013), 3(4): 35–56; and, "The *Qibla*: an Allusion to the *Shemaᶜ*," *Comparative Islamic Studies* (2013), 9(2): 165–194.

consecration (*iḥrām*) and goes back to the Kaᶜbah for another circumambulation (*ṭawāf*) and the *saᶜī* between the hills of Ṣafā and Marwah. The pilgrim then spends two or three nights in Minā, stoning the pillars each day, before making a final farewell circumambulation (*ṭawāf*) of the Kaᶜbah. The final chapter concludes that the Ḥajj rituals are the journey of a soul in search of the Water of Life. In other words, it is the soul's journey from death to eternal life.

WHY ARE ḤAJJ RITUALS PRESCRIBED AS THEY ARE?

Since the emphasis of this study is an exploration of the possible reasons for which the Ḥajj is performed in a certain way, perhaps the first question to address is why this ritual is important. Rituals are a part of most religions. Muslims, for example, engage in ritual prayer, fasting, and Ḥajj, each of which is to be performed using a specific method within a specific timeframe. For over 1400 years, jurists have gone into great depth about every detail of how these rites should and should not be performed, and what measures must be taken to ensure this. The question that remains, however, is *why* they must be performed in a given way and at a given time.

This book is not an investigation into why people have faith from a social or psychological perspective, the social cohesion in which ritual plays a role, or the intentions of individual worshippers.[10] Rather, it attempts simply to identify some of the possible

10. This was famously addressed by Meyer Fortes in "Ritual Festivals and the Social Cohesion in the Hinterland of the Gold Coast," *American Anthropologist* (1936), 38(4): 590–604. Further studies on the matter can be found in Benjamin Beit-Hallahmi and Michael Argyle, *The Psychology of Religious Behaviour, Belief, and Experience* (London: Routledge, 1997). Also see Richard Sosis and Candace Alcorta, "Signaling, Solidarity, and the Sacred: The Evolution of Religious Behavior," *Evolutionary Anthropology* (2003), 12(6): 264–274; Richard Sosis and Eric R. Bressler, "Cooperation and Commune Longevity: A Test of the Costly Signaling Theory," *Cross-Cultural Research* (2003), 37(2): 211–239; Azim F. Shariff and Ara Norenzayan, "God is Watching You: Priming God Concepts Increases Prosocial Behavior in an Anonymous Economic Game," *Psychological Science* (2007), 18(9): 803–809; Ara Norenzayan and Azim F. Shariff, "The Origin and Evolution of Religious Prosociality," *Science* (2008), 322(5898): 58–62; Azim F. Shariff, Ara

reasons for which it has been mandated that the rituals be performed in the way they are.

The New Testament, the Qur'an, and the Hindu scripture - the Bhagavad Gita all invite people to look beyond a ritual's outer performance:

> The law is only a shadow of the good things that are coming—not the realities themselves. For this reason it can never, by the same sacrifices repeated endlessly year after year, make perfect those who draw near to worship. Otherwise, would they not have stopped being offered? For the worshippers would have been cleansed once and for all, and would no longer have felt guilty for their sins. But those sacrifices are an annual reminder of sins. It is impossible for the blood of bulls and goats to take away sins. [Hebrews 10: 1–4]

> Neither their flesh nor their blood will reach God, but the reverence from you reaches Him. Thus has He made them subservient unto you, that you might magnify God for having guided you. And give glad tidings to the virtuous. [Qur'an 22:37]

> The misguided ones who delight in the melodious chanting of the Veda without understanding the real purpose of the Vedas think, O Arjuna, as if there is nothing else in the Vedas except the rituals for the sole purpose of obtaining heavenly enjoyment. They are dominated by material desires, and consider the attainment of heaven as the highest goal of life. They engage in specific rites for the sake of prosperity and enjoyment. Rebirth is the result of their action. The resolute determination of Self-realization is not formed in the minds of those who are attached to pleasure and power, and whose judgment is obscured by ritualistic activities. [Bhagavad Gita 2:42–44]

Norenzayan, and Joseph Henrich, "The Birth of High Gods: How the Cultural Evolution of Supernatural Policing Influenced the Emergence of Complex, Cooperative Human Societies, Paving the Way for Civilization," in *Evolution, Culture and the Human Mind*, eds. Mark Shaller, Ara Norenzayan, Steven J. Heine, Toshio Yamagishi, and Tatsuya Kameda (New York, NY: Psychology Press, 2010), 119–136.

ISLAM'S CONCLUSIVE MESSAGE

Islam's message started with the declaration of God's oneness. For twenty-three years, the message grew from a small seed planted in Mecca and flourished until it had established itself as an independent state.[11] This is the traditional account of the beginning of Islam. Though Islam appears to have started as weak and struggling under the oppression of the local Arab tribes, it grew to a position of power.

Islam's message begins with the oneness of God and concludes with the Ḥajj,[12] a ritual enshrouded in mystery. The Ḥajj performed by the founder of Islam is called the Farewell Ḥajj (*Ḥajj al-Wadāᶜ*), as it was the last ritual Prophet Muḥammad ﷺ taught, and the only time he performed it was before his death. Today, millions of pilgrims from all races and ethnicities and all occupations perform the Ḥajj rituals every year, most of them attempting to ensure that every aspect of the ritual is done precisely as it was meant to be.

As mentioned, the Ḥajj is the most ritualized part of Islam. The five obligatory daily prayers, the second pillar of Islam, are quite simple when compared to the complexity of the Ḥajj. Hence, understanding the Ḥajj, the conclusion of Islam's message, is essential to understanding Islam itself. Its rituals are usually explained as re-enactments of an ancient desert drama in which Abraham leaves some of his family members in the middle of the desert before taking his son to be sacrificed.[13] This study looks beyond the ancient stories to explore the inner significance of the Ḥajj as the ultimate spiritual journey—the journey of humanity.

According to Islamic eschatology, the Ḥajj will be suspended

---

11. I have many reservations about Ibn Isḥāq's *Sīrah*. In this connection, see Andrew Rippin (ed.) *Approaches to the History of the Interpretation of the Qur'ān* (Oxford: Clarendon Press, 1988); Gabriel S. Reynolds, *The Qur'ān and Its Biblical Subtext* (Abingdon: Routledge, 2010); and Fred Donner, *Muhammad and the Believers: At the Origins of Islam* (Cambridge: Harvard University Press, 2010). For comparison, see Ibn Isḥāq, *Sīrah*, ed. Suhayl Zakkār (Beirut: al-Fikr, 1978).

12. Muslim, *Ṣaḥīḥ Muslim*, 1: 45.

13. See Campbell and Moyers, *The Power of Myth*, 103, 228, for the ways in which ritual is a re-enactment of tradition.

at the end of time, when the Ka^{c}bah will be destroyed stone by stone while its treasure is uncovered.[14] The Prophet said: "It is as though I see a black one, whose legs are divergent, destroying it [the Ka^{c}bah] stone by stone,"[15] and, "Leave Abyssinia as they leave you, as no one removes the treasure of the Ka^{c}bah except the one with divergent legs (*dhul-suwayqatayn*) from Abyssinia."[16]

In a similar eschatological account, the Gospels of Matthew and Mark show Jesus foretelling the destruction of the Holy Temple in Jerusalem, which will also be removed stone by stone as a sign of the end times (Matthew 24:1–2, Mark 13:1–2). Some may have regarded this prophecy as fulfilled by the Romans' destruction of Jerusalem in 70 CE.[17] Yet, the Ḥajj is further connected to the End of Days, as the Prophet Muḥammad ﷺ prophesied that Jesus Christ would start to perform the Ḥajj in his Second Coming.[18] As one of the five pillars of Islam, its suspension appears to be unique. Its connection with Islamic eschatology also makes it unique. Because the Ḥajj is not only a re-enactment of ancient drama, but a future transformation as well, one may better understand the spiritual meanings that underlie its rituals.

14. *Ṣaḥīḥ al-Bukhārī*, 2: 149 (#1595), 2: 149 (#1596); Ibn Ḥanbal, *Musnad* (ed. Aḥmad Muḥammad Shākir), Cairo: al-Ḥadīth, 1995, 2: 484 (#2010), 6: 474–475 (#7053), 8: 165–166 (#8080); Abū Dawūd, *Sunan*, ed. Muḥammad Muḥyī-l-Dīn ^{c}Abdulḥamīd, Beirut: al-^{c}Aṣriyyah, 4: 114 (#4309).

15. *Ṣaḥīḥ al-Bukhārī*, 2: 149 (#1595), 2: 149 (#1596); Ibn Ḥanbal, *Musnad*, 2: 484 (#2010), 6: 474–475 (#7053), 8: 165–166 (#8080).

16. Abū Dawūd, *Sunan*, 4: 114 (#4309).

17. David I. Turner, "The Structure and Sequence of Matthew 24:1–41: Interaction with Evangelical Treatments," *Grace Theological Journal* (1989), 10(1): 3–27.

18. *Ṣaḥīḥ Muslim*, 2: 915 (#1252).

THE RITUALS OF THE ḤAJJ

There are three main forms of Ḥajj in Islam: i) *Ḥajj al-Tamattuᶜ*,[19] ii) *Ḥajj al-Qirān*,[20] and iii) *Ḥajj al-Ifrād*.[21] *Ḥajj al-Tamattuᶜ* is the most prominent form of Ḥajj and the type that was performed by the Prophet Muḥammad ﷺ. *Ḥajj al-Tamattuᶜ* occurs when the pilgrim enters the state of ritual consecration (*iḥrām*) for ᶜUmrah,[22] which is known as the Lesser Pilgrimage. The pilgrim is released from *iḥrām* after completion of the ᶜUmrah, and then re-enters the state of *iḥrām* for the Ḥajj (the Greater Pilgrimage) and performs its rituals. *Ḥajj al-Qirān* occurs when the pilgrim enters the state of *iḥrām* for ᶜUmrah, completes the ᶜUmrah, and then remains in the state of *iḥrām* to perform the Ḥajj. As for *Ḥajj al-Ifrād*, it occurs when the pilgrim does not perform the ᶜUmrah but enters the state of *iḥrām* for Ḥajj alone. Unlike the other forms of Ḥajj, this form of the ritual does not require a sacrificial animal.[23]

The pilgrim enters the state of ritual consecration (*iḥrām*) from the *mīqāt*, which is an established entry point for pilgrims. The Prophet Muḥammad ﷺ established five locations of the *mīqāt*,[24] depending on the location from which the pilgrim commences the journey. For ᶜUmrah, after entering the *mīqāt* and therefore the state of *iḥrām*, the pilgrim travels to Mecca and performs the circumambulation (*ṭawāf*) of the Kaᶜbah in seven circuits, starting and ending at the Black Stone, which is on the Eastern Corner.

Once the pilgrim has completed the *ṭawāf*, he prays behind the Station of Abraham (*maqām Ibrāhīm*), after which the pilgrim

19. *Ḥajj al-Tamattuᶜ* is called a *mutᶜah*, or delight, because it relieves the pilgrim from the state of *iḥrām* between the rituals of ᶜUmrah and Ḥajj.

20. *Ḥajj al-Qirān* is called *qirān*, or joining, because the pilgrims join the performance of the ᶜUmrah and Ḥajj in a single state of *iḥrām*.

21. *Ḥajj al-Ifrād* is called *ifrād*, meaning isolation, because pilgrims only perform the Ḥajj without the ᶜUmrah.

22. Details of the difference between the rituals of the ᶜUmrah and Ḥajj are provided later in this section.

23. Muhammad J. Maghniyyah, *The Hajj according to Five Schools of Islamic Law*, vol. iv (Tehran: Islamic Culture and Relations Organization, 1997), 26, 28.

24. Some state that he established only four. For more on this, see Chapter 3.

performs the *saᶜī*, which entails walking and running between the hills of Ṣafā and Marwah seven times. After performing the *saᶜī*, the pilgrim shaves or cuts his hair, known as *taḥlīl*, as he exits the state of *iḥrām*.

For the Ḥajj, or the Greater Pilgrimage, the pilgrim enters the state of *iḥrām*, and then travels to Mecca to circumambulate the Kaᶜbah in what is known as *ṭawāf al-qudūm* if he has not done so already for ᶜUmrah. He then travels to Minā on the eighth of Dhul-Ḥijjah[25] to stay the night. After sunrise, the pilgrim travels to the plain of Mount ᶜArafah, where he/she stands in prayer from noon to sunset. After sunset, the pilgrim travels to Muzdalifah on the eve of the Day of Sacrifice, also known as *al-Mashᶜar al-Ḥarām*. The pilgrim stays the night in Muzdalifah and, after sunrise on the Day of Sacrifice, travels to Minā to stone the pillar called *Jamrat al-ᶜAqabah*—believed to be the location where Satan tempted Abraham not to sacrifice his son, thereby disobeying God's command—seven times.

Unless he/she is performing *Ḥajj al-Ifrād*, the pilgrim then makes his/her sacrifice and either shaves or cuts his/her hair (*taḥlīl*), signifying his/her exit from the state of *iḥrām*. Although pilgrims are no longer bound by the state of *iḥrām*, they are still forbidden to engage in conjugal relations. They then travel to Mecca to perform seven circuits around the Kaᶜbah similar to those done for the ᶜUmrah, but this time while not in *iḥrām*.

Once the seven circuits have been completed, the pilgrim prays behind *maqām Ibrāhīm* and then performs the *saᶜī* between the hills of Ṣafā and Marwah seven times as for the ᶜUmrah, but also this time while not in *iḥrām*. After pilgrims conclude the *sa*ᶜī, they are released from all restrictions, including those on conjugal relations. However, there is a slight variation between Sunnī and Shīᶜī jurisprudence on this matter. According to Shīᶜī jurisprudence, the pilgrim is still not allowed to engage in conjugal relations until another obligatory circumambulation of the Kaᶜbah is performed, known as the circumambulation of women (*ṭawāf al-nisāʾ*). This does not mean that only women

25. The last month of the Islamic calendar.

perform it; rather, it is meant to remove the restriction on conjugal relations, and in Shīʿī jurisprudence, both sexes are obliged to perform it. The inner meaning behind the differences between the Sunnī and Shīʿī jurisprudence will be discussed later in the study.

The pilgrim then returns to Minā and remains there for either two or three days—a period known as *Ayyām al-Tashrīq*. During these days, pilgrims stone three pillars seven times each day. On the last day of Minā, they travel back to Mecca for a final farewell circumambulation (*ṭawāf al-wadāʿ*), thus concluding the Ḥajj. Since Shīʿī jurisprudence requires the additional circumambulation (*ṭawāf al-nisāʾ*) of the Kaʿbah to release the pilgrim from restrictions on conjugal relations, the farewell circumambulation is no longer necessary. Hence, both schools of thought require the same total number of circumambulations; however, they assign them different names and purposes.

Though many Muslims know these rituals and how to perform them, they lack an understanding of what they mean beyond their role as re-enactments of ancient stories. What, then, is the spiritual message that lies behind these rituals?

VIEWS OF ḤAJJ

Many attempts have been made down the centuries to conceptualize the meanings of the Ḥajj. Traditional explanations of the rites' order and manner of performance have been juristic in nature. Muhammad Jawad Maghniyyah, for example, wrote a comprehensive comparison between the Sunnī and Shīʿī juristic views on the rituals of the Ḥajj,[26] but left the mysteries of the rituals themselves unexplained. This is not as strange as one might think; for beyond giving the rituals and establishing their connection with Hagar's desert drama and Abraham's sacrifice of his son as recounted in the books of *ḥadīth*, the Prophet Muḥammad ﷺ did not elaborate any further on their meaning. Interestingly, although the Ḥajj is the most ritualized aspect of Islam, it is associated with the most lenient jurisprudence, since the Prophet Muḥammad ﷺ himself, whenever asked about the order of per-

26. Maghniyyah (1997) *The Hajj*.

formance of the rituals, was almost always flexible and tolerant in his response.[27] For example, when the Prophet ﷺ was asked about one who shaves before completing the sacrifice and other things of this nature, he would say: "no issue, no issue (*lā baʾs, lā baʾs*)."[28]

This suggests that, at least to the Prophet Muḥammad ﷺ, the message embedded in the rituals of the Ḥajj is more important than the manner of their performance. This is not to say that the physical performance is unimportant; rather, it is like saying that the physical body of humans is important, but not more important than the human soul. A person with a handicap, paralysis, or missing limbs can still survive, but a handicapped soul is dead. In the same way, the physical rituals of the Ḥajj are important, but not more important than the spirit of the Ḥajj. Without understanding the spirit of the Ḥajj, its physical performance could be seen as incomplete.

Mysticism is not part of Islamic orthodoxy, and except for Sufism, understanding the symbolism of Ḥajj has not been an integral part of Islamic thought. The elaborate rituals have served only as a traditional way to carry out Ḥajj by linking pilgrims with the Muslim past.[29] In the modern period, by contrast, some scholars have identified the feminine aspect of the Ḥajj, since the rituals honour Biblical women such as Eve (in ᶜArafah) and Hagar (in *saᶜī*).[30]

Some Western scholars, such as Richard Bell,[31] William

27. *Ṣaḥīḥ al-Bukhārī*, 2: 173 (#1721), 2: 173 (#1722), 2: 173 (#1723), 2: 175 (#1734), 2: 175 (#1735), 8: 135 (#6666).

28. *Ṣaḥīḥ al-Bukhārī*, 2: 173 (#1721).

29. Niko Kielstra, "Law and Reality in Modern Islam," in *Islamic Dilemmas: Reformers, Nationalists and Industrialization*, ed. Ernest Gellner (New York, NY: Mouton Publishers, 1985), 12–13.

30. Asma T. Uddin, "The Hajj and Pluralism," *The Review of Faith and International Affairs* (2008), 6(4): 43–47.

31. Richard Bell, "The Origin of the Eid al-Adha." *Muslim World* (1933), 23(2): 117–120.

Graham,[32] and John Bowen,[33] have pointed out the difficulty of explaining the rituals of the Ḥajj to non-Muslims, many of whom believe them to be pagan. Moreover, Muslim traditions indicate that pre-Islamic Arabs also performed the Ḥajj as part of certain deific cults and temple dedications.[34] This might imply a pagan root for the rituals, which the Qur'an subsequently canonized within its fold.

Scholars such as Uri Rubin,[35] Frederick Denny,[36] Martin Jacobs,[37] and Andreas Nordin[38] have advanced many theories on Islamic rituals, especially sacrificial rituals, from an anthropological perspective. Many of these theories attempt to shed light on the cultural aspect of human development through religious rituals, especially since many of the Ḥajj rituals pre-date Islam.[39] However, Abdul Hamid el-Zein has criticized anthropologists for giving a higher degree of credence to folk Islam than they should.[40] Anthropologists generally consider local expressions of Islam to be diluted and corrupted by superstition. This view of Islam implies that there exists a pure and well-defined essence of Islam that cannot be readily found in folk religion. For this

32. William A. Graham, "Islam in the Mirror of Ritual," in *Islam's Understanding of Itself*, eds. Richard G. Hovannisian and Speros Vryonis, Jr. (Malibu, CA: Undena, 1983), 56–59.

33. John R. Bowen, "On Scriptural Essentialism and Ritual Variation: Muslim Sacrifice in Sumatra and Morocco," *American Ethnologist* (1992) 19: 656–657.

34. See K. Conti Rossini (ed.), *Chrestomathia Arabica Meridionalis Epigraphica* (Rome: Istituto per L'Oriente,1931), e.g., 5, 10, 14, 16, 18, 21, 45, 46.

35. Uri Rubin, "The Great Pilgrimage of Muhammad: Some Notes on Sura IX," *Journal of Semitic Studies* (1982) 27(2): 241–260.

36. Frederick M. Denny, "Islamic Ritual: Perspectives and Theories," in *Approaches to Islam in Religious Studies,* ed. Richard C. Martin (Tucson, AZ: University of Arizona Press, 1985), 63–77.

37. Martin Jacobs, "An Ex-Sabbatean's Remorse: Sambari's Polemics against Islam," *Jewish Quarterly Review* (2007), 97(3): 347–378.

38. Andreas Nordin, "Ritual Agency: Substance Transfer and the Making of Supernatural Immediacy in Pilgrim Journeys," *Journal of Cognition and Culture* (2009), 9(3): 195–223.

39. Ian R. Netton, *Ṣūfī Ritual: The Parallel Universe* (Abingdon: Routledge, 2013), 116–123.

40. Abdul Hamid el-Zein, "Beyond Ideology and Theology: The Search for the Anthropology of Islam," *Annual Review of Anthropology* (1977), 6: 241–252.

reason, Talal Asad states that orthodoxy is not just a body of opinion, but also a relationship of power, as it rejects any folklore entering Islam as impure.[41]

Some theologians observe a traditional division between folk Islam and scholarly Islam. Other scholars have done comparative studies of rituals in different religions, such as shaving the hair, while taking into consideration cultural and anthropological perspectives.[42] However, rather than examining the rituals of Ḥajj from a cultural or anthropological point of view, this study views the Ḥajj as a spiritual journey, using comparative intertextual study to understand what the Prophet Muḥammad ﷺ might have meant by his teachings on this rite.[43] In other words, we will be looking not at pilgrims' practices, but at the scriptural meanings of such practices. If the Prophet Muḥammad ﷺ uttered the Qur'an and sanctioned the rituals of the Ḥajj, then it is important to understand what spiritual message he wanted to be conveyed. This is of great importance in studying the Ḥajj rituals because they are not performed locally; rather, Muslims from everywhere converge to perform them collectively in a centralized location.

We cannot go back in time to ask the Prophet Muḥammad ﷺ directly about the inner meaning of this or that ritual—assuming that he could even explain its mysteries in words.[44] Therefore, the method used here is not without its pitfalls: we cannot be certain what the Prophet Muḥammad ﷺ sanctioned and said, as some corruption may have occurred in the transmission of accounts from one generation to the next.

In his book *The Secrets of Pilgrimage* (*Asrār al-ḥajj*), Abu Ḥāmid Muḥammad al-Ghazālī (d. 505/1111) attempted to define the ethics of the Ḥajj, stressing that it should be performed with

---

41. Talal Asad, *The Idea of an Anthropology of Islam* (Washington, DC: Georgetown University Center for Contemporary Arab Studies, 1986), 15–16.

42. Saul M. Olyan, "What Do Shaving Rites Accomplish and What Do They Signal in Biblical Ritual Contexts?" *Journal of Biblical Literature* (1988) 117(4): 611–622.

43. El-Zein, "Beyond Ideology and Theology".

44. Abdulla Galadari, "Psychology of Mystical Experience: Muḥammad and Siddhārtha," *Anthropology of Consciousness* (2019), 30(2): 152–178.

a purity of heart and soul. Although al-Ghazālī[45] referred to the virtues of the lessons learnt from the Ḥajj as "inner deeds," urging pilgrims to ponder the inward meaning of outward rituals, he nonetheless emphasized the *how* of such rituals, and not only their purpose and intended meanings. Ali Shariati, an Iranian Muslim thinker and sociologist of religion, has written a book on the Ḥajj in which he also demonstrates the ethics, virtues, and philosophical and spiritual meanings of the journey and return to God.[46]
In discussing the virtues of the Ḥajj, scholars have drawn upon the related precepts in the Qur'an (Qur'an 2:197),[47] which indicate that all pilgrims, rich and poor alike, visit the House of God as equal guests, without distinction.[48] The Ḥajj teaches patience and endurance, so that the pilgrim may demonstrate that she is ready to overcome anything to visit the House of God.[49] The Ḥajj has been said to weaken the pilgrim's love of the world and transform it into the love of God.[50]

Generally, Sufis have been foremost in focusing on the spiritual meaning of the Ḥajj rituals, while jurists have focused on their correct performance.[51] Some Sufis have even stated that the

45. Al-Ghazālī, *Asrār al-ḥajj*, ed. Mūsā Muḥammad ᶜAlī (Sidon: Al-Maktabah al-ᶜAṣriyyah, no date), 138.

46. Ali Shariati, *Hajj: The Pilgrimage*, translated by Ali A. Behzadnia, and Najla Denny (Costa Mesa, CA: Evecina Cultural and Education Foundation (Jubilee Press), no date).

47. See Muḥammad ibn Aḥmad al-ᶜUtbī (d. 255/869), *Kitāb al-ḥajj*, ed. Miklūsh Mūrānī (Beirut: Ibn Ḥazm, 2007). Also see al-Ṭabarānī (d. 360/918), *Faḍl ᶜashr Dhī al-Ḥijjah* (Sharjah: Al-ᶜUmarayn al-ᶜIlmiyyah, no date); Muḥammad Ibn ᶜAbdulwahhāb (d. 1206/1792), *Mansak al-ḥajj*, ed. Bandar ibn Nāfiᶜ al-ᶜAbdalī (Riyadh: al-Waṭan, 2002); Muṣṭafa Laᶜzūzī, *Thaqāfat al-ḥajj* (Beirut: al-Kutub al-ᶜIlmiyyah, 2006); Muhammad J. Rezae, Muhammad Najafi, Abdul-Majid Mahyger, and S. Masud Keshavarz, "The Role of Pilgrimage to Mecca (Hajj) in Gaining Moral Virtues and Avoiding Moral Vices," *Scientific Journal of Pure and Applied Sciences* (2014), 3(5): 313–317.

48. Shariati, *Hajj*, 7. Laᶜzūzī, *Thaqāfat al-ḥajj*, 37.

49. Shariati, *Hajj*, 83. Laᶜzūzī, *Thaqāfat al-ḥajj*, 57, 59, 63.

50. Shariati, *Hajj*, 83.

51. See Muhammad Khalid Masud, "Sufi Views of Pilgrimage in Islam," in *Sacredscapes and Pilgrimage Systems* (New Delhi: Shubhi Publications, 2011), 95–110; see also Paul R. Powers, "Interiors, Intentions, and the 'Spirituality' of

true Kaᶜbah is the heart, and not a house made of stones.[52] Orthodoxy and mysticism are not usually aligned in Islam, in contrast to Jewish orthodoxy, which as seen in Hasidic Judaism, affirms the mystical nature of the Jewish faith. Hava Lazarus-Yafeh, a scholar, notes that it is as difficult for Muslims to understand the rituals of the Islamic Ḥajj as it is for Christians to comprehend fully the Eucharist, and for Jews to understand the Temple sacrifice.[53] Consequently, she states, al-Ghazālī and Sayyid Quṭb's (d. 1386/1966) exegesis mainly emphasized the pilgrim's character during Ḥajj rather than the rituals' exact meaning.

THE MEANING OF THE WORD ḤAJJ

The Ḥajj is a major pillar of Islam. Its performance is ordained in the Qur'an with a proclamation by Abraham.

> And proclaim the *ḥajj* among humankind:[54] they shall come to thee on foot (*rijālan*) and upon all [manner of] lean beast, coming from all deep and distant mountain highways (*fajj ᶜamīq*). [Qur'an 22:27]

It is interesting to note the reference in this verse to people coming on foot (*rijālan*). The Hebrew Bible has ordained three annual pilgrimages to the Temple in Jerusalem that Jewish men should perform on foot (*rijāl / rĕgālîm*), which is from the same root used in the proclamation of the Qur'an. The word *ḥag* is also used in the Hebrew Bible to mean festival or pilgrimage, although the three pilgrimages (*šālôš rĕgālîm*) in the Pentateuch (Exodus 23:14–17) are known as Passover (*Pesach*), Weeks (*Shavuot*), and Tabernacles (*Sukkot*) (Exodus 34:18–23, Deuteronomy 16).

Islamic Ritual Practice," *Journal of the American Academy of Religion* (2004), 72(2): 425–459.

52. Kerimov G. M. Oglu, "Basic Principles Distinguishing Orthodox Islam from Sufism," *Journal of Muslim Minority Affairs* (1988), 9(2): 245–250. It has been argued that the symbolism of the Kaᶜbah as the heart is even emphasized linguistically in the Qur'an; see Galadari, "The *Qibla*."

53. Hava Lazarus-Yafeh, *Some Religious Aspects of Islam* (Leiden: Brill, 1981), 17–37.

54. In contrast to the *TSQ*, I use "humankind" instead of "mankind" as the translation of *al-nās*, which is more loyal to the Arabic.

The root *ḥ-j-j* contains polysemous meanings. In Arabic, it means an intended destination, pilgrimage, argument, debate, or proof.[55] In Hebrew and Aramaic, it means gathering, festival, and pilgrimage.[56] In Aramaic, an additional meaning is a valley.[57] Some scholars suggest its relationship with the Middle-Egyptian *ḥ3g*, meaning to be glad.[58] In Psalm 107:27, the term is used to mean 'sway'. The *Theological Dictionary of the Old Testament* (*TDOT*) suggests that the root meaning might be to move in a circle, become dizzy, or dance.[59] This type of description would be similar to the circumambulation of Muslims around the Kaᶜbah, but it would not be unique. In Judges 21:19–21, the festival (*ḥag*) comes with dancing (*ḥûl*), a term that also means whirling.[60] It is difficult to ascertain whether the whirling and dancing became associated with the term *ḥag* of the Hebrew Bible due to its ancient use, or if the etymology of the term contains this meaning.[61]

ḤAJJ AND *RĔGĀLÎM*

PASSOVER

Passover (*pāsaḥ*), one of the main pilgrimages ordained in the Pentateuch, commemorates the Exodus of the Israelites from Egypt. It starts on the 15th day of the Hebrew month Nisan (Exo-

55. Ibn Manẓūr (d. 711/1311), *Lisān al-ᶜarab* (Beirut: Ṣādir, 1994), 2: 226–230 on *ḥ-j-j*.

56. Francis Brown, Samuel R. Driver, and Charles A. Briggs, *Enhanced Brown-Driver-Briggs Hebrew and English Lexicon* (*BDB*) (Oak Harbor, WA: Logos Research Systems, 2000), 290–291; see also G. J. Botterweck, H. Ringgren, and H.-J. Fabry (eds.), J. T. Willis (trans.), *The Theological Dictionary of the Old Testament (Revised Edition) (TDOT)* (Grand Rapids, MI: William B. Eerdmans Publishing Company), 2011, 4: 201–203.

57. Stephen A. Kaufman (ed.), *Targum Lexicon: A Lexicon to the Aramaic Versions of the Hebrew Scriptures from the Files of the Comprehensive Aramaic Lexicon Project* (Cincinnati, OH: Hebrew Union College), 2004-2005.

58. See William A. Ward, "Some Egypto-Semitic Roots," *Orientalia* (1962), 31(4): 397–412, 405; see also *TDOT*, 4: 202.

59. *TDOT*, 4: 202.

60. *BDB*, 296–297.

61. John H. Eaton, "Dancing in the Old Testament," *The Expository Times* (1975), 86(5): 136–140.

dus 12). The sacrificial lamb is prepared the day before (the 14th of Nisan) (Exodus 12:6, Numbers 9:11), but should have been taken by the pilgrims on the 10th of Nisan (Exodus 12:1–3). The Festival of Unleavened Bread (*ḥag ha-maṣṣôt*) begins the day after this and continues for seven days. According to Exodus, before the Israelites departed Egypt, God inflicted ten plagues on Egypt; the tenth plague was the killing of all firstborn males, including cattle. In Exodus 11:1–12:36, God instructs Moses to tell the Israelites that they must kill a lamb and sprinkle its blood on their doorposts as a mark so that the Spirit of God will pass over and not afflict them with this plague. The day before Passover, the day of preparation of the sacrificial lamb, is a day of fasting by all the firstborn of Israel, also known as the Fast of the Firstborn.

According to Exodus, after this plague—during which even Pharaoh's son was killed—Pharaoh freed the Israelites. They left their homes so hurriedly that they did not wait for the bread to rise. To commemorate this, Jews are allowed to eat only unleavened bread during Passover. Hence, the week of Passover is also called the Festival of Unleavened Bread. The word for bread used in the Hebrew Bible is *leḥem*. In Arabic, *laḥm* means flesh (or meat),[62] while in Hebrew and Aramaic, it also means bread.[63] According to the Gospels, Jesus was crucified during Passover as the sacrificial lamb, and he was born in Bethlehem (which means House of Bread or House of Flesh). In John 6:22–59, Jesus likened his body to the bread (*leḥem*) of life, which he broke. Arabs widely use the word *khubz* for bread. The Qur'an uses the word *khubz* once and alludes to that the inner meaning (or *taʾwīl*) of bread is crucifixion (the destruction of the body) in the story of the two men jailed with Joseph, where the cupbearer dreams of wine and the baker of bread, which also resembles the Last Supper of Jesus (Qur'an 12:36–41).

The Church Fathers were intrigued by the parallelism between the figures in the Hebrew Bible and the story of Jesus. The Per-

62. *Lisān al-ʿarab*, 12: 535–538 on *l-ḥ-m*.
63. *BDB*, 536–537.

sian sage Aphrahat (d. 345), for example, explicitly shows the parallelism between Joseph and Jesus' story, such as both being betrayed by Judah (or Judas) and both being similarly persecuted.[64] Interestingly, as Joseph entered prison with two other people (Qur'an 12:36, Genesis 40:1–4), Jesus was crucified with two others (Matthew 27:38, Mark 15:27–28, Luke 23:32–33, John 19:18).[65] Further, one of the prisoners survives in Joseph's story and the other dies (Genesis 40:9–18), just as Jesus informs one of the thieves that he will be with him in paradise, while the other, it is assumed, will not (Luke 23:39–43).

Even more interestingly, Joseph tells the cupbearer that he will be restored to his position in three days (Genesis 40:12–13), paralleling Jesus' resurrection on the third day. In Joseph's story, the third day is the birthday of Pharaoh, the king of the land (earth) (Genesis 40:20). In the story of Jesus, the king of heaven, the third day is his resurrection. Additionally, when Joseph asks the cupbearer to remember him to Pharaoh, the cupbearer forgets (Qur'an 12:42, Genesis 40:14, 23), whereas when one of the thieves crucified with Jesus asks Jesus to remember him when he enters his kingdom, Jesus does not forget and tells him that he will be with him in paradise (Luke 23:42–43). Another intriguing connection between Passover, Eucharist, and Joseph's story is that during Passover, only unleavened bread is allowed, which means bread without yeast. Yeast is *ḥāmēṣ* (Hebrew) or *khamīr* (Arabic), from the root *kh-m-r*, which is the same root as wine.[66] If unleavened bread is given with wine (*khamr*), then it is as if it is given with yeast (*khamīr*). The purpose of the wine is to raise the bread (*leḥem*), which also means flesh. Overall, it becomes a symbol of resurrection.

At Passover, the Jews are instructed to perform *Qorban*

64. From 21:9 of Aphrahat's *Demonstrations*; see Philip Schaff and Henry Wace, eds., *A Select Library of the Nicene and Post-Nicene Fathers of the Christian Church* (New York, NY: The Christian Literature Company, 1898), 13:2, 395–396.

65. Abdulla Galadari, "Joseph and Jesus: Unearthing Symbolisms within the Bible and the Qur'an," *The International Journal of Religion and Spirituality in Society* (2011), 1(1): 117–128.

66. *TDOT*, 5: 1.

Pesaḥ, which is the sacrificial lamb. The lamb needs to be sacrificed on the afternoon of Passover (the 14th of Nisan) and eaten in the evening (Exodus 12:6). The lamb must be roasted intact, along with its head, feet, and internal organs, and no bones may be broken (Exodus 12:9–10, 12:46, 23:18). The meat should be completely consumed such that nothing is left of it by morning. If any meat remains, it must be burned with fire (Exodus 12:10). The sacrificial lamb is eaten along with *maṣṣôt* (unleavened bread) and *mĕrōrîm* (bitter herbs) (Exodus 12:8, Numbers 9:11). Nothing leavened shall be eaten with the sacrificial lamb (Exodus 23:18). Similarly, according to the Gospels, Jesus was crucified on Passover in the afternoon, fully intact, and without a broken bone, although the men crucified with him had their legs broken (Matthew 27:45–54, Mark 15:25–39, Luke 23:44–47), which the Gospel of John mentions as a fulfillment of Scriptures (John 19:28–37).

Starting from the second night of the Passover festival (the 16th of Nisan), Jews begin to practice the Counting of the ᶜOmer. The *ᶜōmer* is a unit of dry measure (sheaf) for grain.[67] A *ᶜōmer* of barley (*shaᶜīr* / *śĕᶜōrîm*) was offered to the Temple of Jerusalem. This is practiced each night as a reminder of the approach of the festival of Shavuot, which is the second of the three pilgrimage festivals when an offering of wheat is made. The Hebrew word "*ᶜōmer*" is related to the name of the Lesser Pilgrimage in Islam, called *ᶜUmrah*. The Counting of the ᶜOmer is done each night for seven weeks, starting from the second day of Passover. Therefore, Shavuot starts fifty days from Passover; for this reason, it is called Pentecost in Greek.

According to the New Testament, Jesus was crucified on Passover and resurrected on the third day, after which he stayed with his disciples for forty days, culminating in his ascension to heaven one week before Shavuot (Pentecost) (Luke 24:44–49, Acts 1:1–11). On Pentecost, the Holy Spirit descended in the form of tongues of fire upon Jesus' disciples, which marked the beginning of their active apostleship without their master and

67. *BDB*, 771.

the establishment of the Church of God on earth (Acts 2:1–4). It was during their active apostleship that Christ was no longer with them, but was now *within* them through the power of the Holy Spirit, according to the New Testament. There are six weeks from the Crucifixion to the Ascension of Jesus, which might be symbolic of the six days of creation. On the seventh, which marks the Sabbath, he ascended unto God, and he was established on the Throne.

According to the apostle John, when Jesus was asked during Passover to show a miraculous sign, he told the Jews at the Temple that if they destroyed the Temple, he could rebuild it in three days (John 2:13–22). They mocked him, saying that it had taken forty-six years to build the temple. However, John understands that Jesus was talking about his own body, the temple that was resurrected on the third day. Ironically, Jesus told this story during Passover, the very feast during which he was later crucified (John 2:18–23). The three days it takes Jesus to rebuild the temple (symbolized by the three days between the crucifixion and resurrection) plus the forty-six years it took to rebuild the original temple (paralleling the forty-six days following the resurrection) come to forty-nine days altogether, which equals the seven weeks of Shavuot, with the fiftieth day as Pentecost.

In yet another example of the intrinsic similarity between the message of the Ḥajj and the message of Acts, the apostles were called upon on Shavuot (Pentecost) to establish the Church of God. Once this happened, Luke narrates that Peter proclaimed that everyone should be baptized for the forgiveness of their sins and receive the Holy Spirit as a promise to them, their children, and everyone far off (Greek: *makran*) whom God will call (Acts 2:38–39). This proclamation resembles the proclamation of the Ḥajj by Abraham in the Qur'an, that people who answer the call of God will come through deep and distant mountain highways to the Ḥajj for the forgiveness of their sins (Qur'an 22:27). The Greek term *makran* is used in the Septuagint primarily to translate the Hebrew *r-ḥ-q*,[68] which is cognate to the Arabic *raḥīq* in

68. *TDOT*, 13: 468–469.

Qur'an 83:25 describing how people in heaven will be poured from a "sealed" distance (*raḥīq makhtūm*). Just as the Hebrew Bible frequently uses *r-ḥ-q* (far) and *q-r-b* (near) as antitheses (e.g., Deuteronomy 13:7, Isaiah 33:13, 46:13, 54:14), so does the Qur'an as well in this instance (Qur'an 83:21, 83:25, 83:28).

SHAVUOT

Ḥag Shavuot, known as Pentecost, starts on the sixth of Sivan, after the Counting of the ᶜOmer for seven weeks. This festival commemorates the anniversary of the day God gave the Torah to the Israelites on Mount Sinai after Moses had left them for forty days to receive the Commandments from God. In the Torah, this festival is referred to in different ways, including the Festival of Reaping (*ḥag ha-qāṣîr*) (Exodus 23:16) and the Day of First-fruits (*yom ha-bikkûrîm*) (Numbers 28:26). The word for reaping (*qāṣîr*) seems to be cognate with the Arabic "*q-ṣ-r*" used in the Qur'an to refer to pilgrims' cutting their hair (Qur'an 48:27), signifying release from the state of *iḥrām*. In an interesting coincidence, the Counting of the ᶜOmer concludes with *yom ha-bikkûrîm*, suggestive of the names of the first two Caliphs in Islam, Abū Bakr and ᶜUmar, which use the same roots.

In the Hebrew Bible, the grain harvest, like the Counting of the ᶜOmer, lasts for seven weeks (Deuteronomy 16:9–11, Jeremiah 5:24, Isaiah 9:2), starting with barley harvest (*shaᶜīr / śĕᶜōrîm*; also the root of the word for hair, which is significant in the Ḥajj and ᶜUmrah rituals) on Passover and ending with the harvesting of wheat on Shavuot. The first-fruits (*bikkûrîm*) are brought from seven types of crop: wheat, barley, grapes, figs, pomegranates, olives, and dates (Deuteronomy 8:8). On Shavuot, the *bikkûrîm* are presented to the *kōhēn* (priest) in the Temple of Jerusalem (Deuteronomy 26:1–10). The importance of the number seven in these Jewish festivals is similar to its significance in the Ḥajj and ᶜUmrah rituals, including the seven circumambulations around the Kaᶜbah, the seven traversals between the hills of Ṣafā and Marwah, and the seven stones thrown each time against the pillars situated in Minā.

SUKKOT

Sukkot, which means Tabernacles or Tents, is celebrated on the 15th of Tishrei and lasts for seven days. Different terms have been used for the festival, including the Feast of Ingathering (*ḥag ha-ʾāsip*) (Exodus 23:16, 34:22) and the Festival of the Seventh Month (*ḥāg ba-ḥōdeš ha-šĕbîᶜî*) (Nehemiah 8:14, Ezekiel 45:25).

According to the Book of Deuteronomy, Moses requested that every seven years the Children of Israel read the Torah during Sukkot (Deuteronomy 31:10–11). On the first day of Sukkot, Jews are asked to take the produce of four species of plants—hadar trees, palm trees, leafy trees, and willows of the brook. The Temple in Jerusalem was dedicated by King Solomon on Sukkot (1 Kings 8, 2 Chronicles 7). Sukkot was also the first festival celebrated by the Israelites after the Babylonian captivity (Ezra 3:2–4). For the full duration of Sukkot, Jews are commanded to live in tents for seven days, since God made their ancestors live in tents when He brought them out of Egypt (Leviticus 23:40–43). During the days of the Ḥajj, Muslims also stay in tents, especially on the nights spent at Minā. Zechariah prophesied that Sukkot would become a universal festival celebrated by all nations (Zechariah 14:16–19).

The Festival of Weeks (*ḥol ha-môᶜăd*) refers to the intermediate days of the seven-day festivals of Passover and Sukkot. On those days, Biblical restrictions that are usually applied on Jewish holidays are relaxed, but not eliminated. The word *môᶜăd* has the same root as *mīᶜād*, which means appointed time or promise. This will be seen later in its connection with the Ḥajj, which is a journey from the *Mīqāt* (appointed time) to the Land of *Mīᶜād* (appointed or promised land).

RESEARCH METHODOLOGY

As noted, the main criterion for this research is philological, using intertextual polysemy.[69] This method is not without its pitfalls,[70]

69. For more about intertextual polysemy in the Qur'an, see Galadari, *Qur'anic Hermeneutics*; "The Role of Intertextual Polysemy"; and, "The *Qibla*."

70. Galadari, *Qur'anic Hermeneutics*, 50–51.

as some interpretations are more solid and others are necessarily speculative.[71] Therefore, one needs to proceed cautiously.

Polysemy exists when a word has multiple related meanings. Semitic languages, such as Arabic, are typically very rich in polysemy due to having roots, usually triliteral, which branch into multiple related meanings. Intratextuality and intertextuality are described as looking at keywords and their usage both within the same text and among different texts. In the context of this study, we look primarily at how keywords are used within the Qur'an or between the Qur'an and the Bible. Intertextual polysemy is like putting pieces of a puzzle together, as it can provide a literary device through which an author alludes to a previous text or oral utterance. For example, Michael Fishbane has theorized that some Biblical authors devised literary styles that alluded to previous books through the use of certain keywords or phraseology.[72] Fishbane refers to this style as inner-biblical exegesis. However, this type of literary device is not unique to Biblical literature, as such tools in both oral transmission and written literature are widely known as mnemonic devices.[73] With the Qur'an having been developed primarily in an oral culture dependent on memory, such devices would have been used widely,[74] as indeed they were by ancient Greeks as discussed by Plato.[75]

The Qur'an appears to use both intratextual and intertextual polysemy as a device for inner-Qur'anic and Qur'anic-Biblical allusions.[76] The following are the brief steps for intertextual

71. Ibid., 4–5.

72. Michael Fishbane, *Biblical Interpretation in Ancient Israel* (Oxford: Oxford University Press, 1985).

73. Renate Lachmann, "Mnemonic and Intertextual Aspects of Literature," in *Cultural Memory Studies: An International and Interdisciplinary Handbook*, eds. Astrid Erll and Ansgar Nünning (Berlin: De Gruyter, 2008), 301–310.

74. Jeffrey K. Olick, "From Collective Memory to the Sociology of Mnemonic Practices and Products," in *Cultural Memory Studies: An International and Interdisciplinary Handbook*, eds. Astrid Erll and Ansgar Nünning (Berlin: De Gruyter), 2008, 151–162.

75. Harold Tarrant, "Orality and Plato's Narrative Dialogues," in *Voice into Text: Orality and Literacy in Ancient Greece*, ed. Ian Worthington (Leiden: Brill, 1996), 129–148.

76. Galadari, *Qur'anic Hermeneutics*.

polysemy: keywords of a passage are taken back to their root meanings in the Arabic language, taking into account possible meanings from the root's morphological permutations. The lexical semantics are not only taken from Arabic definitions, but also other Semitic languages, such as Hebrew and Aramaic. The reason for this is that we cannot fully rely on medieval lexicons to understand the Qur'an, as a word might have evolved in response to its use in the Qur'an rather than reflecting the meaning it conveyed in the Prophet's time. Furthermore, medieval Arabic lexicons may define a Qur'anic term based on a particular interpretation of the Qur'an rather than giving us the actual meaning of the word as it was intended. Consequently, comparing the Arabic definitions with their cognates in Hebrew and Aramaic may provide us with a more accurate knowledge of the possible meanings of the words in question, which may have been tainted through medieval lexicographers' interpretations of the Qur'an.

Once all possible meanings from the point of view of lexical semantics have been taken into account, we come to the matter of intertextuality, which takes two forms. The first compares and analyzes how the term and its various morphological permutations are used within the Qur'an and other scriptures. The second form is not always obvious. It involves the intertextuality of comparative meaning or the homophone of the term being analyzed, and not necessarily one that would share the exact same root. An example would be the term *ab*, or father. Possible roots for this term include *awb*, *ayb,* and *abī*. Arab Christians, for example, use the term *āb* for God the Father, which could be rooted in either *awb* or *ayb*. Nonetheless, the term *aba*, which also corresponds to the Aramaic *aba*, could be rooted in the term *abī* or *abū*. Hence, these would be cases in which a full array of possible root meanings is taken into consideration in the analysis. An example of homophone intertextuality would include terms such as *qirān*, which literally means joining, but is usually understood as marriage or partnership, and comparing it with *qur'ān*. Although the term *qirān* is rooted in *qaran*, while the term *qur'ān* is rooted in *qaraʾ*, they are phonetically similar. The second form of intertextuality is not as strong as the first, where sharing the same root is more evident and simpler to compare. Nonetheless, the second form may sometimes provide us with interesting insights during intertextual analysis, and hence, cannot always be ignored.[77]

The hermeneutical method proposed here is based on a linguistic approach to the critical words used for Ḥajj rituals, e.g., *mīqāt*, *ṭawāf*, *hadī*, etc. Each of these Arabic words will be defined based on its root and compared to its usages in the Qur'an, as well as in other Scriptures, such as the Hebrew Bible. After the meaning of the root is established, it is analyzed accordingly. To recover any meanings that may have been forgotten over time, other Semitic languages such as Hebrew and Aramaic are drawn on for definitions of these words.

For example, the word *mīqāt*, which in Ḥajj rituals describes the location at which pilgrims need to consecrate themselves and put on the funeral shroud, has the root *waqt*, which means time. The Ḥajj is describing people wearing funeral shrouds, indicating their death, and then discarding the funeral shrouds, resembling their resurrection as an analogy of the resurrection of the dead. We can observe that in different parts of the Qur'an, the Day of Resurrection is called *yawm al-waqt al-ma*ᶜ*lūm* (Qur'an 15:38, 38:81), which translates as "the Day of the Time Appointed", and in other verses of the Qur'an (e.g., Qur'an 44:40, 56:50, 78:17) the same word, *mīqāt*, is used to describe the Day of Resurrection.

My primary main aim in this research is to link different verses of the Qur'an that describe and relate the Ḥajj rituals to each other. After analyzing the rituals both individually and collectively, I draw out their spiritual dimensions based on demonstrable evidence from within scripture and tradition.[78] In this way, I hope to help readers begin to read Scriptures for themselves in a new

77. Galadari, *Qur'anic Hermeneutics*, 48–49.

78. A review of the scholarly work on this subject will show the significance of this analysis in the context of other studies. See Muhammad A. Quasem, "Understanding the Qur'an and its Explanation by Personal Opinion Which Has Not Come Down by Tradition," *The Recitation and Interpretation of the Qur'an: Al Ghazali's Theory* (Kuala Lumpur, Malaysia: University of Malaya Press, 1979).

and more spiritual light. Readers will then begin to see the Ḥajj rituals not simply as re-enactments of stories from antiquity, but as phases of a deeply meaningful spiritual journey.

2

THE APPOINTED TIME (*MĪQĀT*)

Whether undertaking the Lesser Pilgrimage (ᶜUmrah) or the Greater Pilgrimage (Ḥajj), pilgrims must enter a state of ritual consecration, or *iḥrām*. While in this state, pilgrims wear two white unstitched garments resembling a funeral shroud,[1] as described by al-Ghazālī in his *Iḥyā*ᵓ and alluded to by al-Nawawī (d. 676/1277).[2] The funeral shroud is described in the same way as the garment Jesus wore while on the Cross (John 19:23), seamless and woven in one piece. Throughout the rituals of the Ḥajj, wearing this garment symbolizes death and

1. Shaykh ᶜAlwān (d. 920/1514), *al-Fawātiḥ al-ilāhiyyah wal-mafātiḥ al-ghaybiyyah al-muwaḍḍiḥah lil-kalim al-Qur*ᵓ*āniyyah wal-ḥikam al-furqāniyyah* (Cairo: Rikābī, 1999), 67 on Q. 2:188–189, 205–206 on Q. 5:94–96.

2. Al-Ghazālī, *Iḥyā*ᵓ *ᶜulūm al-dīn* (Beirut: al-Maᶜrifah, no date), 1: 268; al-Nawawī, *al-Minhāj sharḥ ṣaḥīḥ Muslim bin al-Ḥajjāj* (Beirut: Iḥyāᵓ al-Turāth al-ᶜArabī, 1972); Burhān al-Dīn, *al-Mubdi*ᶜ *fī sharḥ al-muqni*ᶜ (Beirut: al-Kutub al-ᶜIlmiyyah, 1997), 2: 245; Ṣiddīq Ḥassan Khān al-Qinnawjī, *Abjad al-ᶜulūm* (Beirut: Ibn Ḥazm, 2002), 270; Ḥassan Ṭurad, *Falsafat al-ḥajj fil-Islām* (Beirut: al-Zahrāᵓ, no date), 224–225; ᶜAbdullah ibn Muḥammad al-Buṣayrī, *al-Ḥajj wal-ᶜumrah wal-ziyārah* (Riyadh: Maktabat al-Malik Fahd al-Waṭaniyyah, 2003), 26; and Laᶜzūzī, *Thaqāfat al-ḥajj*, 37.

its removal symbolizes resurrection.[3] A close relationship thus exists between the pilgrimage and the resurrection of the dead. This chapter shows how one of these symbols, the *mīqāt*, provides us with an insight into the rituals of resurrection.

When undertaking either the Lesser Pilgrimage (ᶜUmrah) or the Greater Pilgrimage (Ḥajj), pilgrims stop at a place known as the *mīqāt*. Beginning from a state of ritual purification, *ṭahārah*,[4] they enter into a state of ritual consecration, or *iḥrām*, and put on the funeral shroud representing their spiritual death.

Time is given great importance in Islam in relation to ritual prayers, fasting, and festivals.[5] Even the obligatory almsgiving (*zakāh*) is time-related, as it is paid on money or certain assets (e.g. gold, cattle) that have been in the individual's possession for a full lunar year. In the event of divorce or the death of a husband, the waiting-period (*ᶜiddah*) that a woman must observe before entering into a new marriage is also time-dependent, whether on the menstrual period (Qur'an 2:228), on a fixed amount of time for non-menstruating women (Qur'an 65:4) or widows,[6] or on the time of pregnancy and childbirth (Qur'an 65:4). Time also has a deeper spiritual meaning.

This chapter portrays the symbolic use of time (*waqt*) within the Qur'an and Islamic rituals. It shows how in Islam, there is a strong relationship between time (*waqt*) and death and resurrection.[7] Although there are various terms for time in Islam, [8] this chapter looks specifically at the term *waqt* and its deep spiritual

3. Jaᶜfar al-Ṣādiq, *Miṣbāḥ al-sharīᶜah* (Beirut: al-Aᶜlamī, 1980), 50.

4. As-Sayyid Sabiq, *Fiqh al-Sunnah: Hajj and ᶜUmrah* (Indianapolis: American Trust Publications, 1985), 27.

5. Ibn ᶜArabī discusses the issue of time under the heading of *mīqāt al-zamān* under Islamic thought in his *Futūḥāt*, and especially the times of the Ḥajj. See Ibn ᶜArabī, *al-Futūḥāt al-Makkiyyah*, ed. A. Shams-ul-Dīn (Beirut: al-Kutub al-ᶜIlmiyyah, no date), 2: 436–437.

6. See Badr al-Dīn al-ᶜAynī (d. 855/1453) *ᶜUmdat al-qārī sharḥ ṣaḥīḥ al-Bukhārī* (Beirut: Iḥyāᵓ al-Turāth al-ᶜArabī, no date), 20: 303.

7. For research on the concept of time (*zaman*) in Islam from philosophical perspectives, see Aziz Ahmed, *Change, Time and Causality, with Special Reference to Muslim Thought* (Lahore: Pakistan Philosophical Congress, 1974); see also Gerhard Böwering, "Ideas of Time in Persian Sufism," *Iran* (1992), 30: 77–89.

8. Al-Khawlānī, *Tārīkh dāryā*, ed. S. al-Afghānī (Damascus: al-Birqī, 1950), 112.

and symbolic meaning within the Qur'an to clarify the symbolism of the *mīqāt* of the Ḥajj.

According to a tradition attributed to God (*ḥadīth qudsī*), God states, "I am the aeon (*al-dahr*)."[9] Gerhard Böwering says that within Islam, there seem to be two levels of time, the time of God, aeon (*dahr*), and the time of human beings, *waqt*.[10] He states that *dahr* is eternal, whereas *waqt* is a mere instant,[11] as Ibn ᶜArabī (d. 638/1240) describes it in his *Meccan Revelations*.[12] This notion that *waqt* is a moment in time exists in traditional Sufi mysticism.[13] To some Sufi mystics, the concept of time (*waqt*) is the time they are absorbed in God, basing it on the tradition (*ḥadīth*) attributed to the Prophet ﷺ, "I have with God a time (*waqt*)."[14] Ibn ᶜArabī calls the *Quṭb*, or spiritual pole of his age, as "master of the moment" (*ṣāḥib al-waqt*),[15] possibly in reference to that during the time of the Prophet ﷺ, he was himself *ṣāḥib al-waqt*, in that he assumed the place of the *Quṭb* of that age.[16] Böwering says, "Breaking through eternity, the mystics relive their *waqt*, their primeval moment with God, here and now, in the instant of ecstasy, even as they anticipate their ultimate destiny."[17] Wein-

9. *Ṣaḥīḥ Muslim*, 4: 1762 (#2246).

10. Gerhard Böwering, "The Concept of Time in Islam," *Proceedings of the American Philosophical Society* (1997), 141(1): 55–66.

11. Ibid., 61.

12. Ibn ᶜArabī refers to *waqt* as the instant of time (*ḥāl*) in which the person finds himself or herself, and to the individual as *ibn al-waqt*, the child of the present moment. Ibn ᶜArabī, *al-Futūḥāt al-Makkiyah*, 2:261 and 3: 199.

13. Ibn ᶜArabī's notion of *ibn al-waqt* is viewed by Böwering as an adaptation from *al-Risālah al-Qushayriyyah*. See al-Qushayrī (d. 465/1074) *al-Risālah al-Qushayriyyah*, eds. ᶜAbdul-Ḥalīm Maḥmūd and Maḥmūd b. al-Sharīf (Cairo: al-Maᶜārif, no date), 1: 151.

14. Al-Naysābūrī, *Gharāᵓib al-Qurᵓān wa-raghāᵓib al-Furqān*, ed. Zakariyyā ᶜUmayrāt (Beirut: al-Kutub al-ᶜIlmiyyah, 1996), 2: 87; see also al-Majlisī, *Biḥār al-anwār*, 18: 360, 79: 243. This *ḥadīth* is also narrated by al-Qushayrī in a slightly different form in his *Laṭāᵓif al-ishārāt*, ed. Ibrāhīm al-Basyūnī (Cairo: al-Hayᵓah al-Miṣriyyah al-ᶜĀmmah lil-Kitāb, 1968-1971), 1: 158 on Q. 2:187.

15. *Quṭb* means axis or pole, which in Sufi tradition is typically a reference to the Perfect Man or Universal Man (*al-insān al-kāmil*). The *quṭb* is considered the leading saint of his time in Sufi tradition.

16. Ibn ᶜArabī, *al-Futūḥāt*, 5: 201.

17. Böwering, "The Concept of Time," 61.

tritt also states that in Islam, the term for a fixed moment in time or period is *waqt,* and therefore, the *mīqāt* is a particular point in time.[18]

In Islamic jurisprudence, the pilgrimage only starts when the pilgrim enters the *mīqāt.*[19] Similarly, the five daily prayers start only when the prayers enter their time (*mīqāt*). Since fasting and the breaking of the fast are dependent on the times of prayers (dawn and sunset), they too are dependent on the concept of entering a sacred time period (*mīqāt*). Evidently, Islam lends great significance to the concept of time (*waqt* and *mīqāt*) in most of its major rituals, and four of its five pillars.

DEFINITION FROM THE QUR'AN

As we have seen, the Arabic word *mīqāt* comes from the root *waqt*, meaning time. In the Qur'an, one of the names for the Day of Resurrection is *yawm al-waqt al-maᶜlūm*, which means the Day of the Known (i.e., Appointed) Time.[20]

Sūrat al-Ḥijr recounts a dialogue between God and Satan (*Iblīs*). When God commands the angels to bow down before the human into whom God has breathed His Spirit, all the angels do so except for Satan who, due to his ego, proudly refuses to obey God's command. In general, this *sūrah* in the Qur'an speaks of death, resurrection, and the Day of Resurrection from a spiritual or mystical perspective (e.g., Qur'an 15:23, 25):

> And [remember] when thy Lord said unto the angels, "Behold! I am creating a human being from dried clay, made of molded mud; so when I have proportioned him and breathed into him of My Spirit, fall down before him prostrating." Thereupon the angels prostrated, all of them together, save Iblīs. He refused to be with those who prostrated. God said, "O Iblīs! What ails

18. Otfried Weintritt, "Interpretations of Time in Islam," in *Time and History: The Variety of Cultures*, ed. Jörn Rüsen (New York, NY: Berghahn Books, 2007), 85–91.

19. Sabiq, *Fiqh al-Sunnah*, 27.

20. See Dalton Galloway, "The Resurrection and Judgement in the Koran," *The Muslim World* (1922), 12(4): 348–372; see also Wahaj D. Ahmad, "An Islamic View of Death and Dying," *Journal of the Islamic Medical Association of North America* (1996), 28(4): 175–177.

> thee that thou art not with those who prostrate?" He said, "I am not one to prostrate to a human being whom Thou hast created from dried clay, made of molded mud." He said, "Go forth from it! Surely thou art outcast, and surely the curse shall be upon thee till the Day of Judgment!" He said, "My Lord! Grant me respite till the Day they are resurrected." He said, "Then verily thou art among those granted respite till the Day of the Moment Known (*yawm al-waqt al-ma*ᶜ*lūm*)." He said, "My Lord! Since Thou hast caused me to err, I shall surely make things seem fair unto them on earth, and I shall cause them to err all together, save Thy sincere servants among them." He said, "This is a straight path unto Me. As for My servants, truly thou hast no authority over them, save for those in error who follow thee. And verily Hell shall be their tryst, all together." Seven gates it has, and for each gate is appointed a separate portion of them. [Qur'an 15:28–44]

In these verses, Satan asks God to grant him a respite until the Day of Resurrection during which he can lead humans astray. God grants this request and informs Satan that he has been granted until the Day of the Time Appointed,[21] the coming of the hour of resurrection. This dialogue, using the same name for the Day of the Time Appointed, is repeated in Qur'an 38:71–85.

The word *mīqāt* is used in various parts of the Qur'an to refer to the Day of Resurrection (e.g., Qur'an 44:40, 56:50, 78:17). Additionally, the word *mawāqīt*, from the same root, is also placed in relationship to the Ḥajj in the following verse:

> They ask thee about the new moons (*ahillah*). Say, "They are markers of time (*mawāqīt*) for humankind and for the *ḥajj*." It is not piety that you should come to houses from their rear (*ẓuhūrihā*), but piety is he who is reverent and comes into houses by their doors. So reverence God, that haply you may prosper. [Qur'an 2:189]

The word used for the new moons is *ahillah*, from the root *h-l-l*. This Arabic root is associated with many meanings, including

21. The day of the time appointed (*yawm al-waqt al-ma*ᶜ*lūm*) in Qur'an 15:38 is a description of Judgment Day (*yawm al-dīn*) in Qur'an 15:35 and the Day of Resurrection (*yawma yub*ᶜ*athūn*) in Qur'an 15:36.

crescent (*hilāl*),[22] as well as the beginning of rain.[23] The word also means to praise, as in *tahlīl*,[24] and according to the *Lisān al-ᶜarab*, it refers to the raising of a pilgrim's voice in *talbiyah* during the Ḥajj or ᶜUmrah.[25] This is based on prophetic traditions that use the terms *ahalla* and *ihlāl* for those starting *tahlīl* for Ḥajj or ᶜUmrah,[26] and specifically the use of *ahillah* to describe those entering the house threshold the *mīqāt* for Ḥajj or ᶜUmrah.[27]

Sharing the same root, *uhilla* in the sense of praising God is mentioned in the context of killing an animal for food in Qur'an 5:3, 6:145, and 16:115. The *ahillah* in reference to the Ḥajj in the Qur'an 2:138 may also be related to the sacrificial animal killed during the Ḥajj rituals, which is done in the name of God (*uhilla li-Llāh*). According to *Lisān al-ᶜarab*, the reason that a crescent is called a *hilāl* is that people raise their voices, giving news of the new lunar month. The root *h-l-l* also means a hunched-over camel, taking its name from the shape of a crescent.[28]

The second topic this verse speaks about is entering houses. As the pilgrim plans to visit and enter the House of God represented by the Sacred Mosque (*al-masjid al-ḥarām*), he is asked to enter it through its 'doors' namely, the *mīqāt*, symbolized in this verse by the plural *mawāqīt*. As the pilgrim enters the *mīqāt*, he also starts praising God (*tahlīl*) symbolized in Qur'an 2:189 by the term *ahillah*.

Notably, the word used for the backs of houses is *ẓuhūrihā*, bearing in mind that the word *ẓuhūr* also means manifestation or appearance as opposed to what is hidden (inner), *bāṭin*. We also find that in another verse, the Qur'an speaks of manifest and hidden doors.

> On the Day when the hypocrites, men and women, will say to those who believe, "Wait for us that we may borrow from your

22. *Lisān al-ᶜarab*, 11: 702–703 on "*h-l-l*."
23. Ibid.
24. Ibid.
25. Ibid.
26. Ibid.
27. Ibid.
28. *Lisān al-ᶜarab*, 11: 703–704 on *h-l-l*.

> light," it will be said, "Turn back and seek a light!" Thereupon a wall with a gate will be set down between them, the inner side (*bāṭinuhu*) of which contains mercy, and on the outer side (*ẓāhiruhu min qibalihi*) of which lies punishment. [Qur'an 57:13]

Qur'an 2:189 states that the true virtue is in the fear of God (*taqwā*), which has the same letters as time (*waqt*) transposed. The word *taqwā* is repeated throughout the Qur'an, as are the themes of the *qiblah*, the direction toward which a Muslim turns for prayer, and sacrifice (Qur'an 2:177, 22:32, 22:37).

Furthermore, in Islam, the revelation of a messenger from God to people is called *biᶜthah*, which comes from the same root as resurrection (*baᶜth*). God 'resurrects' among the people a messenger, that is, 'raises' a messenger from among those who are dead. In *Sūrat al-Mursalāt*, which speaks of the Day of Resurrection, the Qur'an uses the same root of *mīqāt* in the form of *uqqitat*: "And when the apostles are appointed a time (*uqqitat*)[29] for what day is it postponed[30] (*ujjilat*)? For the Day of Division" [Qur'an 77:11].

According to classical exegetes such as al-Ṭabarī (d. 310/923), the appointed time mentioned in Qur'an 77:11 is the Day of Resurrection, which is also the day when God will gather the messengers (Qur'an 5:109).[31] Also, al-Ṭabarī defines the postponement (*ujjilat*) in Qur'an 77:12 as a reference to the *mīqāt* of the Day of Resurrection.[32]

The Qur'an goes on to state that the appointed time has been delayed until the Day of Division (*yawm al-faṣl*) (Qur'an 77:13–15, 77:38), which is the same name used in other verses related to *mīqāt* (e.g., Qur'an 44:40, 78:17), and resembles one of the names for the Day of Resurrection.[33] Thus, the relationship

---

29. The term *uqqitat* is translated as "appointed a time," which is more faithful to the Arabic term than the *TSQ's* "slated."

30. The term *ujjilat* is translated as "postponed," instead of "appointed," as used by the *TSQ*.

31. Al-Ṭabarī, *Jāmiᶜ al-bayān fī ta'wīl al-Qur'ān*, ed. Aḥmad M. Shākir (Damascus: al-Risālah, 2000), 24: 129–130 on Q. 77:11.

32. Al-Ṭabarī, *Jāmiᶜ*, 24: 129–130 on Q. 77:12. See also Q. 15:38 and 38:81.

33. *Ibid.*, 24: 131 on Q. 77:13–15.

between *mīqāt* and the Day of Resurrection is well established in the Qur'an. It is through this door that pilgrims enter the House of God in a state of ritual consecration as dead souls awaiting their resurrection.[34]

THE *MĪQĀT* OF THE SORCERERS WITH MOSES

The word *mīqāt* is also used in the story of Moses and the sorcerers: "So the sorcerers were brought together for the appointed time[35] of an appointed day (*li-mīqāt yawm maᶜlūm*)" [Qur'an 26:38]. This verse is likened to the verse about the Day of Resurrection, which speaks of those who "are gathered for the appointed time of a day appointed (*mīqāt yawm maᶜlūm*)" [Qur'an 56:50]. We may understand from these verses that the sorcerers have entered the *mīqāt*, symbolizing their dead state, and are passing through the gateway to their resurrection. We read:

> So Moses cast his staff, and behold, it was a serpent manifest. Then he drew out his hand, and behold, it was white to the beholders. He said to the notables around him, "Truly this is a knowing sorcerer, who desires to expel you from your land with his sorcery. What would you command?" They said, "Leave him and his brother a while, and send (*ibᶜath*) marshalers (*ḥashirīn*) to the cities to bring to you every knowing sorcerer." So the sorcerers were brought together for the appointed time of an appointed day (*li-mīqāt yawm maᶜlūm*). And it was said unto the people, "Will you gather, that haply we may follow the sorcerers if they are the victors?" Then, when the sorcerers came, they said to Pharaoh, "Shall we truly have a reward if we are the victors?"\ He said, "Yes, and you shall then be among those brought nigh." Moses said to them, "Cast what you would cast!" So they cast their ropes and staffs and said, "By the might of Pharaoh, we shall surely be the victors!" Then Moses cast his staff, and behold, it devours what they make falsely! Then were the sorcerers cast down, prostrating. They said, "We believe in the Lord of the worlds, the Lord of Moses and Aaron." He [Pharaoh] said,

34. Shariati, *Hajj*, 5, 8.

35. I have modified the translation to maintain consistency with the definition of *mīqāt* in the Qur'an as an appointed time, although the *TSQ* renders it as "tryst."

> "Do you believe in Him before I give you leave? He is indeed your chief, who has taught you sorcery. You will surely know! I shall surely cut off your hands and your feet from opposite sides, and I shall surely crucify you all!" They said, "It is no harm. Truly unto our Lord do we turn. Truly we hope that our Lord will forgive us our sins for our having been the first of the believers." Then We revealed unto Moses, "Set forth with My servants by night; you shall indeed be pursued." [Qur'an 26:32–52]

These verses indicate that Pharaoh and his chiefs disbelieved in Moses and the message he brought. They claim that Moses is using sorcery. Hence, they bring in the best of illusionists, the sorcerers. The sorcerers enter the *mīqāt*. Immediately after they enter, it is asked if the other people will enter, implying that the other people have not yet done so. As the sorcerers enter the *mīqāt*, they boast, just as Satan did, that they will win, symbolizing their death and ignorance. During the challenge, the sorcerers understand that their reality is but an illusion, whereas the reality preached by Moses and Aaron is the True Reality. When the sorcerers enter the *mīqāt*, they arrive at the moment of their resurrection, *yawm al-waqt al-maᶜlūm*. As God promises in Qur'an 15:38 and 38:81 that this is the day Satan will no longer be able to deceive people, Satan (the ego) loses his hold on the sorcerers.

The sorcerers' entry into the *mīqāt* symbolizes their dead state. However, it also symbolizes that they are about to be resurrected into the understanding of True Reality which is not available to those who have not yet entered the *mīqāt*. The veils of illusion are torn asunder as the sorcerers are resurrected into genuine awareness. Immediately, they lose their ego, which has been put to death, and unlike Satan, they humbly prostrate themselves and acknowledge their belief in the God whom Moses and Aaron have been proclaiming.

When Pharaoh is asked to send heralds to call the sorcerers from the cities, the word used is *ibᶜath*, which means "resurrect." The word used for those sent to gather them in is *ḥashirīn*, derived from the root *ḥ-sh-r* found in the phrase "the Day of Resurrection" (literally, the day of gathering);[36] the Qur'an uses this term when describing the rituals of Ḥajj (Qur'an 2:203: "and remember that unto Him you will be gathered (*annakum ilayh tuḥsharūn*)"). In Qur'an 26:32–52, Pharaoh becomes a motif for God, who has the power to resurrect and send heralds, just as God sends messengers, using the term *ibᶜath*. Pharaoh is also depicted as having the power to gather people as God does, using the term *ḥāshirīn*. Further, Pharaoh's gathering of the people occurs at the time of the appointed day (*mīqāt yawm maᶜlūm*) just as God promises Satan he shall be given a respite until the day of the appointed time (*yawm al-waqt al-maᶜlūm*). The Qur'an shows that Pharaoh does what God does to differentiate between illusion and truth. In other words, while Pharaoh and his chiefs imagine that he has the power to resurrect and gather the people, the Qur'an illustrates that such power belongs to God alone.

THE *MĪQĀT* OF MOSES AND THE SEVENTY

The Qur'an also describes the appointment between God and Moses at the time of the Torah's writing as a *mīqāt*:

> And We appointed for Moses thirty nights, and We completed them with ten [more]; thus was completed the appointed term (*mīqāt*) of his Lord: forty nights. And Moses said unto his brother, Aaron, "Take my place among my people, set matters aright, and follow not the way of those who work corruption." And when Moses came to Our appointed meeting (*mīqātunā*) and his Lord spoke unto him, he said, "My Lord, show me, that I might look upon Thee." He said, "Thou shalt not see Me; but look upon the mountain: if it remains firm in its place, then thou wilt see Me." And when his Lord manifested Himself to the mountain, He made it crumble to dust, and Moses fell down in a swoon. And when he recovered, he said, "Glory be to Thee! I turn unto Thee in repentance, and I am the first of the believers."

---

36. In a *ḥadīth* that mentions a prayer to be said when a new moon (*hilāl*, plural, *ahillah*, as in Q. 2:189 concerning the *mawāqīt* of the *ḥajj*) is sighted, the Day of Resurrection is referred to as *yawm al-ḥashr*. See Ibn Abī ᶜĀṣim, *al-Sunnah li-Ibn Abī ᶜĀṣim,* ed. Muḥammad Nāṣir al-Dīn al-Albānī (Beirut: al-Maktab al-Islāmī, 1980), 1: 160 (#387).

> He said, "O Moses! Verily I have chosen thee above humankind through My messages and My speaking [unto thee]. So take that which I have given thee, and be among the thankful." And We wrote for him upon the Tablets an exhortation concerning all things, and an elaboration (*tafṣīl*) of all things. "Take hold of them with strength, and command thy people to hold to the best of them. Soon I shall show thee the abode of the iniquitous." [Qur'an 7:142–145]

As described in these verses, the *mīqāt* of Moses is also related to the Day of Resurrection. This may be seen that the name sometimes used for the Day of Resurrection is the Day of Division or Distinction (*yawm al-faṣl*), which is often used in conjunction with the word *mīqāt*. Qur'an 44:40, for example, reads: "Verily, the Day of Distinction is the term appointed for all of them (*inna yawm al-faṣl mīqātuhum ajmaᶜīn*)."[37]

As shown earlier, according to the Qur'an, God's messengers are resurrected among the people, who are represented as dead—hence the term *biᶜthah*. Deuteronomy uses the Hebrew term *aqim* (to raise) when it describes God raising a prophet among the people (e.g., Deuteronomy 18:18), or when stating that no prophet like Moses, who knew God face to face, had arisen in Israel (Deuteronomy 34:10). The root *q-w-m* means to rise or raise in Hebrew, Aramaic,[38] and Arabic[39] and is likened to the word *biᶜthah*. It is the word most commonly used in the Qur'an for the Day of Resurrection (e.g., Qur'an 2:212).

Qur'an 9:36 states that there are twelve months in a year, of which four are sacred, although it does not specify what those four months are. According to a *ḥadīth*, the sacred months are Rajab, Dhul-Qiᶜdah, Dhul-Ḥijjah, and Muḥarram.[40] Only Rajab is not consecutive with the other three. The consecutive months are considered sacred because they are the months during which

---

37. See also Qur'an 44:40, 77:11–14, 78:17). *Tafṣīl,* which means explaining, splitting, or dividing, thereby implying the division between truth and falsehood, is also used in the *mīqāt* of Moses. See *Lisān al-ᶜarab*, 11: 521–524 on *f-ṣ-l*.

38. *BDB*, 877–879.

39. *Lisān al-ᶜarab*, 12: 496 on *q-w-m*.

40. *Ṣaḥīḥ al-Bukhārī*, 6: 66 (#4662), 7: 100 (#5550). *Ṣaḥīḥ Muslim*, 3: 1305 (#1679).

pilgrims typically complete the Ḥajj. Although a pilgrim may enter the *mīqāt* as early as the month of Shawwāl, the month preceding Dhul-Qiᶜdah, it is not a sacred month. The juristic rulings that allow a pilgrim to enter the state of *iḥrām* as early as Shawwāl are not based on any Qur'anic teaching or prophetic tradition; rather, they are based on opinions of the Prophet's companions according to which the months of Ḥajj are Shawwāl, Dhul-Qiᶜdah, and the first ten days of Dhul-Ḥijjah.[41]

However, a pilgrim may enter the *mīqāt* and remain in a state of *iḥrām* during sacred months for the thirty nights of Dhul-Qiᶜdah and the first ten nights of Dhul-Ḥijjah until the Feast of Sacrifice. Extrapolating from the Qur'an, these forty nights might be symbolic of the period of time (*mīqāt*) during which God spoke to Moses and raised him into an understanding of everything written on the Tablets. This is especially the case in how the Qur'an presents this period as thirty nights and added them with ten more (Qur'an 9:142).

The sacredness of the month of Rajab is closely related to the Prophet's Night Journey (*miᶜrāj*), symbolized by the ᶜUmrah, as will be discussed later. Consequently, it sheds light on the old Islamic debate over the performance of ᶜUmrah during Rajab, and whether or not the Prophet ﷺ performed it in that month.[42]

41. *Ṣaḥīḥ al-Bukhārī*, 2: 141.

42. *Ṣaḥīḥ al-Bukhārī*, 3: 2 (#1775), 3: 2 (#1776), 5: 142 (#4253); al-Tirmidhī, *Sunan al-Tirmidhī*, eds. Aḥmad M. Shākir, Muḥammad F. ᶜAbdulbāqī, Ibrāhīm A. ᶜAwaḍ (Cairo: Muṣṭafa al-Bābī al-Ḥalabī, 1975), 3: 265 (#936); al-Maqdisī, *al-Muntaqā min masmūᶜāt maruw* [manuscript], 124; ᶜAbdullāh ibn ᶜUmar claimed that the Prophet performed the ᶜUmrah during Rajab, while ᶜĀiʾshah denied this. According to some Muslim scholars, including Ibn Bāz, it is highly likely that ᶜĀiʾshah did not know of the Prophet's ᶜUmrah during Rajab. See Saᶜīd al-Qaḥṭānī, *Manāsik al-Ḥajj wal-ᶜUmrah fil-Islām fī ḍawʾ al-kitāb wal-sunnah* (al-Qasab: Markaz al-Daᶜwah wal-Irshād, 2010), 596. Ibn Baṭṭūṭah even narrates that the people of Mecca used to prepare for the ᶜUmrah in Rajab. See Ibn Baṭṭūṭah, *Tuḥfah al-nuẓẓār fī gharāʾib al-amṣār wa-ᶜajāʾib al-asfār* (Rabat: Akādīmiyyah al-Mamlakah al-Maghribiyyah, 1997), 1: 400–402. It is also said that pre-Islamic Arabs used to perform the ᶜUmrah during Rajab. On this note, see al-Rāzī, *Mafātīḥ al-ghayb* (Beirut: Iḥyāʾ al-Turāth al-ᶜArabī, 2000), 32: 97 on Q. 106:1–2. According to Shīᶜī teachings, Rajab is the best month in which to perform the ᶜUmrah; see al-Majlisī, *Biḥār al-anwār*, 96: 331–332, 110: 355.

In pre-Islamic Arabia, the consecutive sacred months were those during which the Arabs would travel for pilgrimage, whereas Rajab was designated for the ᶜUmrah.[43]

The Qur'an tells us that when Moses returns to his people, he finds that they have been led astray. He then takes seventy of his people to meet the Lord, which is also described as a *mīqāt*.

> And Moses chose seventy men from his people for Our meeting (*mīqātun*ā). And when the earthquake (*rajfah*) seized them, he said, "My Lord! Hadst Thou willed, Thou wouldst have destroyed them and me beforehand. Wilt Thou destroy us for that which the fools among us have done? It is naught but Thy trial, whereby Thou leadest astray whomsoever Thou wilt, and guidest whomsoever Thou wilt. Thou art our Protector, so forgive us and have mercy upon us, and Thou art the best of forgivers!" [Qur'an 7:155]

The seventy people whom Moses has taken to the *mīqāt* are swallowed up by an earthquake (*rajfah*). The same word is used in various parts of the Qur'an for the earth quaking on the Day of Resurrection (Qur'an 73:14, 79:6). This quaking may not be very different from what Moses experienced earlier during his *mīqāt*, which reduced the mountain to dust and caused him to fall in a swoon or death after he asked God to reveal His face (Qur'an 7:143). Such quakes are also described in other parts of the Qur'an, which speaks of "a day when the earth and the mountains shake (*yawm tarjuf al-arḍ wal-jibāl*)" [Qur'an 73:14] and "the Day when the quaker quakes (*yawm tarjuf al-rājifah*)" [Qur'an 79:6].

---

43. Pre-Islamic Arabs designated the month of Rajab for the ᶜUmrah, which is why the tribe of Muḍar considered Rajab a sacred month. Hence, it is sometimes called the Rajab of Muḍar. See Ibn Rajab al-Ḥanbalī, *Laṭāʾif al-maᶜārif fīmā li-mawāsim al-ᶜām min al-waẓāʾif* (Beirut: Ibn Ḥazm, 2004), 259; see also Muḥammad al-Ṭāhir Ibn ᶜĀshūr, *al-Taḥrīr wal-tanwīr* (Tunis: Al-al-Tūnisiyyah, 1984), 2: 211 on Q. 2:194, 2: 231 on Q. 2:197; Jawād ᶜAlī, *al-Mufaṣṣil fī tarīkh al-ᶜarab qabl al-Islām* (Beirut: al-Sāqī, 2001), 11: 392; al-ᶜUthaymīn, *Majmūᶜ fatāwā wa-rasāʾil faḍīlat al-shaykh Muḥammad ibn Ṣāliḥ al-ᶜUthaymīn*, ed. Fahd al-Sulaymān (Riyadh: al-Waṭan, 2001), 22: 273, 22: 276. On the naming of Rajab as "Rajab Muḍar" in prophetic traditions, see *Ṣaḥīḥ al-Bukhārī*, 4: 107 (#3197).

THE *MĪQĀT* OF JESUS

According to Mark 1:15, Jesus tells his disciples that the time, which is the Greek term *kairos* (*mīqāt*), had come upon them and that, therefore, the Kingdom of God was near. According to John 7:6–8, during the Feast of the Tabernacles, Jesus refused to go out in public, for he said that his time, using the Greek term *kairos* (*mīqāt*), had not yet come. Hence, John goes on to state that even when Jesus was teaching in the temple, the Jews tried to seize him, but they could not, for his hour (*hōra*) had not yet come (John 7:30).

In Luke 9:51, as Jesus' days (*hēmeras*) drew to a close, he set out for Jerusalem. Before the Last Supper, Jesus told his disciples to inform a certain man that his appointed time (*kairos*) (*al-waqt al-maᶜlūm*) was near so that the room in the house could be prepared for the Last Supper (Matthew 26:18). We are told in John 13:1 that Jesus knew his hour (*hōra*) had come before the Last Supper. During the meal, Jesus broke bread and distributed it, proclaiming it his flesh. Then he poured wine in a cup and distributed it, proclaiming it his blood (Matthew 26:26–29). The symbols of the bread and the wine may be interpreted based on both Genesis and the Qur'an as death (crucifixion) and life. This interpretation comes from those scriptures in which Joseph interpreted these symbols in the dreams of the cupbearer and baker who were with him in prison (Qur'an 12:36, 12:41, Genesis 40:9–13, 16–19).[44] The cupbearer, symbolizing wine, was granted life in three days, while the baker, symbolizing bread, was crucified in three days. Perhaps the resurrection of Jesus three days after the wine and bread uses the same motif as the dreams of the cupbearer and baker in Genesis.

The bread may signify that the *mīqāt* has arrived and that the hour of resurrection is near. The wine signifies blood, which is life,[45] and therefore resurrection.[46] In the Gospels, this symbolism shows how Jesus was crucified and then was resurrected three

44. Galadari, "Joseph and Jesus."
45. Compare with Leviticus 17:11–14.
46. Compare with John 6:53–56.

days after the Last Supper. However, this was not the only time in the Gospel of John that Jesus had people drink wine. He also did so at the time of his first miracle during a wedding in Cana when he changed water into wine, which, according to John, occurred on the third day (John 2:1). However, Jesus was reluctant to perform this miracle, perhaps because the symbolism of the wine ordinarily would have meant that his time (*mīqāt)* was near. Hence, when Jesus performed the miracle in Cana, John narrates that Jesus explicitly said that his hour (*hōra*) had not yet come (John 2:4).

According to John 17:1, Jesus states during the Last Supper that his hour (*hōra*) has come and asks God to glorify him (*doxason*). John alludes to the glorification (*doxasei*) of Jesus by describing the method of his death and crucifixion (John 21:19). Hence, one may understand that the *mīqāt* of Jesus in the Gospel of John symbolizes his death and the imminence of his resurrection.

According to the Gospels, Jesus was crucified on Passover. The books of Exodus and Numbers call Passover the appointed time using the Hebrew *môᶜădā* (Exodus 13:10, 34:18, Numbers 9:2–3, 9:7, 9:13). Leviticus 23:4 tells us that all the Feasts (pilgrimages) are considered to have appointed times, just as the Ḥajj is described in the Qur'an (Qur'an 2:197, 22:28).

The son of perdition in 2 Thessalonians 2:6 would come during his time (*kairō*). The time (*kairos*) for the resurrection and judgment of the dead is mentioned in Revelation 11:18 and 22:10. In the Qur'an, the Day of Resurrection (Day of Judgment) is also called the Hour (*al-sāᶜah*), which morphologically may resemble the name of Jesus (*Yasūᶜ* or *Yešuᶜ*).[47] The term *šaᶜătā* also means hour in Aramaic (e.g., Daniel 3:6. 3:15, 4:19, 4:33, 5:5).[48]

However, the Qur'an frequently associates the Day of Resurrection with a sound, in particular, a cry (e.g., Qur'an 36:49, 36:53, 50:42) while the meaning of the root *š-w-ᶜ* in Aramaic and

47. The Arabic name is *Yasūᶜ* from the Aramaic and Hebrew *Yešuᶜ*.

48. Wilhelm Gesenius, *Gesenius' Hebrew and Chaldee lexicon to the Old Testament Scriptures*, trans. Samuel P. Tregelles (Bellingham, WA: Logos Bible Software, 2003), 841.

Hebrew also means a cry, especially for help,[49] besides also meaning (as *y-š-ᶜ*) salvation.[50] As such, the Qur'anic use of *al-sāᶜah* for the Day of Resurrection may mean not just an hour, but also a cry, consistent with the symbolism of the Qur'an. Nonetheless, symbolizing the Day of Resurrection as a time (*waqt*) is also attested, and therefore, the polysemous nature of the term *sāᶜah* might be intended. The following Qur'anic verse brings the terms hour (*sāᶜah*) and time (*waqt*) together.

> They question thee about the Hour (*al-sāᶜah*), when it will set in. Say, "Knowledge thereof lies only with my Lord. None save He shall manifest it at its appointed time (*li-waqtihā*).[51] Heavy shall it weigh upon the heavens and the earth. It shall not come upon you but suddenly." They question thee as if thou knew it well. Say, "Knowledge thereof lies only with God, but most of humankind know not." [Qur'an 7:187]

THE *MĪQĀT* OF PRAYER

Prayer is also described in the Qur'an by the root for *mīqāt*:

> When you have completed the prayer, remember [and invoke] God, standing, sitting, or lying on your sides. Then when you are secure, observe proper prayer, for prayer at fixed hours (*kitāban mawqūtā* / a timed book) is prescribed for the believers. [Qur'an 4:103]

First, to shed light on *mīqāt* and prayers, it should be pointed out how prayer is *itself* resurrected. Throughout the body of the Qur'an, the command to pray is usually conjoined with a word sharing the same root as *qiyām* (e.g., Qur'an 17:78), which is the same root used for the Day of Resurrection (*yawm al-qiyāmah*). *Iqām al-ṣalāh*, which is the raising of prayer, is the second pillar of Islam.[52] The understanding of *iqām al-ṣalāh* as the act of rising *for* prayer is a misnomer. It is not an instruction for people to rise

49. *TDOT*, 14: 532–536; *BDB*, 1002–1003.

50. *BDB*, 221.

51. I translate this as "appointed time", consistent with other instances of *waqt*. The *TSQ* translates it as "proper time."

52. *Ṣaḥīḥ al-Bukhārī*, 1: 11 (#8).

for prayer, but rather, to *raise* or *resurrect* the prayer.[53]

It is noteworthy that five different locations exist for the *mīqāt* of Ḥajj or ᶜUmrah, which is the same as the number of daily obligatory prayers described as a timed book (*kitāban mawqūtā*).[54] This is something that Ibn ᶜArabī also makes a note of in his *Futūḥāt*.[55]

When God instructs Abraham to proclaim the Ḥajj, the word used for this proclamation is *adhdhin*; its root means to make known, to cry out, to give permission, or to give ear.[56]

> And proclaim (*adhdhin*) the *ḥajj* among humankind: they shall come to thee on foot and upon all [manner of] lean beast, coming from all deep and distant mountain highways, [Qur'an 22:27]

The call to prayer is also called *adhān*. The *adhān* announces that the prayer time (*waqt*) has arrived. This is the *mīqāt* of prayer, symbolizing that the prayer is dead and its hour of resurrection (*iqāmah*) is near. The actual prayer is performed after the call for *iqāmah*. Just as in Ḥajj or ᶜUmrah, the pilgrim enters a state of *iḥrām* at the *mīqāt* and, during later rituals, is resurrected, in the same way prayer enters its *mīqāt*, and is resurrected. Thus, a relationship seems to exist between prayer and resurrection, as prayer uses similar motifs to that used for resurrection.

REFLECTIONS ON *WAQT* AND *MĪQĀT*

As discussed, in many instances the terms for time (*waqt*) and hour (*sāᶜah*) in the Bible and the Qur'an are used to denote death and resurrection. When comparing this use in scriptures as well as rituals, the strong relationship between the concept of time

---

53. An example of people rising to pray (as opposed to raising the prayer) is found in Qur'an 4:142, which tells us that "when they [the hypocrites] rise to pray (*wa idhā qāmū ilā al-ṣalāh*), they rise reluctantly (*qāmū kasālā*), only to be seen and praised by people, remembering God but seldom."

54. According to Muslim tradition, the five obligatory daily prayers are gifts from God that were ordained during the Night Journey of the Prophet, which is likened to the rituals of the ᶜUmrah, to be discussed later. See *Ṣaḥīḥ al-Bukhārī*, 5: 52 (#3887).

55. Ibn ᶜArabī, *al-Futūḥāt*, 2: 432–433.

56. *Lisān al-ᶜarab*, 13: 9–14 on *ʾ-dh-n*.

(*waqt*) and death and resurrection becomes highly likely. The pilgrim enters the *mīqāt* to denote his death and later resurrection. Prayers enter the *mīqāt* to denote their death and later resurrection (*iqāmah*). Time (*mīqāt*) is the gateway to death and resurrection.

3

MECCA AND KAᶜBAH: *ṬAWĀF* DURING *IḤRĀM*

After a pilgrim enters the *mīqāt* in a state of *iḥrām*, symbolizing death, she or he then begins the *talbiyah*, which means that she has accepted the call of God to visit His House, the Sacred Mosque (*al-masjid al-ḥarām*). This chapter looks into the details of the rituals of *ṭawāf* around the Kaᶜbah during the state of *iḥrām*.

TALBIYAH

The *talbiyah*, which is uttered during both the Ḥajj and the ᶜUmrah, is usually understood to mean that the pilgrim has heard and answered the call for Ḥajj. According to Khalil Abu-Rahma, the *talbiyah* in pre-Islamic Arabia represented a struggle between Allāh and the inferior deities in Arabia.[1] *Tafsīr al-Qur'ān* (Commentary on the Qur'an) by Muqātil ibn Sulaymān (d. 150/767) and *Kitāb al-aṣnām* (The Book of Idols) by Ibn al-Kalbī (d. 204/819) show how the *talbiyah* in pre-Islamic Arabia was a

1. Khalil Abu-Rahma, "A Reading in Talbiyat of the Jahili Arabs," *Arab Journal for the Humanities* (1987), 7(27).

method for the Arabian tribes to assert Allāh's authority over the inferior Arabian deities, such as al-Lāt, al-ᶜUzza, and Manāt, all of whom are named in the Qur'an (Qur'an 53:19–20).[2]

The *talbiyah* is so named because its first phrase is *labbayk*, which has been understood to mean different things. *Lisān al-ᶜarab* shows that the root of *talbiyah* could be either *l-b-y*, *l-b-ʾ*, or *l-b-b*. The root *l-b-y* means the remnant of a plant,[3] while *l-b-ʾ* means a lioness or the colostrum of a nursing mammal.[4] Although the meaning of the *talbiyah* evolved in Arabic due to its use in the Ḥajj and the ᶜUmrah (even in pre-Islamic Arabia), its polysemous sense might be closely related to the root *l-b-b*, meaning heart (*lubbī* would mean "my heart").[5] The *k* suffix in Arabic grammar means "yours." Hence, from the pronouncement of the *talbiyah*, beginning with *labbayk*, it may be understood that the pilgrim is stating, "My heart is Yours, oh God."

The *lubb* generally means the inside of something, the mind, or the intellect,[6] and not necessarily the physical muscle we today call the heart. Hence, the phrase *labbayk* may mean that the pilgrim's heart belongs to God, (or that the pilgrim's heart is God's heart.) The Kaᶜbah itself is possibly a symbol of the heart in the Qur'an, as it may be seen to be connected with the *Shemaᶜ* passages in Deuteronomy that emphasize the role of the heart:[7]

> Hear O Israel, the Lord our God, the Lord alone. You shall love the Lord your God with all your heart, and with all your soul, and with all your might. Keep these words that I am commanding you today in your heart. [Deuteronomy 6:4–6]

If the *qiblah* is taken to be the heart, and the House of God is in

---

2. Florella Scagliarini, "The Word ṣlm/ṣnm and Some Words for 'Statue, Idol' in Arabian and Other Semitic Languages," *Proceedings of the Seminār for Arabian Studies*, 37: 253–262, 27–29 July 2006, London, UK. The accuracy and reliability of these accounts may be subject to question, as they were written much later in Muslim history.

3. *Lisān al-ᶜarab*, 15: 238-239, on *l-b-y*.

4. *Ibid.*, 1: 15–152, on *l-b-ʾ*.

5. *Lisān al-ᶜarab*, 15: 238–239, on *l-b-y* and 1: 729 on *l-b-b*.

6. *Ibid.*, 1: 729 on *l-b-b*. Also see *BDB*, 523–525; see also *TDOT*, 400–401.

7. For more on the Kaᶜbah as a symbol of the heart, see Galadari, "The *Qibla*."

the heart, the term *labbayk* may be interpreted as meaning that the pilgrim is accepting that his heart should become the *qiblah* by transforming it into the House or Temple of God without any idols or inferior deities. In other words, the House of God, the heart, is freed from ego, which is the major idol or stumbling block in the soul's journey to God.

MECCA

MOTHER OF CITIES

To understand the Ḥajj or the [c]Umrah, we need to understand where the pilgrim intends to go and what he intends to visit. There are three different veils or layers that the pilgrim seeks to penetrate. The pilgrim intends to visit Mecca, also known as Umm al-Qurā (Mother of Cities). In the heart of Mecca (*bi-baṭn Mecca*) (Qur'an 48:24), the pilgrim intends to visit the Sacred Mosque (*al-Masjid al-Ḥarām*). In the heart of the Sacred Mosque, the pilgrim intends to visit the Ka[c]bah. Hence, it can be seen that there are three things enveloped in one another. Like *l-b-b*, the root *b-ṭ-n* means the interior or the inside.[8] Those three covers of Mecca's *baṭn* may be seen as similar to the three layers or veils of darkness in which a foetus is enveloped according to the Qur'an. In the following passage, note the use of the keywords *baṭn* and *buṭūn* along with the term *ummahātikum*, which resonates with Umm al-Qurā (Mecca):

> He created you from a single soul, then made from it its mate, and sent down for you of cattle eight pairs. He creates you in your mothers' wombs (*buṭūn ummahātikum*), creation after creation, in threefold darkness. That is God, your Lord; to Him belongs sovereignty. There is no god but He. How, then, are you turned away? [Qur'an 39:6]

Similarly, the focal point of Jewish prayers is Jerusalem,[9] inside Jerusalem is the Temple, and inside the Temple is the Holy of Holies, three things enveloped in one another. Anyone outside

8. *TDOT*, 2: 94–95.

9. Shubert Spero, "Turning to Jerusalem in Prayer," *Jewish Bible Quarterly* (2003), 31(2): 97–100.

Palestine turns his face towards the land of Israel and recites the prayer. One who is in the Holy Land turns towards Jerusalem. One who is in Jerusalem turns towards the Temple. If one is in the Temple, he turns towards the Holy of Holies. A person, who is blind, unable to determine the right direction, or on a ship, simply directs his heart to the Divine Presence when praying.[10]

MECCA

Mecca is the site of the Sacred Mosque, *al-Masjid al-Ḥarām*, and the Kaᶜbah. The name of Mecca as a city is mentioned only once in the Qur'an:

> He it is Who restrained their hands from you and your hands from them in the valley (*bi-baṭn*) of Mecca, after having made you victorious over them. And God sees whatsoever you do. [Qur'an 48:24]

The Arabic root *makata* means to rise, as in *aqām.*[11] Additionally, it means to fill with *qayḥ*, which is blood.[12] If the root of the word is *m-k-k* instead of *m-k-t*, then it will mean to request fervently.[13] In Aramaic, *mkk* means to humiliate, to subdue, to be low, and to humble.[14] Furthermore, it means to pull or draw (water) in Arabic and Aramaic.[15] In Hebrew and Aramaic, *makka* means to crush, to blow, to slaughter, to wound, a disaster or plague, and it is used as such in the Hebrew Bible.[16] In Aramaic, *makkata* is the feminine form of the word meaning humility.[17]
There are thus various hypotheses on the meaning of the name

10. Hilkot Tefillah 5:3.

11. Murtaḍā al-Zabīdī, *Tāj al-ᶜarūs min jawāhir al-qāmūs*, al-Hidāyah, no date, 5: 96.

12. *Lisān al-ᶜarab*, 2: 90.

13. *Ibid.*, 10: 491. Also in the *ḥadīth*, "Do not request fervently against your debtors (*Lā tumakkikū ᶜala ghuramāᵓikum*)." See Abu ᶜUbayd al-Qāsim ibn Salām, *Gharīb al-ḥadīth* (ed. Muḥammad ᶜAbdul-Muᶜīd Khān), Hyderabad: Dāᵓirat al-Maᶜārif al-ᶜUthmāniyyah, 1964, 3: 122.

14. *BDB,* 568.

15. *Lisān al-ᶜarab*, 10: 490–491; see also *BDB,* 568.

16. Ludwig Koehler and Walter Baumgartner, *The Hebrew and Aramaic Lexicon of the Old Testament* (Leiden: Brill, 2000),579.

17. *Targum Lexicon.*

of Mecca. From the meaning to pull or draw, it could have taken its name from its capacity to draw out the sins of those within it; given its lack of water, it could mean that water has been drawn out of it.[18] The name could also derive from how Mecca draws people in to perform the Ḥajj or the ^cUmrah,[19] or even that it destroys a person, or that its people struggle.[20]

Further, it is possible that the Arabs of the time, returning to the original meaning of *m-k-k*, called the city Mecca because it lies in a valley, which is low ("subdued") ground. In a possible reference to Mecca, the Greco-Egyptian geographer Ptolemy mentioned a place in Arabia called Makoraba.[21] The name may also derive from the Sabaic term *makrab* or *mikrab,* meaning temple.[22] According to Daum, the term *mukarrib* is derived from *hakrabah*, which means to marry a woman.[23] Therefore, he states, Mecca (Makoraba) might have been a pilgrimage place in ancient Arabia where a pilgrim (*mukarrib*) would perform a sacred marriage. Further, Makoraba might have roots in *k-r-b*, meaning to plough or to suffer, or in *q-r-b*, meaning near, or a place of sacrifice. It is possible that the meaning as a place of sacrifice or sacrificial offering (*qurbān*) is what made the name synonymous with any temple in southern Arabia.

There is insufficient evidence to conclude that Ptolemy's Makoraba is Mecca of ancient Arabia. Since it is a Sabaic name from ancient Yemen, it might well have been a location in Yemen. Whether or not Ptolemy's Makoraba is Mecca or any other city in Arabia is irrelevant. If it was, it seems likely that the

---

18. Sirāj al-Dīn al-Nu^cmānī, *al-Lubāb fī ^culūm al-kitāb*, ed. ^cĀdil Mu^cawwaḍ (Beirut: al-Kutub al-^cIlmiyyah, 1998), 5: 398.

19. Ibn al-Jawzī, *Muthīr al-^cazm al-sākin ila ashraf al-amākin*, ed. Marzūq ^cAlī Ibrāhīm (no place: al-Rāyah, 1995), 1: 324 (#191).

20. Ibid.

21. Michael Wolfe, ed., *One Thousand Roads to Mecca: Ten Centuries of Travelers Writing about the Muslim Pilgrimage* (New York, NY: Grove, 1997), xv; see also Ilya P. Petrushevsky, *Islam in Iran* (Albany, NY: State University of New York Press), 1985, 3.

22. Werner Daum, "A Pre-Islamic Rite in South Arabia," *Journal of the Royal Asiatic Society* (1987), 119: 5–14.

23. Ibid., 14.

name Makoraba could be derived from the root *q-r-b* and used to mean the place for a sacrificial offering.

SACRED MOSQUE AND KAᶜBAH

The Qur'an calls the Kaᶜbah *al-Bayt al-Ḥarām*, which means the Sacred House (Qur'an 5:97). However, in matters of the *qiblah*, which is the focal point of Muslim prayers, the Qur'an only refers to *al-Masjid al-Ḥarām*, and not specifically the Kaᶜbah (Qur'an 2:144, 2:149–150). The root name of the Kaᶜbah has many different meanings in Arabic. The simplest meaning is a 'cube' or that which has four corners. Additionally, it means the joints of bones.[24] Thus, in the matters of ablution (*wuḍūʾ*), the Qur'an specifies that the feet be cleansed to the ankle joints (*al-kaᶜbayn*).

> O you who believe! When you rise to perform the prayer, wash your faces, and your hands up to the elbows, and wipe your heads and your feet up to the ankles (*al-kaᶜbayn*). If you are in a state of major ritual impurity, then purify yourselves. But if you are ill, or on a journey, or one of you has come from satisfying a call of nature, or you have touched women, and you find no water, then resort to clean earth, and wipe therewith your faces and your hands. God desires not to place burden upon you, but He desires to purify you, and to complete His Blessing upon you, that haply you may give thanks. [Qur'an 5:6]

The Kaᶜbah has four corners, a) the Eastern Corner (*al-rukn al-sharqī*), also called the Black Corner (*al-rukn al-aswad*), where the Black Stone (*al-ḥajar al-aswad*) resides,[25] b) the ᶜIrāqī Corner (*al-rukn al-ᶜirāqī*), which is toward the north, c) the Western Corner (*al-rukn al-gharbī*), also called the Shāmi Corner (*al-rukn al-shāmī*), and d) the Yamānī Corner (*al-rukn al-yamānī*).[26] These corners are almost the same as the cardinal coordinates.[27] Hence, their names are based on their respective directions.

24. *Lisān al-ᶜarab*, 1: 717–718 on *k-ᶜ-b*.

25. The term ᶜIrāqī Corner is not widely found among early scholars; see Badr al-Dīn al-ᶜAynī, *ᶜUmdah al-qārī*, 3: 26. It does not seem to have much support and is an anomaly.

26. Ibn Jubayr, *Riḥlat Ibn Jubay* (Beirut: al-Hilāl, no date), 53.

27. Ibid., 53.

Being the House of God (Qur'an 5:97), the Kaᶜbah is traditionally believed to be the earthly temple beneath the heavenly temple known as the Built House (*al-bayt al-maᶜmūr*) (Qur'an 52:4).[28] *Al-bayt al-maᶜmūr*, which is said to be similar to the Kaᶜbah in heaven, where the angels and others there worship God, and which the Prophet saw in his Night Journey, [29] is described in a *ḥadīth* as being right below the Throne of God.[30] Hence, it might be compared to the heavenly Jerusalem in the Bible (e.g., Revelation 3:12, 21:2).

If the Kaᶜbah is below *al-bayt al-maᶜmūr*, which in turn is located beneath the Throne of God, then it is well named. Given that the *kaᶜb* is described by the Qur'an as the ankle joint, then the Kaᶜbah may be thought of as the pedestal or footstool of God, being the earthly temple subdued by His Might in Mecca. Compare this to what is written in the Psalms, where we read, "Let us go to his dwelling place; let us worship at his footstool!" (Psalms 137:7), where the term *hădōm raglāy* is used for a footstool, while keeping in mind the term *rěgālîm* that means pilgrimage, which is undertaken by foot (*rijālan*) according to Qur'an 22:27. Similarly, we read in Psalm 99:5, "Exalt the LORD our God and worship at His footstool (*hădōm raglāy*); he is Holy." Isaiah 66:1 asks, seemingly rhetorically, what kind of house will be built for God, since the heavens are His Throne and the earth His footstool: "This is what the LORD SAYS: 'HEAVEN IS MY THRONE, AND THE EARTH IS MY FOOTSTOOL (*hădōm raglāy*). Where is the house you will build for me? Where will my resting place be?'" (Isaiah 66:1). The next verse, Isaiah 66:2, considers these things made by God. It reads, "Has not my hand made all these things, and so they came into being?' declares the Lord." This may

---

28. Al-Ghazālī, *Iḥyāʾ*, 1: 269; see also al-Suyūṭī, *al-Ḥabāʾik fī akhbār al-malāʾik*, ed. Muḥammad Zaghlūl (Beirut: al-Kutub al-ᶜIlmiyyah), 15; Mohsin Akhtar, *Oracle of the Last and Final Message: History and the Philosophical Deductions of the Life of Prophet Muhammad* (Bloomington, IN: Xlibris Corporation, 2008), 353–355.

29. *Ṣaḥīḥ al-Bukhārī*, 4: 109 (#3207), 5: 52 (#3887).

30. Al-Azraqī, *Akhbār Mecca wa-mā jāʾ fīhā min al-āthār*, ed. Rushdī Mulḥis (Beirut: al-Andalus, no date), 1: 35.

imply that no human can build a house for God. In this sense, if the Kaᶜbah is considered the footstool of God's Throne, then it may only symbolize it, since it was made by human hands, and not the hands of God, according to Isaiah 66:1–2.

The pilgrim circles the Kaᶜbah during the *ṭawāf* for the ᶜUmrah, or *ṭawāf al-qudūm* (the circumambulation of arrival) for those performing the Ḥajj without the ᶜUmrah. The root of *qudūm* is *q-d-m*, among whose derivatives is the word *qadam* (foot),[31] as the pilgrim is circumambulating at the foot of the Throne of God, which is the earthly temple. The root *q-d-m* also yields words meaning front, arrive, lead, precede, old, ancient, and bring near.[32] This semantic field also applies to the root *q-d-m* in Hebrew, which means east,[33] as the pilgrim begins the circumambulation at the Eastern Corner.[34]

In classical Jewish thought, the Temple of Jerusalem was similarly considered to be the footstool of God due to the location of the Ark of the Covenant in the Holy of Holies inside the Temple, and is frequently referred to as God's footstool in the Bible (Psalm 132:7–8, Lamentations 2:1, Isaiah 60:13–14).[35] The following passages are illustrative:

> King David rose to his feet (*raglāy*) and said: "Listen to me, my brothers, my people. I had it in my heart to build a house as a place of rest for the ark of the covenant of the LORD, for the footstool (*la-hădōm raglê*) of our God, and I made plans to build it." [1 Chronicles 28:2]

As *al-Masjid al-Ḥarām* is the *qiblah*, this is the pilgrim's focal point. The word *qiblah* is derived from the root *q-b-l*, from which we get the words to receive, to accept, to kiss, front, and

---

31. *Lisān al-ᶜarab*, 12: 470 on *q-d-m*.

32. Ibid., 12: 465–470 on *q-d-m*.

33. *Enhanced Brown-Driver Briggs,* 869–870.

34. Ibid., 870.

35. Elliot R. Wolfson, "Images of God's Feet: Some Observations on the Divine Body in Judaism," in *People of the Body: Jews and Judaism from an Embodied Perspective*, ed. Howard Eilberg-Schwartz (Albany, NY: State University of New York Press, 1992), 143–181, esp. 150.

opposite.[36] In Qur'an 2:127 Abraham and Ishmael ask God to accept (*taqabbal*) their labors toward building the house of worship which we presumed to be the Kaᶜbah.

CIRCUMAMBULATION *(ṬAWĀF)*

ṬAWĀF IN THE WATER OF LIFE

When the pilgrim arrives in Mecca and enters *al-Masjid al-Ḥarām*, he circumambulates the Kaᶜbah seven times, beginning and ending with the Black Stone. Some scholars consider circumambulation to be the most important act to perform when visiting the Kaᶜbah, especially for those not from Mecca.[37] Gerald Hawting provides many examples from classical scholars of Islamic traditions and jurisprudence on the supremacy of circumambulating the Kaᶜbah over entering the Kaᶜbah itself and praying inside.[38] Hence, the status of the *ṭawāf* ritual is considered superior to that of others performed in and around the Kaᶜbah.

Ṭawāf comes from the Arabic root *ṭ-w-f* or *ṭ-y-f* meaning to wander about, the darkness of the night, dream, fantasy, insanity, anger, and spectrum. From it, we derive the word *ṭāʾifah*, meaning part of a group, or a sect.[39] The root *ṭ-f-y*, a transformed and permuted morphology, means to float or to immerse.[40] The meanings of the root *ṭ-f-y* in Arabic are related to the meanings of the Aramaic roots of *ṭ-w-p* meaning to flow over.[41] In Aramaic, the root *ṭ-w-p* also means to float, to immerse, to overflow, to swim, to be flooded, to sail, to wander, or stream.[42] Moreover, pilgrims might be said to be "floating" around the Kaᶜbah. As previously stated, the Kaᶜbah is understood symbolically to be

36. *Lisān al-ᶜarab*, 11: 536–547 on *q-b-l*.

37. This is based on the opinions of Ibn ᶜAbbās, Saᶜīd ibn Jubayr, ᶜAṭāʾ, and Mujāhid. See al-Nawawī, *al-Īḍāḥ*, 392.

38. Gerald R. Hawting, " 'We Were Not Ordered with Entering It but Only with Circumambulating It.' Ḥadīth and fiqh on Entering the Kaᶜba," *Bulletin of the School of Oriental and African Studies* (1984) 47(2): 228–242.

39. *Lisān al-ᶜarab*, 9: 225-228 on *ṭ-w-f* and *ṭayyāf*.

40. *Ibid.*, 10: 15 on *ṭ-f-y*.

41. *The Hebrew and Aramaic Lexicon of the Old Testament*, 373.

42. *Targum Lexicon*, on *ṭ-w-p*.

below *al-bayt al-maᶜmūr*, which is in turn below the Throne of God that the Qur'an tells us was upon water. Qur'an 11:7 reads:

> He it is Who created the heavens and the earth in six Days--and His Throne was over the waters—that He might try you, which of you is best in conduct. But if you were to say to them, "You shall indeed be raised up after death", the Unbelievers would be sure to say, "This is nothing but obvious sorcery!"

In the Islamic tradition, the act of *ṭawāf* mirrors that of the angels in heaven as they circumambulate the Throne of God or *al-bayt al-maᶜmūr*.[43] Asma T. Uddin explains that circumambulation not only mirrors the angels in heaven, but also heaven itself as the whole universe revolves: moons around planets, planets around stars, solar systems around the center of galaxies, and the revolution of galaxies as well.[44] Similarly, electrons revolve around the atomic nucleus and the maximum number or the highest number of energy levels in an atom discovered so far is seven, the same as the number of circuits the pilgrim makes around the Kaᶜbah. Uddin quotes Abdul Hakim Murad as explaining that with its black cover the Kaᶜbah resembles a black hole around which the whole galaxy circumambulates.[45] He states,

> Blackness recalls the blackness of the night sky, of the heavens, and hence the pure presence of the Creator ... recent astronomy affirms that the spiral galaxies are revolving around black holes. A powerful symbol, written into the magnificence of space, of the spiritual vortex which beckons us to spiral into the unknown, where quantum mechanics fail, where time and space are no more.[46]

Each circuit of *ṭawāf* is called a *shawṭ*,[47] the Arabic root of which (*sh-w-ṭ*) means to travel, to run to a destination.[48] It also means a long trip, which would morphologically relate it to the meaning

43. Uddin, "The Hajj and Pluralism."

44. Ibid., 44.

45. Ibid.

46. Abdal Hakim Murad, "The Sunnah as Primordiality," http://www.masud.co.uk/ISLAM/ahm/sunnah.htm.

47. This definition is based on a *ḥadīth*. See *Ṣaḥīḥ Muslim*, 2: 923 (#1266).

48. *Lisān al-ᶜarab*, 7: 337 on *sh-w-ṭ*.

of *shaṭṭ*.[49] The Hebrew and Aramaic meanings of the root *š-w-ṭ* are also to move about, to go around, to rove over, to stroke, to row, to swim, or to sail.[50] In Arabic, the term *shāṭiᵓ* or *shaṭṭ* is a beach, shore, or riverbank.[51] In Aramaic, besides meaning to swim, it also means to guide or to fly.[52] Since *ṭawāf* means to float and to swim, while *shawṭ* may have similar associations, these are noticeably related to the rituals of the pilgrim.

The dead pilgrim might thus be understood to be floating or swimming in the waters below the Throne of God, which Qur'an 21:30–35 describes as the Water of Life:

> Have those who disbelieve not considered that the heavens and the earth were sewn together and We rent them asunder? And We made every living thing from water. Will they not, then, believe? And We placed firm mountains in the earth, lest it shake beneath them, and We made wide tracts between them as paths, that haply they may be guided (*fijājan subulan laᶜallahum yahtadūn*). And We made the sky a canopy preserved; yet they turn away from its signs. He it is Who created the night and the day, the sun and the moon, each gliding in an orbit (*wa kullun fī falakin yasbaḥ*ūn). We have not ordained perpetual life for any human being before thee. So if thou diest, will they abide forever? Every soul shall taste death. We try you with evil and with good, as a test, and unto Us shall you be returned.

The Qur'an seems to be saying that everything lives via water (21:30). It goes on to state that no physical flesh (*bashar*) has eternal life (21:34) and that every soul (*nafs*) tastes death (21:35). Since the Qur'an is talking about life and death in these passages, the water mentioned in Qur'an 21:30 could refer to the Water of Life, which is received not by the physical flesh (*bashar*) (21:34), but by the soul that is dead (21:35).[53]

49. *Ibid.*; see also 7: 333–344 on *sh-ṭ-ṭ*.

50. *BDB*, 1001–1002.

51. *Lisān al-ᶜarab*, 1: 100 on *sh-ṭ-ᵓ*.

52. *Targum Lexicon*, on *sh-w-ṭ*.

53. Much of the discussion on Qur'an 21:30–35 is found in Galadari, *Qur'anic Hermeneutics*, 128–136.

COMING FROM DEEP MOUNTAIN HIGHWAYS

Qur'an 21:31 talks about the mountains standing firm and the broad highways (*fijāj*) that have been made within it. The same term is used for the proclamation of Ḥajj.

> And proclaim the *ḥajj* among humankind: they shall come to thee on foot and upon all [manner of] lean beast, coming from all deep and distant mountain highway (*fajj*), [Qur'an 22:27]

Even in some classical books of *tafsīr*, the interpretation of the foregoing verse concerning the Ḥajj relates a tradition that all souls in the heavens and the earth and all of creation that has heard the call have accepted and uttered the *talbiyah*. According to Ibn ᶜAbbās:

> After Abraham finished building the house, he was told: "Call the people to Ḥajj," and he [Abraham] said: "My Lord! And what would allow my voice to be heard?" [God] said: "Call and I will make it heard." So Abraham called: "O people, it is decreed that you perform the Hajj to the ancient house, so perform it." And so those between the heaven and the earth heard it. Do you not see the people coming from the limits of the earth accepting the call (uttering the *talbiyah*)?[54]

The Qur'an says that God has made broad mountain highways for people to find their way (*fijājan subulan laᶜallahum yahtadūn*) (Qur'an 21:31). Similarly, God has established means by which human beings can find their way to the Ḥajj:

> Truly the first house established for humankind was that at Bakkah, full of blessing and a guidance (*hudā*) for the worlds. Therein are clear signs: the station of Abraham, and whosoever enters it shall be secure. Pilgrimage to the House is a duty upon humankind before God for those who can find a way (*man istaṭāᶜa ilayhi sabīlā*). For whosoever disbelieves, truly God is beyond need of thc worlds. [Qur'an 3:96–97]

The fifth pillar, the Ḥajj, is incumbent upon those who can make the journey (*man istaṭāᶜa ilayhi sabīlā*). In the Qur'an, God tells Abraham to proclaim the Ḥajj and that people will come from

54. Al-Ṭabarī, *Jāmiᶜ*, 18:605–608 on Q. 22:27.

deep broad mountain highways, while elsewhere, God proclaims that the Pilgrimage is a duty for those who can undertake the journey.

The Qur'an also states that these broad mountain highways (*fijājan subulan*) have been created so that people may receive guidance (*la*ᶜ*allahum yahtadūn*) (Qur'an 21:31). The term *fijāj* in Qur'an 21:31 is likened to the term *fajj* in Qur'an 22:27 in reference to the Ḥajj. The term *yahtadūn* in Qur'an 21:31 is likened to the term *hudā* (guidance) in Qur'an 3:96, which is also a reference to the Ḥajj. According to the Qur'an, the journey of the Ḥajj is about guidance (*hudā*) and offering sacrifice (*hadī*) (Qur'an 3:96), with both terms sharing the same root, *h-d-y*.

The water from the heavens that is brought down to resurrect the dead earth might be a reference to Genesis 2:5–6. Genesis 2:7 goes on to state that God created man from the earth and breathed life into him. The dead earth in Qur'an 2:164 might be an allusion to the dead human who is made of earth, and the water that comes down from heaven that resurrects the dead earth an allusion to the Spirit of God (Qur'an 15:29, 32:9, 38:72), which in itself is a parallel reference to the Spirit of God hovering over the waters in Genesis 1:2. As such, Qur'an 21:30–35 and Qur'an 2:164 are linked, as they both discuss death and life, and the water that brings forth eternal life. The Jewish *midrash* states that the prayer for rain is also inserted in the prayer for the resurrection of the dead, hence connecting the water that comes from heaven with the resurrection of the dead.[55] It links the opening of heaven with rain and the opening of the graves.[56] This further suggests the possibility that the dead earth in Genesis 2:5–6 and Qur'an 2:164 are allusions to the dead state of humans and their resurrection. Interestingly, Qur'an 2:165 discusses the love of God using the term *ḥubb*. Since the term for love (*ḥubb*) and seed (*ḥabb*) share the same root (*ḥ-b-b*), the context of Qur'an 2:164–165 may be that a person is dead as dead earth, but if the love (*ḥubb*) of God, which is the seed (*ḥabb*), in her heart, and the water from the

55. *Genesis Rabbah*, 13:6, 102.
56. Ibid.

heavens (Spirit of God) comes down to it, then that person is resurrected just as plants and fruits are also brought forth. In other words, if the dead soul has the love (*ḥubb*) of God, then good works will be its fruits.

Qur'an 2:164 mentions not only water coming from heaven, but also seas and clouds. The *midrash* mentions the role of clouds in distilling salty water from the seas as well as the different types of clouds.[57] Hence, this Qur'anic passage may be similar not only to Genesis 2:5–6 but also to its interpretation in the *midrash*.

The creatures mentioned in Qur'an 2:164 might be likened to those mentioned in the creation story of Genesis (Genesis 1:20–25). Qur'an 2:164 talks about the division of the night and the day and states that these are signs (*āyāt*), not unlike Genesis, which states that the creation of the sun and moon are signs for knowing seasons and days (Genesis 1:14), an idea which, in itself, is linked to the Ḥajj, as discussed earlier, in particular to the *ahillah*, or new moons.

The word used for the celestial bodies swimming in space is *yasbaḥūn*. Besides meaning to swim, the root *s-b-ḥ* is also related to the act of praising and glorifying.[58] Hence, the reference to the celestial bodies floating or swimming (*yasbaḥūn*) in Qur'an 21:33 is lent additional nuance by the following verse.

> He is God, the Divider [Creator] (*al-Khāliq*), the Maker (*al-Bāriʾ*), the Fashioner; unto Him belong the Most Beautiful Names. Whatsoever is in the heavens and the earth glorifies (*yusabbiḥu*) Him, and He is the Mighty, the Wise (*al-Ḥakīm*). [Qur'an 59:24]

This passage uses the term *al-Bāriʾ*, which is rooted in *b-r-ʾ*, the same verb used for creation in Genesis. It goes on to state that everything in the heavens and the earth glorifies (*yusabbiḥ*) God, connecting with Qur'an 21:33, which uses the term *yasbaḥūn*.

The Qur'an describes the day, night, sun, and moon as all

57. *Genesis Rabbah*, 13:10–12, 105–107.

58. *Lisān al-ʿarab*, 2: 471–474 on *s-b-ḥ*. See also *Gesenius' Hebrew-Chaldee Lexicon to the Old Testament*, 800–801, and *The Hebrew and Aramaic Lexicon of the Old Testament*, 1387.

floating in their orbit (*kull fī falak yasbaḥūn*) (Qur'an 21:33). The root *f-l-k* means the rounded course of celestial bodies,[59] as well as ark, a meaning also used by the Qur'an (e.g., Qur'an 2:164, 14:32). Qur'an 21:30–35 is connected to the Ḥajj in that it describes celestial bodies praising and glorifying or "swimming" (*falak yasbaḥūn*). This might be compared to the Ark (*fulk*) of Noah floating in the waters, just as celestial bodies floating in the heavens, and as the pilgrim "floats" while doing the circumambulation (*ṭawāf*). Perhaps the Qur'an is suggesting that the whole cosmos is singing praises (*yusabbiḥūn*) to God while floating (*yasbaḥūn*) on its course. A Hindu observing the circumambulation might recall the Naṭarāja or Cosmic Dance of Shiva.[60]

Qur'an 21:35 states that every soul shall taste death; it does not state every "body," but specifically every soul. We all know the birth and death of the body, but that is not the death seemingly alluded to in the Qur'an.[61] When the pilgrim is circumambulating the Kaᶜbah, his wearing a funeral shroud does not symbolize the death of the body but the death of the soul that is entombed in that body. The Qur'an describes those who cannot hear its message as being in graves. The Qur'an describes the body as that grave.

> Not equal are the living and the dead. Truly God causes whomsoever He will to hear, but thou canst not cause those in graves to hear. Thou art naught but a warner. [Qur'an 35:22–23]

The passage describes how the dead in their graves cannot hear. Abraham called people to the Ḥajj in Qur'an 22:27, using the term *adhdhin*, which means to give ear. According to Qur'an 35:22, God could make whomever He wills to hear, but we human beings cannot. Since souls are described as dead in Qur'an 21:35,

59. *Lisān al-ᶜarab*, 10: 478–479 on *f-l-k*. This term does not seem to have a Hebrew or Aramaic cognate. Hence, the meaning of the term from *Lisān al-ᶜarab* might be a form of exegesis (*tafsīr*) and not the root meaning of the term.

60. Wolf-Dieter Storl, *Shiva: The Wild God of Power and Ecstasy* (Rochester, VT: Inner Traditions, 2004), 138–141.

61. For more on the concept of death and resurrection in the Qur'an, see Abdulla Galadari, *Metaphors of Death and Resurrection in the Qur'an: An Intertextual Approach with Biblical and Rabbinic Literature* (London: Bloomsbury Academic, 2021).

then it is God who can make them hear the call, and not us. Abraham is thus merely a warner, for it is God alone who can cause the dead to hear, as described in Qur'an 35:23.

The *ṭawāf* is done counter-clockwise. The reason for the counter-clockwise movement is not the physical revolution of the planets around the sun or the rotation of the earth, as that depends on the angle at which it is being viewed. However, the pilgrim is representing herself as being on the right hand of the House of God. When you are revolving counter-clockwise, you are always to the right of the centre. Being at the right hand of the Throne of God (House of God) seems to have significance in both the Qur'an and Bible, as shown in the following passages:

> And if one be among the companions of the right, then peace unto thee from the companions of the right. [Qur'an 56:90–91]

> The LORD says to my Lord: "Sit at My right hand until I make your enemies a footstool for your feet (*hădōm raglêkā*)." [Psalm 110:1]

> After the Lord Jesus had spoken to them, he was taken up into heaven and he sat at the right hand of God. [Mark 16:19]

THE CORNERS OF THE KAᶜBAH

In his *Meccan Revelations*, Ibn ᶜArabī suggests that each of the four corners of the Kaᶜbah corresponds to a "corner" of the heart.[62] He identifies the Eastern Corner, where the Black Stone is, as the place of divine thoughts.[63] The ᶜIrāqī Corner is the place of satanic thoughts,[64] perhaps because it is northern (*shamāl*), meaning left, which is usually associated with wickedness in the Qur'an. The Shāmī Corner is described as the locus of the self or soul (*al-nafsī*),[65] while the Yamānī Corner symbolizes the angelic thoughts.[66] In this section, we will look at each corner, starting from the Eastern Corner, where the pilgrim commences circumambulation and then traverses to the Northern, Western,

62. Ibn ᶜArabī, *al-Futūḥāt*, 2: 332.
63. Ibid.
64. Ibid.
65. Ibid.
66. Ibid.

and Southern corners, then returning to the Eastern Corner.

Based on the Prophet's ﷺ example, the pilgrim is encouraged to kiss the Black Stone after arriving at the Kaᶜbah and making the circumambulation (*ṭawāf*).[67] If she cannot, she raises her hand to greet it. According to tradition, to greet the Black Stone is to greet God.[68] The word for a kiss in Arabic is *qublah.*[69] When the pilgrim arrives at the *qiblah*, she gives it a *qublah.* As *qabila* means to accept, the pilgrim and the stone "accept" one another. As the verb *qābala* means to face,[70] so are both facing each other. Moreover, as *qabīl* means to follow God's commandments,[71] so is the pilgrim following God's call.

The Black Stone, known as *al-ḥajar al-aswad*, is located on the Eastern Corner of the Kaᶜbah. The pilgrim starts circumambulation at the Eastern Corner, where the sun rises. According to Ibn ᶜArabī, the stone's black colour symbolizes spiritual detachment and poverty (*faqr*) and the extinction of the ego in the journey toward God. The term "east" in Hebrew and Aramaic is *qedem.*[72] The root *q-d-m* in Arabic, Hebrew, and Aramaic is in some ways a synonym for the root *q-b-l* in that they both mean to be in front, before, or facing.[73] The pilgrim comes to the *qiblah* and starts circumambulating from the east, *qedem.* In Arabic, the term *qadam* also means foot, similar to *rijl*,[74] which is associated with the Ḥajj. The pilgrim comes to the Ḥajj (*rijālan*) and starts circumambulating from the east (*qedem*). According to Muslim tradition, one of God's names is *al-Muqaddim*, and one of His descriptions is the Ancient One (*al-Qadīm*).[75] As one of the meanings is ancient, it would be synonymous with *ᶜatīq.*[76] When speaking of

---

67. *Ṣaḥīḥ al-Bukhārī*, 2: 149 (#1597)

68. This is a weak tradition (see al-Rāzī, *Mafātīḥ*, 22: 9 on Q. 20:1–8 and 26: 410 on Q. 38:71–85), but otherwise it is a non-prophetic tradition based on Ibn ᶜAbbās; see al-Ghazālī, *Iḥyā*ʾ, 1: 269.

69. *Lisān al-ᶜarab*, 11: 544 on *q-b-l.*

70. Ibid., 11: 537–540 on *q-b-l.* Also see BDB, 867.

71. Ibid., 11: 539 on *q-b-l.*

72. *BDB,* 869–870.

73. *Lisān al-ᶜarab*, 12: 465–469 on *q-d-m. BDB,* 869–870.

74. Ibid., 12: 470 on *q-d-m.*

75. Ibid., 12: 465 on *q-d-m.*

76. Ibid.; see also *Targum Lexicon*, The Comprehensive Aramaic Lexicon.

the Ḥajj rituals, especially those associated with circumambulation (Qur'an 22:29, 22:33), the Qur'an describes the Ka^c^bah as the Ancient House (*al-Bayt al-^c^Atīq*). The root *^c^-t-q* also means to free a slave or servant (*^c^abd*).[77] Perhaps the pilgrim who is a servant (*^c^abd*) is coming to *al-Bayt al-^c^Atīq* to be freed.

> Then let them be done with their untidiness, and fulfill their vows, and circumambulate (*wa-liyaṭṭawwafū*) the Ancient House (*al-bayt al-^c^atīq*). [Qur'an 22:29]

Based on much of the intertextuality described thus far, this verse describes circumambulation at the Ancient House, where the term *^c^atīq* (ancient) is related to *qadīm* (eternal or timeless), the term *qadam* is related to *rijl*, which is itself related to Ḥajj (Qur'an 22:27), while *qedem* is also related to east, where the circumambulation starts.

Northern Corner

From the east, the pilgrim proceeds to circumambulate towards the ^c^Irāqī Corner, which is the Northern (*shamāl*) Corner. In Arabic, the root *^c^-r-q* is associated with various meanings, such as sweat, a blood vessel, a well-bred person, a shore, among others.[78] In Aramaic, the root is associated with gnawing, fleeing,[79] or keeping something hidden.[80] The term *shamāl* means both left and north in Arabic, Hebrew, and Aramaic.[81] Additionally, it means human nature in Arabic. The root *sh-m-l* conveys meanings related to the concepts of containing or comprising, as well as outer garments such as a cloak or a mantle (perhaps so-called because it 'contains' a person inside it).[82] The Qur'an typically uses the term *shamāl* as a negative symbol. The Qur'an classes the people of the left (*aṣḥāb al-shimāl*) (e.g., Qur'an 56:41) or those who receive their book with the left hand (*shimāl*)

77. *Lisān al-^c^arab*, 10: 234–238 on *^c^-t-q*.
78. Ibid., 10: 240–250 on *^c^-t-q*.
79. *BDB,* 792.
80. *Targum Lexicon*, The Comprehensive Aramaic Lexicon.
81. *Lisān al-^c^arab*, 11: 364 on *sh-m-l*. *BDB,* 1332–1333.
82. Ibid., 11: 365, 367, 368 on *sh-m-l;* and *BDB,* 1337-1338.

(e.g., Qur'an 69:25) among those who go to Hell. Hence, the Northern Corner may be thought of as symbolizing wickedness.

The Western Corner

From the Northern Corner, the pilgrim moves to the Western Corner (*al-rukn al-gharbī*). The word *gharb* means west.[83] In Arabic, its root *gh-r-b* yields words such as sunset (*ghurūb*), strange/stranger (*gharīb*), travel to a strange land (*ightirāb*), and crow (*ghurāb*),[84] with similar meanings derived from the corresponding cognate in Hebrew and Aramaic.[85]

The Western Corner is also known as *al-rukn al-shāmī*, meaning the Levantine Corner, which might lead one to assume that it faces towards *al-Shām*, or the Levant, whereas in fact, the Levant is not to the west of Mecca. This suggests that the corners are named not simply for their directions, but rather based on the meanings associated with these names. (It has been suggested that people coming from the Levant would pray next to this corner of the Kaᶜbah, but there is no evidence to support this notion).[86] The root *sh-w-m* is associated with meanings such as nature or disposition (*shīmah*), to hide, dust, and placenta (*mashīmah*). It also means a mark on the skin (*shāmah*) in both Arabic and Aramaic.[87]

Al-gharb is the place where the sunset (*ghurūb*) occurs on the horizon. The Qur'an contains various references to occurrences happening on the west side (*al-gharbī*), such as God speaking to Moses on the western side of the mountain:

> And indeed We gave unto Moses the Book—after We had destroyed the former generations (*qurūn*)—as a [source of] insight for humankind, and guidance and mercy, that haply they may reflect. And thou wast not on the western side (*al-gharbī*) when We decreed (*qaḍaynā*) unto Moses the Commandment

83. *Lisān al-ᶜarab*, 1: 637 on *gh-r-b*.

84. Ibid., 1: 638–648 on *gh-r-b*.

85. *BDB*, 787–788.

86. This conjecture is narrated in al-Sarkhasī, *al-Mabsūṭ* (Beirut: al-Maᶜrifah, 1993), 10:191.

87. Ibid., 12: 329–331 on *sh-w-m*.

> (*al-amr*), and thou wast not among the witnesses. But it is We Who brought into being the generations (*qurūn*), and lives (*al-ᶜumur*) grew long for them. And thou dwelt not among the people of Midian, reciting unto them Our signs. But it is We Who sent. And thou wast not on the side of the Mount when We called out. But [thou sent as] a mercy from thy Lord that thou mayest warn a people unto whom no warner has come before thee, that haply they may remember. [Qur'an 28:43–46]

Regarding the western side in the story of Moses in the Qur'an, the text seems to be alluding to the following passage from Exodus, which recounts the first encounter between God and Moses in the west:

> Now Moses was keeping the flock of his father-in-law, Jethro, the priest of Midian, and he led his flock to the west side (*ʾaḥar*) of the wilderness (*midbār*) and came to Horeb, the mountain of God. [Exodus 3:1]

In contrast to the east, which is *qedem*, also meaning front, the west is *ʾaḥar,* also meaning back or behind.[88] Thus, the left (*shamāl*) is north, and the right (*yamīn*) is south.[89] The keywords in the intertextuality between Qur'an 28:44 and Exodus 3:1 are not only the term for the western side but also the Qur'anic use of *qaḍaynā al-amr* (We decreed the matter). The Qur'an connects the phrase *qaḍā amr* with the command *kun fa-yakūn* (Be, and it shall be) (e.g., Qur'an 2:117, 3:47, 19:35, 40:68), which is described as related to the Word of God or the Messiah, and as such is related to the term *yudabbir al-amr* (Qur'an 10:3, 10:31, 13:2, 32:5).[90] In Exodus 3:1, the term used to mean wilderness is *midbār*, which also means mouth, and is rooted in *d-b-r*.[91] The term *dabar* also means behind, and so does *akhar*. Another point of intertextuality between Qur'an 28:44 and the story of Moses in Exodus is the use of the phrase *qaḍaynā ilā Mūsa al-amr* in the

---

88. *BDB,* 29–31; see also N. M. Sarna, *The JPS Torah Commentary: Exodus* (Philadelphia, PA: The Jewish Publication Society, 1991), 14 on Exodus 3:1.

89. *Quddām* (in front of) is the antonym of *khalf* (behind), and *yamīn* (right) is the antonym of *shimāl* (left). See *Lisān al-ᶜarab*, 13: 463 on *y-m-n*.

90. Galadari, *Qur'anic Hermeneutics*, 100–101, 131–136.

91. *BDB,* 184–185.

Qur'anic passage. Exodus also uses the root *ᵓ-m-r* for both God and Moses speaking to each other (e.g., Exodus 3:4–7). As such, the Qur'an associates God's speech to Moses with the western side, based on the story from Exodus. The Qur'an describes some details of what has been described earlier in the same *sūrah*, which also has intertextualities with the story from Exodus.

> He said, "I desire to marry you to one of these two daughters of mine, on condition that you hire yourself to me for eight years (*ḥijaj*/pilgrimages). But if you complete ten, that will be of your own accord. And I desire not to be hard upon you. You shall find me, if God wills, to be among the righteous." He said, "So let it be between you and me. Whichever of the two terms (*al-ajalayn*) I complete (*qaḍayt*), let there be no enmity toward me. And God is Guardian (*wakīl*) over what we say." Then when Moses had completed (*qaḍā*) the term (*al-ajal*) and set out with his family (*wa-sār bi-ahlih*), he perceived a fire on the side of the Mount. He said to his family (*li-ahlih*), "Stay here. I perceive a fire. Perhaps I will bring you some news therefrom, or a firebrand, that haply you may warm yourselves." And when he came upon it, he was called from the right (*al-ayman*) bank of the valley, at the blessed site, from the tree, "O Moses! Truly I am God, Lord of the worlds!" and, "Cast thy staff!" Then when he saw it quivering like a serpent, he turned in retreat without returning. "O Moses! Approach and fear not! Truly, thou art of those who are secure." [Qur'an 28:27–31]

Although the Qur'an states that Moses went to the west side (*al-gharbī*), it also specifically states that Moses was spoken to by God from the right side (*al-ayman*) (Qur'an 28:30). This reference is not found in Exodus. Interestingly, the right (*yamīn*) is also another term for south.[92] In the Qur'an, the terms *qaḍā* and *ajal* are also associated with death.

> God takes (*yatawaffā*) souls at the moment of their death, and those who do not die, during their sleep. He withholds those for whom He decreed (*qaḍā*) death, and sends forth the others till a term appointed (*ajal*). Truly in that are signs for a people who reflect. [Qur'an 39:42]

---

92. *Lisān al-ᶜarab*, 13: 464 on *y-m-n*. Also see *BDB*, 411–412.

Before and after discussing Moses going to the west side, Qur'an 28:43 and 28:45 use the term *qurūn* to describe generations. The term *qurūn* is rooted in *q-r-n*. There is a Qur'anic relationship between the west, the setting of the sun, and Dhul-Qarnayn from the Qur'an as well.

> And they question thee about Dhul-Qarnayn. Say, "I shall recite unto you a remembrance of him." Truly We established him in the land, and gave him the means to all things. So he followed a means, till when he reached the place of the setting (*maghrib*) sun, he found it setting in a murky (*ḥamiʾah*) spring, and there he found a people. We said, "O Dhul-Qarnayn! Thou mayest punish, or thou mayest treat them well." He said, "As for the one who has done wrong, we shall punish him. Then he shall be brought back to his Lord, whereupon He will punish him with a terrible punishment. But as for the one who believes and works righteousness, he shall have a reward, that which is most beautiful, and we shall speak unto him that which is easy from our command." Then he followed a means, till he reached the place of the rising sun. He found it rising over a people for whom We had not made any shelter from it. Thus [it was], and We encompassed that which lay before him in awareness. Then he followed a means, till he reached the place between the two mountain barriers. He found beyond them a people who could scarcely comprehend speech. They said, "O Dhul-Qarnayn! Truly Gog and Magog are workers of corruption in the land. Shall we assign thee a tribute, that thou might set a barrier between them and us?" He said, "That wherewith my Lord has established me is better; so aid me with strength. I shall set a rampart between you and them. Bring me pieces of iron (*zubar al-ḥadīd*)." Then, when he had levelled (*sāwā*) the two cliffs, he said, "Blow!" till when he had made it fire. He said, "Bring me molten copper to pour over it." Thus they were not able to surmount it, nor could they pierce it. He said, "This is a mercy from my Lord. And when the Promise of my Lord comes, He will crumble it to dust (*dakka*). And the Promise of my Lord is true." [Qur'an 18:83–98]

When Dhul-Qarnayn arrived at the setting of the sun, he found it setting on a spring of murky (*ḥamiʾah*) water. The word *ḥamaʾ* is the same word used in the Qur'an for the creation of humanity from earth (mud) (Qur'an 15:26, 15:28, 15:33). Dhul-Qarnayn judged the people in the west, where the sun set below the murky water; those who are good are rewarded, and those who are not good are punished. It seems like the setting of the sun in the west is a symbol of death, when a soul is judged. In contrast, when Dhul-Qarnayn arrives at the location of the sunrise, he finds people who do not have any covering from it, and the Qur'an does not state what he does to them. This may represent that they are the people of the east, symbolizing life and resurrection. They do not have veils between them and the sun. They are full of understanding. They are not judged like those who dwell by the setting of the sun, but pass through judgment into life. The pilgrim in *iḥrām*, symbolizing his death, nevertheless does not cover his head, for he shall have no cover other than the Throne of God, according to Muslim tradition.

The Western Corner symbolizes death, the judgment of the dead, and the state of souls at death. When Cain killed Abel, the Qur'an states that a raven (*ghurāb*) was sent (resurrected / *baᶜath*) to show Cain what he had done (Qur'an 5:31). In Islam, Cain is called *Qābīl*, which has the same root as *qiblah*. The word for raven in Arabic is *ghurāb*, which has the same root as west (*gharb*). In ancient Egypt, the sunset was a symbol of death. Yet, though the sun sets, it rises the next morning, from which the ancient Egyptians concluded that resurrection of the dead or rebirth occurs, just as the sun is reborn every day.[93]

The raven, which symbolizes death and judgment, has been widely used as a symbol of death in Near Eastern literature.[94] Through the actions of the raven, Cain understood what to do. As a result, he was judged by the raven (*ghurāb*), as Dhul-Qarnayn judged those at the setting (*maghrib*) of the sun. The raven shows Cain how to bury his brother in the earth. Interestingly, if the soul is symbolized as dead, it is as if it is buried

93. Ronald A.Wells, "The Mythology of Nut and the Birth of Ra," *Studien zur Altagyptischen Kultur* (1992), 19: 305–321; see also James P. Allen, *The Ancient Egyptian Pyramid Texts* (Leiden: Brill, 2005, 1991), 8–10.

94. Arthur De Vries, *Dictionary of Symbols and Imagery* (Amsterdam: North-Holland, 1874), 382.

in the earth (*ḥamaʾ*) of the body.

The raven serves as an interesting symbol in the Hebrew Bible. In the story of Noah's Ark, Noah sends a raven to see if the waters have dried up (Genesis 8:7) before later sending a dove. In another verse, God commands the ravens to feed Elijah, when he travels east, and bring him water and flesh every morning and every evening, but after a time, the waters dry up, reminiscent of the story of the raven that Noah had sent forth. Later, in a story that resembles that of the Last Supper of Jesus, Elijah goes to a widow's house for water, and remains as a guest there in the upper chamber, giving life to the dead (1 Kings 17:1–24). Jesus himself alluded to this story very early in his ministry (Luke 4:24–26).

Perhaps there are two possible meanings of Moses going to the western side (Qur'an 28:44). As the raven was a symbol of teaching Cain how to bury the dead, Moses' going to the western side might symbolize the dead state of his own soul. As the raven was a symbol of the waters drying up in the Hebrew Bible and as the waters are a symbol of the Spirit in Genesis, Moses going to the western side might symbolize his lack of the Spirit of God and, hence, his yearning for the Water of Life. The pilgrim's circling to the Western Corner may thus correspond to the lifeless state of his or her soul.

The Southern Corner

The pilgrim then proceeds to the Southern (right) Corner (*al-rukn al-yamānī*). According to the Qur'an, it was on the right side that God spoke to Moses (Qur'an 19:52, 20:80, 28:30). It is "the people of the right" (*aṣḥāb al-yamīn*) who occupy Paradise according to the Qur'an, and according to Muslim tradition, the Prophet ﷺ touched "the right corner" (*al-rukn al-yamānī*).[95] This is perhaps to show some status of significance over the Northern and Western Corners; after all, besides meaning south and right, the root *y-m-n* also means blessing.[96] The Qur'an thus dis-

95. *Ṣaḥīḥ al-Bukhārī*, 2: 151 (#1606), (#1609), 2: 158 (#1644).
96. *Lisān al-ʿarab*, 13: 458 on *y-m-n*.

tinguishes three different groups: the foremost (*al-sābiqūn*), the people of the right (*aṣḥāb al-yamīn*), and the people of the left (*aṣḥāb al-shimāl*) (Qur'an 56:7–57).

The Eastern Corner

If the Western Corner symbolizes death, then the Eastern Corner (*al-rukn al-sharqī*), would symbolize life or resurrection. The root *sh-r-q* means to rise (specifically concerning the sun). Hence, east is called *sharq* because the sun rises from this direction. As such, the sun is also called *al-sharqah*.[97] The term also means a red colour,[98] perhaps taking its name from the sun's hue while rising. East and west as symbols of life and death may be reflected in the following Qur'anic passages:

> God is the Protector of those who believe. He brings them out of the darkness into the light. As for those who disbelieve, their protectors are the idols, bringing them out of the light into the darkness. They are the inhabitants of the Fire, abiding therein. Hast thou not considered him who disputed (*ḥājja*) with Abraham about his Lord because God had given him sovereignty? When Abraham said, "My Lord gives life and causes death," he said, "I give life and cause death." Abraham said, "Truly God brings the sun from the east. Bring it, then, from the west." Thus was he who disbelieved confounded. And God guides not (*lā yahdī*) wrongdoing people. Or [think of] the like of him who passed by a town as it lay fallen upon its roofs. He said, "How shall God give life to this after its death?" So God caused him to die for a hundred years, then raised him up. He said, "How long hast thou tarried?" He said, "I tarried a day or part of a day." He said, "Nay, thou hast tarried a hundred years. Look, then, at thy food and thy drink—they have not spoiled. And look at thy donkey. And [this was done] that We may make thee a sign for humankind. And look at the bones, how We set them up, then clothe them with flesh." When it became clear to him he said, "I know that God has power over all things." And when Abraham said, "My Lord, show me how Thou givest life to the dead," He said, "Dost thou not believe?" He said, "Yea, indeed, but so that my heart may be

97. *Lisān al-ᶜarab*, 10: 173, 175 on *sh-r-q*.
98. *Ibid.*, 10: 177–178 on *sh-r-q*.

> at peace." He said, "Take four birds and make them be drawn to thee. Then place a piece of them on every mountain. Then call them: they will come to thee in haste (*saᶜyā*). And know that God is Mighty, Wise." [Qur'an 2:257–260]

These passages, which discuss life and death, or death and resurrection, appear to be connected with the Ḥajj through: i) the term *ḥājj*; ii) guidance or sacrifice through use of the term *hudā*; iii) the running between the hills of Ṣafā and Marwah, which is called *saᶜī*; and iv) the rising of the sun in the east and setting in the west symbolizing death and resurrection. *Saᶜī* will later be discussed in detail in connection to the meaning of the Ḥajj rituals.

As discussed, the Eastern Corner symbolizes the resurrection of the soul entombed in the body. In many churches, especially Orthodox churches, the altar is located on the eastern side.[99] In ancient Egypt, the sunrise is represented by the symbol called the *ankh*, also known as the key of life, representing eternal life.[100] The *ankh* is also used to symbolize sunrise, which is resurrection.[101] Ancient Egyptians symbolize death and the journey of the soul in the netherworld as the sun sets and journeys below the horizon until it rises the next morning, symbolizing resurrection and rebirth.

The books of the afterlife of the ancient Egyptians, such as the *Book of Gates* and its predecessor, *Amduat*, depict the details of the death of the soul, represented by the sunset in the west, as well as every moment the soul experiences until rebirth or resurrection symbolized by the sunrise in the east.[102] It is important to

---

99. See B. L.Gordon, "Sacred Directions, Orientation, and the Top of the Map," *History of Religions* (1971), 10(3): 211–227; see also H. M. Taylor, "The Position of the Altar in Early Anglo-Saxon Churches," *The Antiquaries Journal* (1973), 53(1): 52–58; and Eric Fernie, "The Use of Varied Nave Supports in Romanesque and Early Gothic Churches," *Gesta* (1984), 23(2): 107–117.

100. Reginald E.Witt, *Isis in the Graeco-Roman World* (London: Thames and Hudson, 1971), 39.

101. Matthias Seidel, and Regine Schulz, *Egypt Art and Architecture* (New York, NY: Barnes and Noble Books, 2005), 584.

102. Erik Hornung, *The Ancient Egyptian Books of the Afterlife*, trans. David Lorton (Ithaca, NY: Cornell University Press, 1999), 59; see also John C. Darnell,

note that in the northern hemisphere, as the sun sets in the west, it goes below the horizon and travels north, until rising again from the east. Hence, north (*shamāl*) is depicted as midnight or where the sun is at midnight. Perhaps this is why the Qur'an describes the left hand (*shimāl*) as the torment of Hell. Easter service in many churches is known as the sunrise service. Since Easter is the celebration of the resurrection of Jesus, the sunrise service on Easter Sunday uses the symbol of sunrise for the resurrection.[103] Jesus' defeat of death is likened to descriptions, in ancient Egyptian texts, of Pharaoh's journey through the afterlife, a journey viewed as being responsible for the sun's rising in the east.[104]

The Qur'an uses the symbolism of resurrection and life in ways that are similar to those of the ancient Egyptians. When the Qur'an discusses the Day of Resurrection, it describes how the earth shines (*ashraqat*), sharing the same root as the word for east, with God's light. In the following verses, the metaphor of the earth shining with the light of the sun from the east is describing how the body made from earth shines with the Light of God:

> They did not measure God with His true measure. The whole earth shall be but a handful to Him (*qabḍatuhu*) on the Day of Resurrection (*yawm al-qiyāmah*), and the heavens will be enfolded in His right Hand. Glory be to Him, exalted is He above the partners they ascribe. And the trumpet will be blown, whereupon whosoever is in the heavens and on the earth will swoon, save those whom God wills. Then it will be blown again, and, behold, they will be standing (*qiyām*), beholding The earth will shine (*ashraqat*) with the Light of its Lord, the Book will be set down, and the prophets and the witnesses will be brought forth. Judgment will be made between them in truth, and they shall not be wronged. [Qur'an 39:67–69]

The Enigmatic Netherworlds Books of the Solar-Osirian Unity: Cryptographic Compositions in the Tombs of Tutankhamun, Ramesses VI and Ramesses IX (Fribourg: Academic Press, 2004), 282.

103. L. T. W. Baruti, *The Practice of Easter Morning Service and Its Theological Implication into Christian Faith: In North-Eastern Diocese of Lutheran Church of Tanzania*, Master's Thesis, Norwegian School of Theology, 2011, 1.

104. Darnell, *The Enigmatic Netherworlds Books*, 282.

Ibn ᶜArabī suggests that this verse is about the Age of the Mahdī, and therefore not necessarily about the Day of Resurrection unless he considers both to be the same.[105] Since the Light of God can be related to the creation story of Genesis, and since Proverbs 8:22–31 relates the creation story to wisdom, then perhaps the Qur'an here is giving us an allegory for enlightenment: that is, as the soul is resurrected, it achieves divine wisdom.

In Genesis, the Garden of Eden is in the east (Genesis 2:8). The Tree of Life is also placed in the east (Genesis 3:24). Proverbs 3:18 likens wisdom to a tree of life, while Proverbs 3:19–20 connects wisdom with the creation story of Genesis by referring to the foundation of the earth and the establishment of the heavens. Qur'an 39:67–69 also appear to have some similarities with Ezekiel's vision of the Temple:

> Then the man brought me to the gate facing east (*ha-qādîm*), and I saw the glory of the God of Israel coming from the east (*ha-qādîm*). His voice was like the roar of rushing waters, and the land was radiant with his glory. The vision I saw was like the vision I had seen when he came to destroy the city and like the visions I had seen by the Kebar River, and I fell facedown. The glory of the LORD ENTERED THE TEMPLE THROUGH THE GATE FACING EAST (*ha-qādîm*). Then the Spirit lifted me up and brought me into the inner court, and the glory of the LORD FILLED THE TEMPLE. While the man was standing beside me, I heard someone speaking to me from inside the temple. He said: "Son of man, this is the place of my throne and the place for the soles of my feet (*raglay*). This is where I will live among the Israelites forever. The people of Israel will never again defile my holy name—neither they nor their kings—by their prostitution and the funeral offerings for their kings at their death." [Ezekiel 43:1–7]

The earth shining with the light of its Lord using the same root as east in Qur'an 39:69 can be likened to Ezekiel's vision in that the glory of God was coming from the east and the land was radiant with His glory (Ezekiel 43:2). Apparently, the Qur'anic use of east, the point of sunrise as having significance for worship

105. Ibn ᶜArabī, *Tafsīr*, on Q. 3:69.

in the temple is similar to its use in ancient Egypt, Judaism, and Christianity.

THE *ṬAWĀF* OF THE DEAD PILGRIM

Wearing a funeral shroud, the pilgrim arrives at the Kaᶜbah for *ṭawāf al-qudūm* or ᶜUmrah as a dead soul. While floating on the Water of Life, the soul passes the four corners of the Kaᶜbah to experience his or her own history, be transformed from death into true life, and understand its own mysteries from God and True Reality.

The pilgrim starts at the east, symbolizing her original state in its full purity (*fiṭrah*). From there she travels to the ᶜIrāqī Corner, derived from the root *ᶜ-r-q*, from which we get the word for sweat (*ᶜaraq*), as the soul is born into suffering in the physical realm. This is followed by an encounter with the Western Corner, which symbolizes death and judgment. The Qur'an frequently suggests that at the judgement, there are people of the right (the righteous) and people of the left (the wicked). If the soul is judged as being evil, it is returned to the Northern (left, *shimāl*) Corner, where suffering abides. However, if it is judged among the good, it travels to the Yamānī (right) Corner.

If the soul travels to the right, God speaks to it, making her realize her state of death and ignorance, and restoring her to her pure state at the Eastern Corner. This is the state of the soul that judgment has passed over, that has returned from death into life; the symbolism is perhaps similar to that found in Jesus' saying, according to John, that some souls are not judged, but pass from death into life (John 5:24). In the Qur'an, perhaps those whom judgment has passed over are of neither the right nor the left, but rather, the foremost who are drawn near (*al-sābiqūn ulāʾika al-muqarrabūn*):

> And you shall be of three kinds: the companions of the right; what of the companions of the right? And the companions of the left; what of the companions of the left? And the foremost shall be the foremost (*al-sābiqūn al-sābiqūn*). They are the ones brought nigh (*al-muqarrabūn*) [Qur'an 56:7–10]

These are the people of the east. Apparently, the Qur'an symbolizes them as the people that Dhul-Qarnayn found in the place of the rising sun and who are not veiled from it. That is the Eastern Corner of the Kaᶜbah, where the Black Stone (*al-ḥajar al-aswad*) resides. Since we have seen that the Ḥajj passages in the Qur'an are related to the Water of Life, the stone may be seen as pouring out the river of the Water of Life.

> Then your hearts (*qulūbikum*) hardened thereafter, being like stones (*kal-ḥijārah*) or harder still. For indeed among stones (*al-ḥijārah*) are those from which streams gush forth (*yatafajjar*), and indeed among them are those that split and water issues from them, and indeed among them are those that crash down from the fear of God. And God is not heedless of what you do. [Qur'an 2:74]

The 'dead' pilgrim circumambulates (*yaṭūf*) around the Kaᶜbah seven times. The first six circumambulations might possibly symbolize the creation of the heavens and the earth in six days (e.g., Qur'an 7:54, 10:3, 25:59, 32:4, 57:4). On the seventh circuit, God established (*istawā*) His Throne, just as He establishes His Throne in the human being (*sawwaytuhu*) (Qur'an 15:29, 38:72), with both of these verbs sharing the same root *s-w-y*.[106] God breathes from His Spirit into the human, making him or her His Temple and resurrecting their dead souls into life. Alternatively, it might be a symbol for God establishing (*sawwāhā*) the seven heavens, again using the root *s-w-y* (Qur'an 2:29).

106. Galadari, *Qur'anic Hermeneutics*, 117–128.

4

MAQĀM IBRĀHĪM

After completing the circumambulation (*ṭawāf*) of the Ka^cbah, the pilgrim prays behind the station of Abraham (*maqām Ibrāhīm*).[1] Qur'anic commentators have had various opinions of what constitutes *maqām Ibrāhīm*.[2] Al-Ṭabarī, al-Rāzī (d. 606/1210), Ibn Kathīr (d. 774/1373) and others viewed the entire place of pilgrimage, including ᶜArafah, Muzdalifah, and Minā, as *maqām Ibrāhīm*. Nonetheless, another view holds that *maqām Ibrāhīm* is the stone in *al-Masjid al-Ḥarām*, which the Prophet prayed behind after he performed circumambulation (*ṭawāf*). In this chapter, we shall look into the significance of praying behind *maqām Ibrāhīm* before traversing between the hills of *Ṣafā* and *Marwah*.

---

1. *Ṣaḥīḥ al-Bukhārī*, 1: 88 (#395), (#397), (#398).

2. M.J. Kister, "*Maqām Ibrāhīm*: A Stone with an Inscription," *Le Muséon* (1971) 84: 477–491.

ABRAHAM

To understand the symbolism of praying behind *maqām Ibrāhīm*, it is necessary to understand first who Abraham was and his connection to the Kaᶜbah according to the Qur'an. Abraham, whose name in Hebrew means "father of a multitude" (*ᵓab hămôn*) according to Genesis,[3] is considered a patriarch in Judaism, Christianity, and Islam. Islam reveres him as the epitome of the meaning of *islām*; the Qur'an describes him as the foremost *muslim* and the one who first called the believers *muslims*, or those who surrender to God (Qur'an 22:78). The Qur'an frequently connects Abraham with *islām*, self-surrender to God (e.g., Qur'an 2:128–133). To understand the *islām* of the Qur'an, one needs to understand Abraham, who is sometimes referred to as the Friend of God (Qur'an 4:125).

The Qur'an argues that some Jews and Christians may tell others to become one of them, but the Qur'an states that one should follow instead the way of Abraham (Qur'an 2:135, 3:95, 4:125, 6:161, 16:123). Qur'an 3:95, which invites people to follow the way of Abraham, saying, "Say: 'God has spoken the truth: follow, then, the creed of Abraham, who turned away from all that is false,' " is specifically within the context of the House presumed to be the Kaᶜbah, *maqām Ibrāhīm*, and the Ḥajj. Qur'an 6:161 also uses the term *mustaqīm* ("straight"), which shares the same root as *maqām*, concerning the way of Abraham.

The Qur'an says that Abraham was neither a Jew nor a Christian, but a *muslim*, for how could he have been either a Jew or a Christian if the Torah and Gospel only came after him (Qur'an 3:67)? According to this same logic, it is equally important to understand what it means for Abraham to be called *muslim*, since the Qur'an also was revealed only after him.

According to the Qur'an, Abraham first surrendered to God (*aslam*) before he knew who Prophet Muḥammad ﷺ would be or even knew where Mecca was, as he seems to have taken his family there in a later account (Qur'an 14:37). Therefore, if he

3. See *BDB*, 4; see also *Gesenius' Hebrew-Chaldee Lexicon to the Old Testament*, 9.

prayed in his own way to God, it was not toward Mecca or even Jerusalem. Nonetheless, Abraham gave to charity, and per Genesis 14:20, he gave one-tenth as a tithe to Melchizedek after having been blessed by him. There is no evidence from the Qur'an that Abraham instituted any special fast to God.

In other words, Abraham was a *muslim* according to the Qur'an even though the five pillars had not yet been instituted in the manner in which Muslims observe them today.[4] Hence, perhaps one can distinguish the term *islām* in the Qur'an from the term *sharī^{c}at Muḥammad* (the path or laws of Muḥammad). This being the case, what does it mean to be a *muslim* according to the Qur'an? The Qur'an refers to Lot's household as *muslim* (Qur'an 51:36) and describes the sorcerers who challenged Moses as having become *muslims* (Qur'an 7:126). The Qur'an says that the Torah was revealed in order for the Hebrew prophets, who were *muslims*, to judge the Jews by it (Qur'an 5:44). There is no evidence that any of the Jewish prophets went to Mecca to perform the Ḥajj or fasted Ramadan, yet the Qur'an still calls them *muslims*. Similarly, the Qur'an tells us that Solomon invited the Queen of Sheba to become a *muslim* (Qur'an 27:31, 27:38, 27:42, 27:44), and Jesus' disciples also called themselves *muslims* (Qur'an 3:52, 5:111).

Even the Prophet Muḥammad ﷺ was a *muslim* before he knew the method of prayer, fasting, Ḥajj, or the percentage to be paid in charity per present-day Islamic jurisprudence. If the Qur'an says that Muḥammad is like Abraham in the sense that the Torah and the Gospel were only revealed after him (Qur'an 3:65–68), then it may be concluded that *islām* is not the Qur'anic *sharī^{c}ah*, but rather, a path that pre-dates the revelation of the Qur'an itself. Therefore, it is imperative first to understand what *islām* is as described in the Qur'an.

Islam has its root in *s-l-m*, which yields terms with various meanings: to be innocent, complete, or whole, to be full, to finish, to conclude, to perish, to heal, to surrender, to be sacrificed,

4. See my discussion of the meaning of *muslim* in Galadari, *Qur'anic Hermeneutics*, 68–71.

to be handed over, to be delivered, to be perfect, to be fulfilled, to be paid, to be fitting, to be safe, and to be peaceful, among other meanings.[5] Perhaps the Qur'an portrays Abraham as a *muslim* because he searched for God, and when he could not find Him, he surrendered to Him (Qur'an 6:74–79). Hence, Abraham did not surrender to the Will of God because he followed someone who showed him the way; he surrendered to God alone so that God would show him the way.

Similarly, perhaps the Qur'an is alluding to the idea that Prophet Muḥammad ﷺ did the same—that is, he searched for the truth until he surrendered to it. Not satisfied with what he saw his people worshiping, he meditated in the cave of Ḥirāʾ in his search for God. When he did not find Him, he perhaps surrendered to Him and then told the people that the way to find God is by surrendering to Him, as Abraham had done.

Perhaps the prayer behind the station of Abraham (*maqām Ibrāhīm*) is to remind the pilgrim to surrender to the will of God by being ready to shed all his personal beliefs in order to understand the True Reality of God. The Qur'an seems to portray the *islām* of Abraham as the supreme surrender, to obey God in even the most apparently irrational matters, as Abraham did in his readiness to sacrifice his son (Qur'an 37:102–103). The Qur'an shows that Abraham did not question God, but did so in full surrender, using the term *aslam* in Qur'an 37:103. Even before the Qur'an discusses Abraham being asked to sacrifice his son, it states in Qur'an 37:101 that Abraham was given the good news that he would have a son. Abraham had longed for a son, and when he was granted one, he was asked to sacrifice the thing he so loved and desired. Perhaps the pilgrim is being reminded to sacrifice all his desires and passions for the sake of deep surrender to God.

The pilgrim knows of the state of death. The dead soul is, therefore, *dying* of thirst, wanting to drink from the Water of Life and to be resurrected, knowing that it has been dead. It

5. *Lisān al-ʿarab*, 12: 289–301 on *s-l-m*; see also *BDB*, 1022–1025; and *The Hebrew and Aramaic Lexicon of the Old Testament*, 1532–1541.

is *dying* to live by sacrificing itself (Luke 9:24, John 12:25). It is dying, completely surrendering to the will of God (Qur'an 2:132, 3:102), and foregoing all of its feeble desires. Its ego (false self) is dying so that the soul may be resurrected.

The dead pilgrim, who now thirsts to drink from the fountain of life, stands behind *maqām Ibrāhīm*. The Station of Abraham is important because the dead soul understands that, for it to be resurrected, it must follow the approach and faith of Abraham (*millah Ibrāhīm*). It has to surrender itself to the will of God, as Abraham did.

AL-MAQĀM

The word *maqām* has the same root as resurrection, *q-w-m*. As *mīqāt* represents that the hour of resurrection is near, *maqām* (station, or place of standing or rising) may represent that the place of resurrection is near. The Qur'an uses the word *maqām* (station) several times. Noah speaks to his people of his *maqām* (station), stating that he is a *muslim*, a person who has surrendered to God.

> And recite unto them the story of Noah, when he said to his people, "O my people! If my presence (*maqāmī*) is grievous to you, and [so too] my reminding of the signs of God, then in God do I trust. So decide on your plan, you and your partners; then let there be no doubt concerning your plan, but carry it out against me, and grant no respite! And if you turn your backs, I have not asked of you any reward. My reward lies only with God, and I am commanded to be among those who submit (*al-muslimīn*)." [Qur'an 10:71–72].

Elsewhere, the Qur'an uses *maqām* for God's "station":

> Their messengers said unto them, "We are but human beings like yourselves, but God is gracious unto whomsoever He will among His servants. And it is not for us to bring you an authority, save by God's Leave (*bi-idhn illāh*); so in God let the believers trust. And why should we not trust in God, when He has guided us in our ways (*hadānā subulanā*)? And we shall surely endure patiently, however you may torment us. And let those who trust,

> trust in God." But those who disbelieved said to their messengers, "We shall surely expel you from our land, or you shall revert to our creed." So their Lord revealed unto them, "We shall surely destroy the wrongdoers. And We shall surely make you to dwell in the land after them. This is for those who fear My Station (*maqāmī*) and fear My Threat." [Qur'an 14:11–14]

In these verses, the messengers use the word *idhn* for God's permission for their message. The same word is used for the *adhān* of prayers when prayer arrives at its *mīqāt* and for the proclamation of Ḥajj (Qur'an 22:27). Then, the messengers say that God guided (sacrificed) them to their paths (*hadānā subulanā*), which are the same words used for guidance and sacrifice (*hadī*) concerning the Ḥajj (Qur'an 2:196). Additionally, *subulanā* is the root used in the Qur'an for God's creation of broad mountain highways for people to pass through (Qur'an 21:31), and for those capable of performing the Ḥajj (Qur'an 3:97). These words are even repeated when Noah explains the ways of God to his people (Qur'an 71:20), a passage that uses not only the term "*subul*" but also "*fijāj,*" which also appears in the Ḥajj passage that states people will be coming from deep and distant "*fajj*."

The term *maqām* is also found in the Jewish understanding of the Divine Place or Presence, which is referred to in Hebrew as *ha-Maqom*. It is even one of the divine names.[6] Since the term *maqām* has as its root *q-w-m*, meaning to rise, or resurrection,[7] this reference may be interpreted to mean that since God is life, He is the Place of Resurrection (*al-Maqām* or *ha-Maqom*). The ascription of 'place' to God (*ha-Maqom*) is related to the Kabbalistic notion of *tzimtzum*[8] according to which, although God is infinite, God's Presence (the *Shekhinah* / *al-Sakīnah*) chooses to contract in such a way as to 'fit into' a space.

In the Qur'an, believers are urged to perform prayers throughout the night to attain a praiseworthy station (*maqām*), bearing in mind that from the time the sun sets in the west until it rises

6. *Genesis Rabbah*, 68:9.

7. *Lisān al-ᶜarab*, 12: 496–506 on *q-w-m*. *BDB,* 877–879.

8. The concept of *tzimtzum* is based on Isaac Luria's teachings that the infinite God contracted Himself so as to fit into a finite space.

again in the east, it is night, and the sunrise is seen as a symbol of resurrection:

> Resurrect[9] (*aqim*) the prayer at the declining of the sun till the darkening of the night. And the recitation at dawn (*al-fajr*)—truly, the recitation at dawn (*al-fajr*) is ever witnessed! And keep vigil in prayer for part of the night as a supererogatory act for thee. It may be that thy Lord will resurrect thee (*yab*ᶜ*athuka*) in a praiseworthy station (*maqāman maḥmūdā*). [Qur'an 17:78–79]

In another verse, the word *maqām* is used when people ask each other who has been resurrected in a better station (*maqām*) on the Day of Resurrection (Qur'an 19:73). Hell is described in the Qur'an as a bad location (*maqām*) to be resurrected into (Qur'an 25:66), whereas heaven is a good location (*maqām*) to be resurrected into (Qur'an 25:76, 35:35, 55:46, 79:40–41).

Solomon is also referred to in the Qur'an as having a station (*maqām*) when he asks for the throne of the Queen of Sheba (Qur'an 27:39). Solomon is told that the Queen of Sheba's throne will be brought to him before he rises from his station (*maqām*). However, another who has knowledge of the Book tells him that he can bring him the throne before he blinks his eyes (Qur'an 27:40), employing the same words (*yartadd ilayk ṭarfuk*) used to describe those who cannot blink on the Day of Resurrection (Qur'an 14:43).

Additionally, the Qur'an explains how Pharaoh and his hosts were in gardens, rivers, and high stations (*maqām*), but God had the Israelites inherit them instead (Qur'an 26:57–60, 44:25–28). Ibn ᶜArabī's interpretation of these passages emphasizes their spiritual nature as opposed to their physical reality.[10]

The Qur'an describes how the God-fearing (*al-muttaqīn*) are in a safe place (*maqām amīn*) (Qur'an 44:51). Similarly, we are told in Qur'an 3:97 that "[It is] the place whereon Abraham once stood; and whoever enters it finds peace (or safety) (... *maqām ibrāhīm wa man dakhalah kān āminā*)." Moreover, concerning the term *maqām*, the angels are described in the Qur'an as having

9. The *TSQ* translates *aqim* as "perform".

10. Ibn ᶜArabī, *Tafsīr*, on Q. 26:41–60 and Q. 44:17–42.

a Station Known (*maqām maᶜlūm*): "There is none among us, but that he has a known station (*maqām maᶜlūm*)" [Qur'an 37:164].[11] As the speaker is not defined by the above Qur'anic passage, classical exegetes interpreted the speakers to be angels.[12] Al-Ṭabarī supports his assumption with a prophetic tradition (*ḥadīth*) on the authority of ᶜĀᵓishah that states that every place in the heavens and the earth has an angel standing or prostrating.[13]

Qur'an 17:79 asks that prayers be performed through the night so that one may be resurrected to a praiseworthy station (*maqām maḥmūdā*). Although the Qur'an does not specify whom it is addressing in Qur'an 17:79, classical exegetes suggest that it is possibly addressing Prophet Muḥammad ﷺ.[14] According to tradition, during the Night Journey of the Prophet ﷺ, he saw several of the prophets in different stations of heaven.[15] The Station of Abraham (*maqām Ibrāhīm*) was at the seventh heaven.[16] It could even be imagined that circumambulating seven circuits marks the seven heavens; after completing the seventh circuit, one prays behind the Station of Abraham (*maqām Ibrāhīm*) marking his station in the seventh heaven.

GARMENT OF GOD

The act of praying behind the Station of Abraham (*maqām Ibrāhīm*) might even have the following symbolic meaning. The

---

11. The word *maᶜlūm*, which has its root in *ᶜ-l-m*, is important for understanding the Qur'anic concept of the Ḥajj. The Qur'an speaks about those established in knowledge (*al-rāsikhūn fil-ᶜilm*) (Qur'an 3:7, 4:162). It also talks about the Ḥajj as "known" months or days (*ayyām maᶜlūmāt*) (Qur'an 2:197, 22:28), and the Day of Resurrection is called *yawm al-waqt al-maᶜlūm* (the day of the known time) (Qur'an 15:38, 38:81).

12. Al-Ṭabarī, *Jāmiᶜ*, 21: 125–126 on Q. 37:161–164.

13. Ibid. However, it is uncertain whether this prophetic tradition comes from the Prophet or not, with Ibn Kathīr stating that it is not a prophetic tradition but, rather, originated with Ibn Masᶜūd. See Ibn Kathīr, *Tafsīr al-Qurᵓān al-ᶜaẓīm*, ed. Sāmī M. Salāmeh (Riyadh: Ṭaybah, no date), 7: 43 on Q. 37:164. Nor does the Qur'an identify the speaker, though it might be the Prophet Muḥammad describing how each prophet has a station (*maqām*).

14. Al-Ṭabarī, *Jāmiᶜ*, 17: 523–533 on Q. 17:79.

15. *Ṣaḥīḥ al-Bukhārī*, 5: 52 (#3887).

16. Ibid.

pilgrim surrenders completely to the will of God in *islām* (see the definition of *islām* described earlier) in the same way that Abraham did. This is the epitome of true surrender to God regardless of how difficult His commandments may appear to be, even if the individual has to shed all his beliefs—and even himself. To know the truth, the garments of falsehood need to be taken off, and the pilgrim must be "naked", waiting to be covered in the garments of God.[17] Adam and Eve were naked in the Garden of Eden, perhaps because they were clothed in "God's garments" before the Fall (Qur'an 7:27, Genesis 2:25). Such complete surrender to God is also portrayed in other scriptures such as the *Bhagavad Gita*:

> This divine power (Maya) of Mine, consisting of three states of matter or mind, is very difficult to overcome. Only those who surrender unto Me easily cross over this Maya. (7.14)
>
> Anybody can attain the Supreme Abode by just surrendering unto My will with loving devotion, O Arjuna. (9.32)
>
> My devotees remain ever content and delighted. Their minds remain absorbed in Me, and their lives surrendered unto Me. They always enlighten each other by talking about Me. (10.09)
>
> Therefore, focus your mind on Me, and let your intellect dwell upon Me alone through meditation and contemplation. Thereafter you shall certainly attain Me. If you are unable to focus your mind steadily on Me, then long to attain Me by practice of any other spiritual discipline; such as a ritual, or deity worship that suits you. If you are unable even to do any spiritual discipline, then be intent on performing your duty just for Me. You shall attain perfection by doing your prescribed duty for Me—without any selfish motive—just as an instrument to serve and please Me. If you are unable to do your duty for Me, then just surrender unto My will, and renounce the attachment to, and the anxiety for, the fruits of all work—by learning to accept all results as God's grace—with equanimity. (12.08–12.11)

17. The *midrash* interprets the light in Genesis 1:3 as a garment of God, citing Psalm 104:2. See *Genesis Rabbah*, 3:4, 20–21.

The "dead" pilgrim, wearing a funeral shroud, is about to meet his Maker and travel the seven heavens, to reach the unknowable, unimaginable, infinite Supreme Being. The pilgrim sheds all his imagined ideas about Whom he is about to meet. He remains completely naked of beliefs, removing the worthless, earthly, selfish garments (*libās*) from his heart, surrendering to the will of God and waiting to be covered by the garments of God. (This may explain why the ancient Arabs appear to have taken such symbolism literally and, in so doing, performed the Ḥajj nude.[18])

The root of *libās* (*l-b-s*) has various meanings, including a cover or a garment;[19] confusion or ambiguity;[20] insanity.[21] These meanings are found in the Qur'an: "Did We then weary in the first creation? Nay, but they are in doubt (*labs*) regarding a new creation" [Qur'an 50:15].

The root of *libās* also means covering a partner through copulation, as in Qur'an 2:187,[22] where we read: "It is lawful for you to go in unto your wives during the night preceding the [day's] fast: they are as a garment for you, and you are as a garment for them." Perhaps this is why, in this verse, which discusses the permission to be intimate with one's partner on the night of fasting, even though each partner is a "garment" (*libās*) for the other, it is still forbidden to do so if people are in retreat (*iᶜtikāf*) in a mosque (Qur'an 2:187), which is considered a house of God. In His House, only He shall be the worshipper's garment (*libās*). The garments (*libās*) of falsehood are also explained in the Qur'an.

> And confound (*talbisū*) not truth with falsehood, nor knowingly conceal the truth. [Qur'an 2:42]

> Those who believe and who do not obscure (*yalbisū*) their belief through wrongdoing, it is they who have security, and they are rightly guided. [Qur'an 6:82]

---

18. Implied from the prophetic tradition (*ḥadīth*) that forbids performance of the circumambulation nude. See *Ṣaḥīḥ al-Bukhārī*, 1: 79, 82 (#369), 2: 153 (#1622), 4: 102 (#3177), 5: 167 (#4363), 6: 64 (#4655), (#4656), 65 (#4657).

19. *Lisān al-ᶜarab*, 6: 202–204 on *l-b-s*. *BDB*, 527–528.

20. Ibid., 6: 204 on *l-b-s*.

21. *Targum Lexicon*, on *l-b-š*.

22. *Gesenius' Hebrew-Chaldee Lexicon to the Old Testament*, 428.

> Likewise have their partners made the slaying of their children seem fair unto many of the idolaters, that they may ruin them and confound (*liyalbisū*) them in their religion. Had God willed, they would not have done so. So leave them and that which they fabricate. [Qur'an 6:137]

The Qur'an also explains the garments (*libās*) of God, saying:

> O Children of Adam! We have indeed sent down upon you raiment (*libās*) to cover your nakedness, and rich adornment. But the raiment (*libās*) of reverence, that is better. This is among the signs of God, that haply they may remember. O Children of Adam! Let not Satan tempt you, as he caused your parents to go forth from the Garden, stripping them of their raiment (*libāsahumā*) to show them their nakedness. Surely he sees you—he and his tribe (*qabīluh*)—whence you see them not. We have indeed made the satans the friends of those who do not believe. [Qur'an 7:26–27]

> For such as these, theirs shall be the Gardens of Eden with rivers running below. Therein they shall be adorned with bracelets of gold, and shall wear (*yalbasūn*) green garments of fine silk and rich brocade, reclining upon couches. Blessed indeed is the reward, and how beautiful a resting place! [Qur'an 18:31]
> Truly God will cause those who believe and perform righteous deeds to enter Gardens with rivers running below, adorned therein with bracelets of gold and pearl, and therein their clothes (*libāsuhum*) will be of silk. [Qur'an 22:23]

> Gardens of Eden which they will enter, adorned therein with bracelets of gold and pearls; and their garments (*libāsuhum*) therein will be of silk. [Qur'an 35:33]

> Wearing (*yalbasūn*) fine silk and rich brocade, facing one another (*mutaqābilīn*). [Qur'an 44:53]

As the root from which *islām* is derived, *s-l-m*, also yields the word for ladder (*sullam*), the pilgrim is now ready to go up the ladder. Having been stripped naked of his beliefs by fully surrendering to God, the pilgrim waits for God's garments to cover him (e.g., Exodus 20:26, Job 26:6, Isaiah 47:3, Ezekiel 16:8, Hosea 2:3, Amos 2:16, Mark 14:52, 2 Corinthians 5:1–5,

Revelation 3:17–18, Revelation 16:15).

In the early chapters of the Book of Ezekiel, God confronts Jerusalem (which may be seen as a metaphor for people's bodies) for its aversion to God. Although God has clothed it in a pure state (*fiṭrah*), it has become like a prostitute, just as in the story of the Fall of Adam, who was also clothed by God's garments but took them off in pursuit of selfish desires:

> The word of the LORD came to me: "Son of man, confront Jerusalem with her detestable practices and say, 'This is what the Sovereign LORD says to Jerusalem: Your ancestry and birth were in the land of the Canaanites; your father was an Amorite and your mother a Hittite. On the day you were born your cord was not cut, nor were you washed with water to make you clean, nor were you rubbed with salt or wrapped in cloths. No one looked on you with pity or had compassion enough to do any of these things for you. Rather, you were thrown out into the open field, for on the day you were born you were despised." Then I passed by and saw you kicking about in your blood, and as you lay there in your blood I said to you, "Live!" I made you grow like a plant of the field. You grew up and developed and became the most beautiful of jewels. Your breasts were formed and your hair grew, you who were naked and bare. Later I passed by, and when I looked at you and saw that you were old enough for love, I spread the corner of my garment over you and covered your nakedness. I gave you my solemn oath and entered into a covenant with you, declares the Sovereign LORD, and you became mine. I bathed you with water and washed the blood from you and put ointments on you. I clothed you with an embroidered dress and put leather sandals on you. I dressed you in fine linen and covered you with costly garments. I adorned you with jewelry: I put bracelets on your arms and a necklace around your neck, and I put a ring on your nose, earrings on your ears and a beautiful crown on your head. So you were adorned with gold and silver; your clothes were of fine linen and costly fabric and embroidered cloth. Your food was fine flour, honey and olive oil. You became very beautiful and rose to be a queen. And your fame spread among the nations on account of your beauty, because the splendor I had given you made your beauty perfect, declares the Sovereign LORD. [Ezekiel 16: 1–9]

Just as Jerusalem is clothed in God's garment, the Qur'an also describes how a city (*qaryah*)[23] may be clothed in a negative sense: "God sets forth a parable: a town (*qaryah*) secure and at peace, its provision coming unto it abundantly from every side. Yet, it was ungrateful for the blessings of God; so God let it taste the garment (*libās*) of hunger and fear for that which they had wrought" [Qur'an 16:112].

The pilgrim, dead from thirst and stripped of his garments, is now ready to go up the ladder (*sullam*) to the seventh heaven, to the Station of Abraham (*maqām Ibrāhīm*), just below the Throne of God. The pilgrim cries out to God in full surrender to His Will, asking he be granted a sip of the Water of Life and that his nakedness be covered with the divine garments that clothed Adam and Eve before the Fall.

23. The use of city (*qaryah*) might be significant, as the Qur'an allegedly describes Mecca as the Mother of Cities (*Umm al-Qurā*).

5

JACOB'S LADDER (*SA^{c}Ī*)

After praying behind *maqām Ibrāhīm*, the pilgrim is now in complete surrender and, stripped of all garments of falsehood, and waits to be clad in the garment of God that clothed Adam and Eve before the Fall (Qur'an 7:27, Genesis 2:25). Knowing herself to be dead, she longs for the Water of Life to resurrect her and is ready to ascend the ladder (*sullam*) above the seven heavens and meet her Maker.

THE DESERT DRAMA

BARREN DESERT

According to Islamic tradition, walking and running between the hills of Ṣafā and Marwah is a re-enactment of Hagar's search for water to quench the thirst of her dying child, Ishmael. This happened when Abraham left Hagar and his son Ishmael in the barren desert.[1]

We read in the Book of Genesis that God commanded Abraham to leave Hagar and his son Ishmael in a barren desert at

1. Al-Ṭabarī, *Jāmi^{c}*, 17: 19–20 on Q. 14:37.

the request of his wife Sarah (Genesis 21:8–21). This is similar to God having previously commanded Abraham to leave the household of his father, his people, and his country to move to another land (Genesis 12:1). This commandment might be seen as an allegory for the act of leaving everything behind (*hājar*) for the sake of God:[2]

> Our Lord! Verily I have settled some of my progeny in a valley without cultivation by Thy Sacred House, our Lord, that they might perform the prayer. So cause the hearts of some men to incline toward them, and provide them with fruits, that haply they may give thanks. [Qur'an 14:37]

When Hagar and Ishmael were in the barren desert, having already consumed their provisions of water, Ishmael starts to thirst. According to Islamic tradition, Hagar rushes between the hills of Ṣafā and Marwah in search of water. She does so seven times, and after the seventh, the well of Zamzam gushes out from below an angel's foot.[3] According to Genesis, God hears the voice of the boy and opens the eyes of the mother weeping over her dying child so that she can see the water (Genesis 21:17–19).

The name Ishmael, which means God hears, was given to the boy by an angel when Hagar was pregnant with him (Genesis 16:11). Interestingly, the angel also tells Hagar that he will increase her descendants so that they become too numerous to count (Genesis 16:10). Then the angel describes Ishmael as a wild donkey of a man (Genesis 16:11–12). Hagar does not seem to be offended but reacts as if it were a blessing (Genesis 16:13). The Hebrew word for wild donkey is *pereʾ*, whose root is possibly *p-r-y*, meaning fertility, progeny, generation, and fruitful. Although people usually understand the term wild donkey as a pejorative term,[4] it is possible to understand that the angel is describing Ishmael as a fruitful man who will have many

2. This is a play on words, as Hagar's name (*hājar*) means to "migrate." Another play on words using Hagar's name is found in *Genesis Rabbah*, 380, where Hagar is noted as Pharaoh's daughter, in which Pharaoh tells Sarah, "Here is thy reward (*agar*)," as Pharaoh presents Hagar as a reward (*agar*) to Sarah.

3. Al-Ṭabarī, *Tarīkh al-rusul wal-mulūk* (Beirut: al-Turāth, 1967), 1: 255–256.

4. *BDB*, 826.

descendants (Genesis 16:10). Interpreting it as a blessing to be fruitful fits more logically with the Biblical text. Although in *Genesis Rabbah* it is interpreted to mean that Ishmael will live in the wilderness or will be a savage person in the literal sense,[5] nothing in Hagar's response indicates that she has taken any offense or that the angel means the boy will be a savage. Clare Amos also highlighted another polysemous linguistic translation in the angel's words, which describes Ishmael as living in hostility toward his brethren, using the term *pĕnê*.[6] The root of the word, however, also means face,[7] which, like the Arabic term for face (*wajh*), can mean either to confront with hostility (*yuwājih*)[8] or to instruct (*yuwajjih*).[9] In English, for example, if a king says, "I need to face my people," it may mean that he needs to be in their presence, whereas if he says, "I need to face my enemies," it may mean that he needs to confront them.

Hagar has fled from her mistress, Sarah (or Sarai at the time), and is near a well (Genesis 16:7, 16:14), not to be confused with Zamzam. Since Hagar saw God and remained alive after seeing God, she refers to God as the One Who Sees Me (Genesis 16:11–13). This is the first instance in the Bible in which God is referred to as the One Who Sees. Hence, God is the One Who both hears and sees (*al-samīᶜ al-baṣīr*), as God heard the cries and saw. This passage in Genesis describes God's hearing and seeing, in this order. This is significant because the running between Ṣafā and Marwah (*saᶜī*) will be discussed as an allusion to the Prophet's Night Journey (*al-Isrāʾ wal-Miᶜrāj*), which is alluded to in a chapter of the Qur'an that bears the same name, *Sūrat al-Isrāʾ* and whose first verse refers to God as the One Who Hears and Sees—*al-samiᶜ al-baṣīr*—in the same order: "Glory be to Him Who carried His servant by night (*asrā bi-ᶜabdih laylā*) from the Sacred Mosque to the Farthest Mosque, whose precincts We

5. *Genesis Rabbah*, 49.9, 386.

6. Clare Amos, "Incomplete without the Other: Isaac, Ishmael and a Hermeneutic Diversity," *Islam and Christian-Muslim Relations* (2009), 20(3): 247–256.

7. *BDB*, 815–819.

8. *Lisān al-ᶜarab*, 13: 557 on *w-j-h*.

9. *Ibid.*, 556–557 on *w-j-h*.

have blessed, that We might show him some of Our signs. Truly He is the Hearer, the Seer (*al-samīᶜ al-baṣīr*)" (Qur'an 17:1).

The root of the name Hagar (*h-j-r*) means to emigrate, to leave, and to abandon. In Arabic, it also means ill-speaking, greatness, or midday.[10] A pilgrim traversing the hills of Ṣafā and Marwah wearing a funeral shroud (*iḥrām*) represents a dead soul that is abandoning the earthly world and emigrating (*hājar*) to God to seek the Water of Life, as Hagar searched for water in the wilderness. To do so, however, the dead pilgrim needs to abandon even herself. It is noteworthy that Hagar did not seek water for herself, but her son. This might represent the dead soul abandoning (*hajr*) its ego, seeking the Water of Life not for itself, but all other dead and dying souls. Perhaps when Hagar fled from Sarah, the angel of God asked her to return because she should not be fleeing for her own sake, but for the sake of others, as she did when searching for water for her dying son. It is interesting to note that Hagar knew through God's promise that her descendants would multiply, and that therefore, the child could not die (Genesis 16:6–10).

Another reference to the desert drama from Genesis is that Hagar wept (*tēbk*) as the boy was dying (Genesis 21:16). Weeping in Arabic and Hebrew is from the root *b-k-y* or *b-k-h*.[11] The Qur'an refers to the House of God being located in a place called Bakkah (Qur'an 3:96), which might mean weeping, although in Arabic the root *b-k-k* might mean crowding,[12] while its root means to crush.[13] Al-Ṭabarī states that among various reasons Bakkah was so named is that men and women crowd into it.[14] As a result, it is difficult to state whether *Lisān al-ᶜarab*'s definition might be an interpolation from classical *tafsīr* or not. Nonetheless, the Arabic definition of crushing might be its root meaning.[15]

10. *Lisān al-ᶜarab*, 13: 250–257 on *h-j-r*; BDB, 212.

11. Ibid., 14: 82–83 on *b-k-y*; *BDB*, 113–114; and Wolf Leslau, *Comparative Dictionary of Geᶜez* (Wiesbaden: Harrassowitz, 2006), 94.

12. *Lisān al-ᶜarab*, 10: 402 on *b-k-k*.

13. *Ibid.*

14. Al-Ṭabarī, *Jāmiᶜ*, 6: 24 on Q. 3:96.

15. See *Comparative Dictionary of Geᶜez*, 94, where its meanings include crushing, emptying, or fading away.

There may be a relationship between Bakkah as mentioned in the Qur'an and the valley mentioned in Psalm 84:6.[16] If so, then we might conclude that people need to make their bodies and hearts into a temple or dwelling place for God. It then becomes a place into which God breathes His Spirit—the divine presence that the Jews call *Shekhinah* and the Muslims call *al-Sakīnah*. Indeed, the root *sakan* means house or dwelling place.

> How lovely is Your dwelling place (*miškĕnôtêkā*), O LORD Almighty! My soul yearns, even faints, for the courts of the LORD; my heart and my flesh (*bĕšāriy*) cry out for the living God. Even the sparrow has found a home, and the swallow a nest for herself, where she may have her young—a place near Your altars (*mizbĕḥôtêkā*), O LORD Almighty, my King and my God. Blessed are those who dwell in Your house; they are ever praising you (*yĕhallûkā*). Selah. Blessed are those whose strength is in you, who have set their hearts on pilgrimage (highways / *mĕsillôt*). As they pass through the Valley (*ᶜēmeq*) of *Baka* (weeping), they make it a place of springs; the autumn rains also cover it with pools. They go from strength to strength, till each appears before God in Zion. Hear my prayer, O LORD God Almighty; listen to me, O God of Jacob. Selah. Look upon our shield, O God; look with favour on Your anointed (*mĕšiḥekā*). Better is one day in Your courts than a thousand elsewhere; I would rather be a doorkeeper in the house of my God than dwell in the tents of the wicked. For the LORD God is a sun and shield; the LORD bestows favour and honour; no good thing does He withhold from those whose walk is blameless. O LORD Almighty, blessed is the man who trusts in You. [Psalm 84:1–12]

Several points of intertextuality may be interpolated and extrapolated from this Psalm concerning the Ḥajj.[17] The Psalm may describe the true Temple of God in our bodies. Psalm 84:2 states that the soul yearns for God and that the heart and flesh cry out for God. Since it discusses the heart and soul, it also suggests a connection to the *Shemaᶜ*, which is a reference to the *qiblah*.[18]

16. For more details, see Galadari, *Metaphors of Death.*
17. Ibid.
18. Galadari, "The *Qibla*."

The *qiblah* passages are found to be engaging with the *Shemaᶜ* passages in Deuteronomy and its rabbinic commentary, suggesting the *qiblah* passages to be alluding to the *Shemaᶜ*.[19] This is the first point of intertextuality.

The second point of intertextuality is found in this Psalm's description of God's sacrificial altars using the word *mizbĕḥôtêkā*, from the root *z-b-ḥ* in Hebrew and Aramaic, which is cognate to *dh-b-ḥ* in Arabic, meaning to slaughter or sacrifice,[20] especially the sacrifice during the pilgrimage. The same root is used in the Qur'an to describe the sacrifice of Abraham's son and his sacrificial replacement by God (Qur'an 37:101, 37:107), events to which the Ḥajj ritual is related. Psalm 84:4 describes the praises (*yĕhallûkā*), which may be related to the *ahillah* of Ḥajj, as discussed earlier in Qur'an 2:189, making it the third point of intertextuality. Psalm 84:6 also uses the word *ᶜēmeq* to describe the valley of Baka. This shares the root, *ᶜamīq*, which is used in the Qur'an during the proclamation of the Ḥajj, as people will be travelling from deep (*ᶜamīq*) and distant mountain highways (Qur'an 22:17), which might be conjoined with the term *mĕsillôt* in Psalm 84:5, which itself means highway or path;[21] these make the fourth and fifth points of intertextuality respectively. The name Baka in this Psalm and Bakkah in the Qur'an is the sixth point of intertextuality. Psalm 84:10 states how a day with God is better than a thousand years elsewhere, which has a similar resonance with a passage in the Qur'an described in *Sūrat al-Ḥajj*, making it the seventh point of intertextuality:

> Yet they ask you to hasten on the Punishment! But Allah will not fail in His Promise. Verily a Day in the sight of your Lord is like a thousand years of your reckoning. [Qur'an 22:47]

Psalm 84 displays the pilgrim's longing to experience the divine presence.[22] The notion of seeing God, a recurring motif in the

19. Ibid.

20. *Lisān al-ᶜarab*, 2: 436–440 on *dh-b-ḥ*; *BDB*, 256–259.

21. *BDB*, 700.

22. Mark S. Smith, "The Near Eastern Background of Solar Language for Yahweh," *Journal of Biblical Literature* (1990), 109(1): 29–39.

Psalms (e.g., Psalms 11:7, 17:15, 27:4, 27:13, 42:3, 63:3), might be linked to Hagar's description of God as the Him Who Sees (Genesis 16:13). Similarly, Psalm 42 describes the soul's thirst for God. Therefore, a link between Psalms 84 and 42 could also establish that the pilgrim is actually the dead soul that is thirsty for God and the Water of Life: "As the deer pants for streams of water, so my soul pants for you, my God. My soul thirsts for God, for the living God. When can I go and meet with God?" [Psalm 42:1–2].

The name Zion (*ṣiyyôn*), in Psalm 84:5 and 84:7, perhaps has its root in "*ṣ-y-n*" or "*ṣ-w-n*" meaning the marking of a grave or a funerary monument in Hebrew and Aramaic.[23] The same root has been used for such meaning in the Hebrew Bible (2 Kings 23:17, Jeremiah 31:21, Ezekiel 39:15). The term "*ṣahwah*" in Arabic means a fortress on top of a mountain.[24] In Psalm 48:2–3, Zion is explicitly described as a mountain and a fortress. Therefore, the root of the meaning for "*ṣahwah*" would fit such a description. Putting it into perspective, perhaps the dead pilgrim wearing a funeral shroud (*iḥrām*) is Zion (the dead soul in a grave of the body).

ṢAFĀ, MARWAH, AND ZAMZAM

To understand the walking and running between the hills of Ṣafā and Marwah, it may be useful to apply intertextual polysemy to the meanings of these names. In Arabic, *ṣafā* means to be clear, to make clear, to drink, to filter, and to be chosen, as in *muṣṭafā*, an epithet of the Prophet Muḥammad ﷺ meaning "chosen" or "elect."[25] Similarly, the root *ṣ-f-y* in Hebrew and Aramaic means to look out, to spy, to face, to filter, to clarify, to make to drink, a watchman, or a watchtower.[26]

One possible root of Marwah is *m-r-w*, meaning a fragrant

23. *BDB*, 846.

24. *Lisān al-ᶜarab*, 14: 471 on "*ṣ-h-w-h*." The Hebrew and Arabic terms may be related. See Robinson, A. (1974) "Zion and Saphon in Psalm XLVIII 3," *Vetus Testamentum*, 24(1): 118–123.

25. *Lisān al-ᶜarab*, 14: 462 on *ṣ-f-y*.

26. *BDB*, 859–860.

tree, or to come out.[27] In Aramaic, it means dominion or domination.[28] However, if it is considered to be derived from the root *r-w-y*, it means the place where thirst is quenched (*marwā*), as *r-w-y* means to give drink, to quench thirst, or to irrigate.[29] According to Genesis 22:2, Abraham was to sacrifice Isaac on Mount Moriah, a name similar to Marwah, while according to 2 Chronicles 3:1, Mount Moriah is the location of the Temple of Jerusalem. As for Ṣafā, it bears a resemblance to Mount Ṣophīm (Mount Scopus), which played a role in the pilgrimage to Jerusalem. After the destruction of the Temple, Jewish pilgrims were eventually allowed to visit Jerusalem. In an insightful study entitled *Four Paths to Jerusalem: Jewish, Christian, Muslim, and Secular Pilgrimages, 1000 BCE to 2001 CE*, Hunt Janin states,

> By the middle of the third century they [the Romans] had given the Jews permission to return to Jerusalem and climb Mount Scopus [Ṣophīm] or the Mount of Olives to mourn the Temple [on Mount Moriah] from afar. At some later point they were also allowed to enter the ruins of the Temple [on Mount Moriah] itself …[30]

A manuscript of unknown date, but from after the Temple's destruction, offers the following instructions to Jewish pilgrims to Jerusalem:

> If you are worthy to go up to Jerusalem, when you look at the city from Mount Scopus [Ṣophīm] [you should do as follows]. If you are riding on a donkey, step down; if you are on foot, take off your sandals, then rending your garments say: "This sanctuary was destroyed" … When you arrive in the city, continue to rend your garments for the Temple [on Mount Moriah] and the people and the house of Israel. Then pray saying, "May the Lord our God be exalted" and "Let us worship at his footstool … We give you thanks, O Lord our God, that you have given us life, brought us to this point, and made us worthy to enter your

27. *Lisān al-ᶜarab*, 15: 276–277 on *m-r-w*.

28. *Targum Lexicon*.

29. *Lisān al-ᶜarab*, 14: 345 on *r-w-y*; *BDB*, 924.

30. Hunt Janin, *Four Paths to Jerusalem: Jewish, Christian, Muslim, and Secular Pilgrimages, 1000 BCE to 2001 CE* (Jefferson, NC: McFarland, 2006), 56.

> house" … Then return and circle all the gates of the city and go around all its corners, make a circuit and count its towers.[31]

Thus, the names of hills of Ṣafā and Marwah have homophonic parallels with Mount Scopus [Ṣophīm] and Mount Moriah in Jerusalem, both of them destinations for Jewish pilgrimage to Jerusalem.

SAᶜĪ

HEAVENLY LADDER

Walking and running between the hills of Ṣafā and Marwah appears to represent an ascent from death to life, as the dead pilgrim, who is dying of thirst ("dying to live") takes a ladder (*sullam*) up to the seven heavens seeking God and the Water of Life in a kind of resurrection. The Qur'an describes how God has created seven heavens above one another, saying:

> He it is Who created for you all that is on the earth. Then He turned (*istawā*) to heaven and fashioned them[32] (*fa-sawwāhunna*) into seven heavens, and He is the Knower of all things. [Qur'an 2:29]

Here, the Qur'an describes the creation of the heavens using the same root *s-w-y* used for God establishing (*istawā*) His Throne and fashioning the human (*sawwaytuhu*) (Qur'an 15:29, 38:72).[33] According to the Qur'an, each of the seven heavens is established (*sawwāhunna*) as God creates the human in seven stages or levels. The Qur'an describes the seven stages of human development by considering the beginning of creation from clay, then sperm, then a clinging clot, then a lump, then bones, then flesh, then a different development (new human) (Qur'an 23:12–14). The Qur'an further details that after the new development come death and resurrection (Qur'an 23:15–16). Although the Qur'an initially talks about the seven stages of human development,

---

31. Quoted by Janin in *Four Paths to Jerusalem*, 57.

32. The *TSQ* uses the singular because the subject, heaven, is singular. However, though the subject is singular, the Arabic uses a plural suffix in this case, as the singular heaven becomes seven.

33. For further details, see Galadari, *Qur'anic Hermeneutics*, 117–128.

it then makes an apparent link to the seven heavens (Qur'an 23:17). It is also important to note that in these verses the Qur'an describes death first and then resurrection or life. This may also be compared with the following verses:

> Who created death and life that He may try you as to which of you is most virtuous in deed, and He is the Mighty, the Forgiving, Who created seven heavens one upon another (*ṭibāqā*); no disproportion dost thou see in the Merciful's creation. Cast thy sight again; dost thou see any flaw (*fuṭūr*)? Then cast thy sight twice again; thy sight will return (*yanqalib*) to thee humbled and wearied. [Qur'an 67:2–4]

It is usually said that the body lives and then dies. In these verses, however, the Qur'an mentions death before life. This reversal is significant. Perhaps it represents the death of the soul, which comes before its life, as the 'dead' soul is entombed within the living body. Then the verses discuss how God created the seven heavens above each other, asking people to see if there is any flaw (*fuṭūr*), using the same root for the pure state of the soul, *fiṭrah*:[34] "seeing that He has created you in stages (*aṭwārā*), have you not considered how God created the seven heavens one upon another (*ṭibāqa*)?" [Qur'an 71:14–15].

In this passage and the one cited earlier, the word used for creating the heavens above each other is *ṭibāqā* (Qur'an 67:3, 71:15). The root *ṭ-b-q* means to cover, to layer, to adhere, and to be similar.[35] Perhaps these verses explain how humans are created in diverse stages, with their souls ascending from one level to another.[36] Each layer (*ṭabaq*), up to seven layers, is covered by a heaven. A different verse in the Qur'an describes how humans mount from one level (*ṭabaq*) to another, saying, "thou wilt surely journey (*la-tarkabunna*) from stage to stage (*ṭabaqan ᶜan ṭabaq*). [Qur'an 84:19]

Al-Ṭabarī relates that the meaning of this passage is to mount one level after another or one stage after another, and in at least

---

34. *Lisān al-ᶜarab*, 12: 275 on *f-ṭ-r*.
35. *Ibid.*, 10: 209 on *ṭ-b-q*.
36. Another possibility is evolutionary creation; see Galadari, "*Creatio ex Nihilo*."

one interpretation, ascending from one heaven after another.[37] The word used for travel is *tarkabunna*, of which the root is *r-k-b*. The root *r-k-b* means to mount, to ride, or anything that is mounted, whether animal, car, boat, etc.[38] The Qur'an uses this meaning when Noah enters or mounts into the ark (Qur'an 11:41–43, 36:41–42), when people board the boat of salvation (*al-khalāṣ*) (Qur'an 29:65), as Moses and the mysterious righteous fellow board a boat (Qur'an 18:71), or when animals are created to be mounted and ridden (Qur'an 16:8, 40:79). Moreover, the Qur'an also uses the root to describe God forming the human being: "Who created you, then fashioned you (*sawwāk*), then proportioned you, assembling (*rakkabak*) you in whatever form (*ṣūrah*) He willed?" [Qur'an 82:7–8].

The root *r-k-b* also means chariot or that which is mounted, as well as the knee.[39] Hence, in the *rukūᶜ*, which is the bow, the hands are placed on top of the knees (*rukbah*), as perhaps the person praying mounts from one level to another (*ṭabaqan ᶜan ṭabaq*). Then, the person praying straightens (*yastaqīm*) from the bowing position (*rukūᶜ*) as he mounts the new level, just as he prays before the *rukūᶜ*, saying, "Guide us to the path that is straight (*al-mustaqīm*)" [Qur'an 1:6]. Once he is standing (*istawā*) on the new level (*ṭabaq*), he falls down in prostration (*sujūd*), just as in the Qur'an God commands the angels to fall in prostration after He forms (*sawwaytuhu*) the human being and breathes into him from His Spirit (Qur'an 15:29).

There is a connection between Ishmael, which means "God hears", and the bow (*rukūᶜ*). As discussed, every time the person praying bows, he symbolizes the soul mounting up a level (*ṭabaq*). Similarly, the pilgrim travels between Ṣafā and Marwah, mounting seven heavenly levels. Hagar was running between the hills to search for water for Ishmael. When the person praying stands up after the *rukūᶜ*, he does not say "God is greater" (*Allāh akbar*) as he does between other parts of the prayer ritual, but

37. Al-Ṭabarī, *Jāmiᶜ*, 24: 322–326 on Q. 84:19.
38. *Lisān al-ᶜarab*, 1: 428 on *r-k-b*.
39. Ibid., 1: 433 on *r-k-b*.

instead says, "God hears he who praises Him" (*samiʿ Allāhu li-man ḥamidah*). *Samiʿ Allāh*—God hears—is the meaning of Ishmael's name. This is what the person praying says every time he mounts a level, just as a pilgrim does between Ṣafā and Marwah, re-enacting the desert drama of Hagar and Ishmael. There needs to be a reason why a person praying would say *samiʿ Allāh li-man ḥamidah* when rising from a bow (*rukūʿ*), while between all other pairs of actions he says *Allāhu akbar*. The answer may be simpler than it seems. Before bowing, the person praying recites the Fātiḥah, also known as *al-ḥamd*, since it begins with *al-ḥamdulillāh*. Hence, the person praying praises God (recites *al-ḥamdulillāh*), then performs the bow (*rukūʿ*); hence, God has heard the person praying, for he has praised Him (*samiʿ Allāh li-man ḥamidah*).

The night prayers, both *maghrib* and *ʿishāʾ*, have seven *rakʿāt* (prayer cycles) combined, since the person praying is mounting seven levels at night, whereas morning prayers (*fajr*) and daytime prayers, both *ẓuhr* and *ʿaṣr*, have ten *rakʿāt* combined, since the person praying is mounting ten levels. Even those who missed coming to the prayer from the beginning need to be sure that the number of *rakʿāt* are the same for them, in that they must perform the bow (*rukūʿ*), putting their hands on their knees (*rukbah*) to mount from one level to another the correct number of times. Every time the person praying mounts one level, he prostrates in adoration (*sujūd*).

The root *r-k-b* is likewise used in 2 Kings for the chariot (*rekeb*) that takes Elijah up to the heavens (2 Kings 2:11–12). The word *merkabah*, which comes from the same root, is also used by Jewish Kabbalah as the Chariot of the Throne of God, which is described as having four wheels and being driven by four living creatures, each of which has four faces and four wings (Ezekiel 1:4–26).[40] However, in the Qur'an, the Throne of God is described as being carried by eight (Qur'an 69:17). Since res-

---

40. For more information on the Merkabah in Jewish mysticism, see Timo Eskola, *Messiah and the Throne: Jewish Merkabah Mysticism and Early Christian Exaltation Discourse* (Philadelphia, PA: Coronet Books, 2001).

urrection is symbolized by the sun, the *ẓuhr* (noon) and ^{c}*aṣr* (mid-afternoon) prayers are comprised of a total of eight cycles (*rak^{c}āt*) which are performed while the sun is up; perhaps these prayer cycles are "the eight" that carry the Throne of God.

When the Qur'an speaks of God raising some people above others in rank (Qur'an 43:32), it invokes images of God raising Mount Sinai (*al-Ṭūr*) above the Israelites (Qur'an 2:63, 2:93, 4:154). Although Qur'an 43:33 describes people as being one, each person is above another in rank according to Qur'an 43:32 with each rank denoting a different spiritual level (Qur'an 5:48, 10:19, 11:118). The word used for stairways in Qur'an 43:33 is *ma^{c}ārij*, which shares the same root of *mi^{c}rāj* as in the Prophet's Night Journey and his ascension to the heavens. Qur'an 43:34 goes on to describe how the blessed will have doors to their houses and thrones on which to recline. This is similar to the ascension (*mi^{c}rāj*) of the Prophet in the Night Journey in which the Prophet Muḥammad ﷺ travelled up the heavens, each having a door, until he reached the heavenly temple (*al-bayt al-ma^{c}mūr*) and eventually the Lote Tree of the Utmost Boundary (*sidrat al-muntahā*).[41] Mount Sinai (*al-Ṭūr*), the heavenly temple (*al-bayt al-ma^{c}mūr*), and the heavenly ceiling are also brought together in the Qur'anic passage which reads: "By the Mount (*wal-Ṭūr*), and by a Book inscribed on parchment outspread; by the house inhabited (*wal-bayt al-ma^{c}mūr*), by the canopy (*wal-saqf*) raised, and by the sea swelling over" (Qur'an 52:1–6).

Since the Ḥajj or ^{c}Umrah is about the dead pilgrim who comes with the virtue of the fear of God, he is now to understand the secret mysteries of his soul. As the dead pilgrim ascends the staircase (*sullam*) from one level to another (*ṭabaqan ^{c}an ṭabaq*), he knocks in turn on the door of each of the seven heavens just as the Prophet ﷺ did during his nocturnal *mi^{c}rāj*, or ascent, to the heavens. Qur'an 43:43 describes the thrones (*surur*) on which people in heaven recline. The root from which *surur* is derived—*s-r-r*—also yields the word for mystery or secret (*sirr*)

41. *Ṣaḥīḥ al-Bukhārī*, 4: 109–110 (#3207), 5: 52 (#3887).

and, hence, that which is hidden.[42] The belly is called *baṭn*, just as *sirr* means secret, and *bāṭin* means hidden. Additionally, as the Qur'an describes, within it (*bāṭinuhu*) is mercy (*raḥmah*); it is also understood that the embryo grows in the mother's womb (*raḥim*), in her belly (*baṭn*).[43] After all, the pilgrim is believed to emerge pure from the Ḥajj rituals as a newborn emerges from his mother's womb.[44]

SOARING OR FLOATING UP THE LADDER

Although the *sa*ᶜ*ī* between Ṣafā and Marwah is a prominent pillar of both the Ḥajj and the ᶜUmrah, it is mentioned only once in the Qur'an (Qur'an 2:158), where it is treated almost as though it were a practice in need of justification: "Behold, As-Safa and Al-Marwah are among the symbols set up by God; and thus, no wrong does he who, having come to the Temple on pilgrimage or on a pious visit, strides to and fro between these two" [Qur'an 2:158]. This apparent contradiction was understood by classical exegetes, such as al-Ṭabarī, in light of the circumstances surrounding the revelation of this verse.[45] According to tradition, ancient Arabs used to have two idols, *Isāf* on Ṣafā and *Nā*ᵓ*ilah* on Marwah, for whom they showed their reverence by going back and forth between these two hills; consequently, early Muslims considered it blasphemous to run between the two hills, because it would appear as if they were imitating a polytheistic practice. Therefore, this verse is said to have been revealed to dissociate the ritual from idol worship; Muslim exegetes have attempted to show that the verse actually emphasizes the importance of the ritual. However, there might also be another explanation of the emphasis placed on this ritual:

Truly Ṣafā and Marwah are among the rituals of God; so whoso-

---

42. *Lisān al-*ᶜ*arab*, 4:356–357 on *s-r-r*; it is the same root used for the navel (*surrah*) (Ibid., 4:360).

43. On spiritual birth in the Qur'an, see Galadari, *Qur'anic Hermeneutics*, 55.

44. This is based on the prophetic *ḥadīth*, "Whoever performs the *ḥajj* while committing no obscenity or evil will be restored to the state he was in on the day his mother bore him." See *Ṣaḥīḥ al-Bukhārī*, 2: 133 (#1521), 3: 11 (#1819), (#1820).

45. Al-Ṭabarī, *Jāmi*ᶜ, 3: 224–248 on Q. 2:158.

> ever performs the *ḥajj* to the House, or makes the *ᶜumrah*, there is no blame (*fa-lā junāḥ*) on him in going to and fro (*yaṭṭawwaf*) between them. And whosoever volunteers (*taṭawwaᶜ*) good, truly God is Thankful, Knowing. [Qur'an 2:158]

Since, as we have seen, the seven-fold repetition of the *saᶜī* between Ṣafā and Marwah could represent the pilgrim passing through the seven heavens, this verse needs to be analyzed more closely. Beginning with the phrase rendered "there is no blame" (*fa-lā junāḥ*), its root, *j-n-ḥ*, means to bend; hence, since a bird flaps its wings, *j-n-ḥ* also yields the word for wing (*janāḥ*),[46] as well as the word *junḥah*, meaning a sin or a crime, which involves bending or inclining away from what is right.[47]

To understand the meaning of *j-n-ḥ*, however, it is important to understand how the Qur'an relates it to the word *taṭawwaᶜ*. The word *taṭawwaᶜ*, which has its root in *ṭ-w-ᶜ*, meaning to volunteer, to agree, or to obey,[48] is used here to mean to obey one's impulses for good. (The same root is used in a contrasting sense in the Qur'anic story of Cain, which describes how Cain obeyed his soul's impulse to kill his brother (Qur'an 5:30)). The following verses describe the obeisance (*ṭawᶜ*) to the surrender of God, sharing the same root:

> Do they seek other than God's religion, while whosoever is in the heavens and on the earth submits (*aslam*) to Him, willingly (*ṭawᶜan*) or unwillingly, and unto Him they will be returned? Say, "We believe in God and what has been sent down upon us, and in what was sent down upon Abraham, Ishmael, Isaac, Jacob, and the Tribes, and in what Moses, Jesus, and the prophets were given from their Lord. We make no distinction among any of them, and unto Him we submit (*muslimūn*)." Whosoever seeks a *dīn*[49] other than submission (*islām*), it shall not be accepted of him, and in the Hereafter he shall be among the losers (*al-khāsirīn*). [Qur'an 3:83–85]

46. *Lisān al-ᶜarab*, 2: 428–429 on *j-n-ḥ*.

47. *Ibid.*, 2: 430.

48. *Ibid.*, 8: 240–243 on *ṭ-w-ᶜ*.

49. Although the word *dīn* is typically understood to mean "religion," it is also associated with *dayn*, meaning "loan" or "debt," thus symbolizing that surrender (*islām*) is one's debt to God; see Galadari, *Qur'anic Hermeneutics*, 137–145.

The Qur'an describes here how everything in the heavens and the earth has surrendered (*aslam*) to the Will of God, whether voluntarily (*ṭawᶜan*) or otherwise (cf. 13:15). Those who have surrendered (*muslimūn*) to the will of God believe in all the prophets and what was revealed to them. Furthermore, surrendering to the Will of God (*islām*) is the only acceptable "religion" (*dīn* / repayment, *dayn*) and anyone choosing anything else has lost, just as Cain lost when he obeyed his soul's urge to kill his brother (Qur'an 5:30). In short, the heavens and the earth come to God in obedience, willingly or unwillingly, to His Will.

> Say, "Do you indeed disbelieve in the One Who created the earth in two days, and do you set up equals unto Him? That is the Lord of the worlds." He placed firm mountains therein rising above it, blessed it, and apportioned its means of sustenance therein in four days, alike for all who ask. Then He turned (*istawā*) to heaven while it was smoke and said unto it and unto the earth, "Come willingly (*ṭawᶜan*) or unwillingly!" They said, "We come willingly (*ṭāʾiᶜīn*)." Then He decreed (*fa-qaḍāhunna*) that they be seven heavens in two days and revealed to each heaven its command. And We adorned the lowest heaven with lamps and a guard. That is the Decree of the Mighty, the Knowing. [Qur'an 41:9–12]

These verses describe how God created the earth and placed mountains on it, just as in other verses the Qur'an describes these mountains as having paths to help people find their way (Qur'an 16:15, 21:31). He then asks the heavens and the earth to come to His Will, willingly (*ṭawᶜan*) or unwillingly, and they obey (*ṭāʾiᶜīn*).

Hence, it is understood from the Qur'anic verse, which mentions the passage between Ṣafā and Marwah for those performing Ḥajj or ᶜUmrah, that if anyone does not have a wing (*janāḥ*) to fly between the seven heavens, then he must do so floating (*yaṭṭawwaf*). Additionally, it is better for those who perform this willingly, obeying the Will of God (*taṭawwaᶜ*) (Qur'an 2:158). The verse may be understood and translated as follows:

> Truly Ṣafā and Marwah are among the rituals of God; so who-

> soever performs the *ḥajj* to the House, or makes the *ᶜumrah*, if he has no wing [to fly] (*falā junāḥ*) on him, then he needs to float (*yaṭṭawwaf*) between them. And whosoever volunteers (*taṭawwaᶜ*) good, truly God is Thankful, Knowing. [Qur'an 2:158]

JACOB'S LADDER

As discussed earlier, another name for a heavenly ladder is *miᶜrāj*. The Qur'an discusses how His angels and His Commands go up to the heavens through the *miᶜrāj*, just as the Prophet ascended to the heavens during the Night Journey (Qur'an 32:5, 34:2, 57:4, 70:3–4). The angels are described as having wings (*ajniḥah*), from the singular *janāḥ* (Qur'an 35:1).

There are interesting linkages between Ṣafā and Marwah and Jacob's Ladder mentioned in Genesis. A pilgrim traverses the ladder for his resurrection, symbolized by the east. Similarly, Jacob has been described as having gone to sleep when the sun set, symbolizing death, only to dream of a heavenly ladder:

> Jacob left Beersheba and set out for Haran. When he reached a certain place, he stopped for the night because the sun had set. Taking one of the stones there, he put it under his head and lay down to sleep. He had a dream in which he saw a stairway (*sullām*) resting on the earth, with its top reaching to heaven, and the angels of God were ascending and descending on it. There above it stood the LORD, and He said: "I am the LORD, the God of your father Abraham and the God of Isaac. I will give you and your descendants the land on which you are lying. Your descendants will be like the dust of the earth, and you will spread out to the west and to the east, to the north and to the south. All peoples on earth will be blessed through you and your offspring. I am with you and will watch over you wherever you go, and I will bring you back to this land. I will not leave you until I have done what I have promised you." When Jacob awoke from his sleep, he thought, "Surely the LORD is in this place, and I was not aware of it." He was afraid and said, "How awesome is this place! This is none other than the house of God; this is the gate (*šaᶜar*) of heaven." Early the next morning Jacob took the stone he had placed under his head and set it up as a pillar and poured

> oil on top of it. He called that place Bethel, though the city used to be called Luz. Then Jacob made a vow, saying, "If God will be with me and will watch over me on this journey I am taking and will give me bread (*leḥem*) to eat and clothes to wear so that I return safely to my father's house, then the LORD will be my God and this stone (*ha-ᶜeben*) that I have set up as a pillar will be God's house, and of all that you give me I will give you a tenth." [Genesis 28:10–22]

In his vision, Jacob sees the angels of God ascending and descending by a ladder to heaven. This seems to be similar to the depiction of Ṣafā and Marwah, as pilgrims ascend to the heavens while wearing a funeral shroud (their *iḥrām*) during the *saᶜī* of the ᶜUmrah and, as will see later, descend while not wearing the *iḥrām* during the *saᶜī* of the Ḥajj.

Jacob's vision might also be likened to the ascension of the Prophet during the Night Journey when he traversed the heavens and then came back down. Jacob calls the place where he saw the vision Bethel, which means the House of God in Hebrew.[50] Jacob goes on to say that God will provide him with bread, using the word *leḥem*, which also means flesh. Jesus was born in Bethlehem, which means the House of Bread or Flesh. Such parallelism with Jesus is notable, as the Gospels show Jesus likening his body to the Temple of God (John 2:21) and himself to Jacob's Ladder: "He then added, 'I tell you the truth, you shall see heaven open, and the angels of God ascending and descending on the Son of Man.' " [John 1:51]

The stone that Jacob sets up as a pillar for the House of God is important. According to Deuteronomy, it is prohibited to erect a stone pillar: "And do not erect a sacred stone, for these the Lord your God hates" [Deuteronomy 16:22]. Nonetheless, Jacob does so, but whether he violated the prohibition is dependent on how the prohibition is understood. Was it prohibited to make a stone pillar because God hated all such pillars, or was it prohibited simply to erect a stone pillar that God hated? In other words, it might have been permissible under certain conditions. Fur-

50. *BDB*, 110–111.

thermore, Jacob calls the place Bethel, which is etymologically similar to the Semitic Baetylus,[51] which is a name for a sacred stone believed to be the place where God abides. In Phoenician mythology, Baetylus was a son of the gods Uranus and Ge. Uranus had put life into what were called Baetylia, that is, large conical stones that were worshipped in many temples of Greece and Asia Minor; many were minted on ancient coins in the Asiatic provinces of the Roman Empire.[52] Ancient Semites anointed Baetylia with oil as well. Hence, Jacob's action was consistent with Semitic practices prevalent at the time, the difference being that he had consecrated the stone to what he believed to be the one and only God. Joshua also erected a stone pillar under an oak in violation of the Deuteronomic prohibition (Joshua 24:26–27), an action which Jewish commentators had difficulty rationalizing.[53]

The word for stone shares the same root as son (*ibn*). Hence, Jacob sets the stone (son or *ʾeben*) as a pillar for the Temple of God. The stone (*ʾeben*) that Joshua places as a witness might be an allusion to Jesus as the Son (*ibn*) of God. Jesus' claim to be the son (*ibn*) might simply mean that he is the Temple of God in the flesh (Luke 22:70).[54]

Jesus informed Simon, his disciple, that he would make him Cephas (Peter), meaning rock (John 1:42). This perhaps indicates that since Jesus is the Temple of God in the flesh, so also did he make his disciples Temples of God, a term that may be interpreted to mean sons of God:

> For you did not receive a spirit that makes you a slave again to fear, but you received the Spirit of sonship. And by him we

51. George F. Moore, "Baetylia," *American Journal of Archaeology* (1903), 7(2): 198–208.

52. Massimo D'Orazio, "Meteorite Records in the Ancient Greek and Latin Literature: Between History and Myth," in *Myth and Geology*, eds. L. Piccardi and W. B. Masse (London: Special Publications, The Geological Society of London, 2007), 215–225.

53. S. David Sperling, "Joshua 24 Re-examined," *Hebrew Union College Annual* (1987), 58: 119–136.

54. Galadari, *Qur'anic Hermeneutics*, 84–95.

> cry, "Abba, Father." The Spirit himself testifies with our spirit that we are God's children. Now if we are children, then we are heirs—heirs of God and co-heirs with Christ, if indeed we share in his sufferings in order that we may also share in his glory. [Romans 8:15–17]

Paul testifies that he and those who truly have the Spirit are the Temples of God. It is as if they are resurrected pilgrims. Hence, when the Qur'an rejects the notion of sonship and rebukes the people who claim it with their mouths (Qur'an 9:30), it may be because the Temple of God has to be their own bodies and flesh when the Spirit of God dwells in their hearts.[55] Many times, the Qur'an condemns saying something with the mouth when it is supposed to be in the heart (e.g., Qur'an 3:167, 5:41, 9:8, 9:32, 14:9, 18:5, 61:8). In other words, the Qur'an is not rejecting the notion of sonship, but rejects it as a notion that is only uttered with the mouth.

> and that He may know the hypocrites (*nāfaqū*). And it was said unto them, "Come, fight in the way (*qātilū fī sabīl*) of God or defend [yourselves]." They said, "Had we known there would be fighting (*qitālan*), we would have followed you." That day they were closer to disbelief than to belief, saying with their mouths what was not in their hearts (*qulūbihim*). And God knows best what they conceal. [Qur'an 3:167]

The reference in this verse to those who say with their mouths what is not in their hearts is similar to Qur'an 9:32, which uses the term *ibn Allāh*.[56] The root for hypocrite is *n-f-q*, which means death,[57] as these people are dead souls entombed in their bodies.[58] Though they are asked to kill in the way (*sabīl*) of God, as just described for the Ḥajj, which means to kill their egos, they refuse to do so. Jacob's name in Arabic is *Ya*ᶜ*qūb,* whose root, ᶜ*-q-b*, also yields

55. Ibid.

56. For more details, see Ibid.

57. *Lisān al-*ᶜ*arab*, 10: 357 on *n-f-q*.

58. The root of the term *n-f-q* means to exit. It is used to mean dead, as in the soul's exiting of the body. The verb *yanfuq* means to pay, which involves the outward movement of money. See Gesenius' Hebrew-Chaldee Lexicon to the Old Testament, 558.

the name of the first pillar to be stoned during the Ḥajj, namely, *Jamrat al-ᶜAqabah*. Its relationship with Jacob's Ladder will be discussed later. Jacob was later called Israel. As discussed earlier, the Qur'an describes a heavenly ladder using the word *maᶜārij*. The name of Israel means the one who struggled with God, as described in Genesis 32:28. When combined, the root of Israel and the root for the heavenly ladder is *al-Isrāʾ* (Israel) and *al-Miᶜrāj* (Jacob's Ladder). This is the same name as the Prophet's Night Journey and Ascension, which is described by the rituals of ᶜUmrah. *Al-Isrāʾ wal-Miᶜrāj* is the Prophet's Night Journey from Mecca to Jerusalem followed by his ascension to the heavens; Jacob's Ladder is otherwise known as Israel's Heavenly Ladder, *al-Isrāʾ wal-Miᶜrāj*.

In the Qur'an, *Sūrat al-Isrāʾ* (Chapter of the Night Journey) is also known by another name, Sūrat Banī Israel (Chapter of the Children of Israel).[59] The word used for children (*banī*) is polysemous from the root (*ibn*), meaning son or building.[60] Hence, the name of Sūrat *Banī Israel* also means Temple of Israel, perhaps describing the temple that Jacob built as a pillar from the place in which he saw the dream of the heavenly ladder.

PASSING BETWEEN ṢAFĀ AND MARWAH

MEANING OF *SAᶜĪ*

The ritual of passing through Ṣafā and Marwah is called *saᶜī*, whose root, *s-ᶜ-y*, means to go.[61] Similarly, the Hebrew *s-ᶜ-h* means to rush or to go about quickly.[62] The Qur'an uses this word to mean people striving for a goal, either constructively (e.g., Qur'an 17:19) or destructively (e.g., Qur'an 2:113, 2:205). The Qur'an has also used the word to describe Judgment Day when every soul will be rewarded or reprimanded based on what it has striven for (e.g., Qur'an 20:15, 53:39–40, 79:35).

59. Muqātil bin Sulaymān, *Tafsīr Muqātil* (Beirut: Iḥyāʾ al-Turāth, 2003), 2: 512 on Q. 17:1.

60. Galadari, *Qur'anic Hermeneutics*, 87–89.

61. *Lisān al-ᶜarab*, 14: 385 on *s-ᶜ-y*.

62. *BDB*, 703.

*SA*ᶜ*Ī* OF THE SNAKES WITH MOSES

When God commands Moses to throw down his rod and it turns into a snake, the Qur'an uses a word rooted in *sa*ᶜ*ī* to describe how the snake moves, perhaps suggesting that the snake had an intention or a goal to reach. Sūrat ṬaHa begins with the statement that the Creator of the heavens and the earth, the Most Compassionate (*al-Raḥmān*), is the author of the Qur'an, and that He was established (*istawā*) on His Throne. It continues by stating that it is He Who knows all secrets and all that is hidden. The sūrah then relates the story of Moses, how he sees a fire and goes to it so that he might receive some light and guidance (*hudā*). When Moses arrives in the sacred valley, God speaks to him with the famous Exodus quote, *ʾehĕye ʾăšer ʾehĕye* (Exodus 3:14), which the Qur'an translates as *innī anā*, meaning "I am (who) I am" (Qur'an 20:1–14). This is followed by the description of the snake:

> "Surely the Hour is coming. I would keep it hidden, that every soul might be recompensed for its endeavours (*tas*ᶜ*ā*). So let not he who believes not and follows his caprices turn thee away from it, or thou wilt perish. And what is that in thy right hand, O Moses?" He said, "It is my staff. I lean upon it (*atawakkaʾ* ᶜ*alayhā*) and beat down leaves for my sheep. And I have other uses for it." He said, "Cast it (*alqihā*), O Moses!" So he cast it, and behold, it was a serpent (*ḥayyah*), moving swiftly (*tas*ᶜ*ā*). He said, "Take hold of it, and fear not! We shall restore it to its former way."" [Qur'an 20:15–21]

These verses start by discussing how every soul will be rewarded according to what it has striven for (*tas*ᶜ*ā*) and continue with how Moses should not follow the disbelievers' vain desires, implying that he should follow only the will of God. Then God asks Moses what is in his right hand. Moses replies that it is his rod, which he uses for various things. The first use he mentions is that he leans on it, using the word *atawakkaʾ*, which is derived from the same root used in the Qur'an to refer to the divine reward of leaning (*muttakiʾīn*) on thrones in heaven (e.g., Qur'an 18:31, 36:56, 38:49, 52:20, 55:54, 55:76, 56:16, 76:13, 83:23, 83:35).

God asks Moses to throw down (*alqihā*) his rod. This is as God casts His Word into Mary (Qur'an 4:171), as Joseph asks that his coat be cast onto his father's face to bring back his vision (Qur'an 12:93–96), and as God throws mountains on the earth making broad highways through which people pass and receive guidance, as in the description of Ḥajj discussed earlier (Qur'an 16:17, 31:10). Moses throws his rod, and it becomes alive (*ḥayyah*), where the word for 'snake' is the same as that for 'living', *ḥayyah.* Another word, *thuᶜbān*, is used in other verses to refer to the snake of Moses (Qur'an 7:107, 26:32). However, in Qur'an 20:20, the word used is *ḥayyah.*[63]

The life that comes into the rod, turning it into a snake, is described using the verb *tasᶜā*. Similarly, the dead pilgrim performs *saᶜī* between Ṣafā and Marwah in his striving for a sip of the Water of Life. Qur'an 7:117 describes how Moses' snake devours the sorcerers' deceptions (*yaʾfikūn*): "And We revealed unto Moses, 'Cast thy staff!' And, behold, it devoured all their deceptions (*yaʾfikūn*)." The terms 'snake' (*ḥayyah*) and 'deceptions' (*yaʾfikūn*) resonate with the following passage, which asks how people are deluded and kept from truth, using the word *tuʾfakūn*:

> Truly God is the Cleaver of the grain and the fruit stone. He brings forth the living (*al-ḥayy*) from the dead, and He is the One Who brings forth the dead from the living (*al-ḥayy*). That is God—how, then, are you perverted (*tuʾfakūn*)—[Qur'an 6:95]

As discussed earlier, the Qur'an shows how Pharaoh is a motif for God, since he is shown to gather people and resurrect, and has physical splendor, while in contrast, the Qur'an promises spiritual splendor. As such, the Qur'an goes on to contrast the physical with the spiritual, showing how the sorcerers appeared to have made their ropes and rods as if they were snakes, while Moses' rod ate up these falsehoods:

> They said, "O Moses! Either you cast, or we shall be the first to cast." He said, "Nay, you cast." Then, behold, their ropes

63. *Lisān al-ᶜarab*, 14: 220 on *ḥ-y-y*.

> (*ḥibāluhum*) and their staffs appeared to him, through their sorcery, to move swiftly (*tasᶜā*), whereat Moses conceived a fear in his soul. We said, "Fear not! Truly thou art uppermost. Cast that which is in thy right hand; it will devour what they have produced. They have produced only a sorcerer's trick. And the sorcerer prospers not, wheresoever he may go." Then the sorcerers were cast down (*fa-ulqiyā*) in prostration. They said, "We believe in the Lord of Aaron and Moses." He said, "Do you believe in Him before I give you leave? He is indeed your chief, who has taught you sorcery. Now I shall surely cut off your hands and your feet on alternate sides, and I shall surely crucify you on the trunks of palm trees. And you will surely know which of us [inflicts] a more severe and lasting punishment!" They said, "We shall never prefer you to the clear proofs that have come to us, nor to Him who originated us (*faṭaranā*). So decree (*f-qḍi*) whatsoever you decree (*qāḍ*); you only decree (*taqḍī*) in the life of this world. Truly we believe in our Lord, that He may forgive us our sins and the sorcery that you compelled us to perform. And God is better and more lasting!" [Qur'an 20:65–73]

Not only is the symbolism of the snake, connected with the term *saᶜī* in the Qur'an, relevant to the term used for the ritual of passing between Ṣafā and Marwah but it is also connected with the symbolism of life in general. According to the Book of Numbers, Moses lifted a bronze snake in the wilderness through God's instruction to heal and give life to those who were bitten by snakes:

> The Lord said to Moses, "Make a snake and put it up on a pole; anyone who is bitten can look at it and live (*wā-ḥay*)." So Moses made a bronze (*nĕḥōšet*) snake (*nĕḥaš*) and put it up on a pole. Then, when anyone was bitten by a snake (*nāḥāš*) and looked at the bronze (*nĕḥōšet*) snake (*nĕḥaš*), they lived (*wā-ḥay*). [Numbers 21:8–9]

In the Gospel of John, Jesus also refers to this event after discussing spiritual rebirth and may be likening himself to the snake. In Christian theology, Christ undoes what Adam had done by breaking the curse of sin, which was caused by the serpent's deception of Eve. Since Moses' bronze serpent in the wilderness was used to heal people from serpent bites, the Gospel may be inferring here that like the snake, Jesus heals those who are bitten by the serpent (Satan), healing them from sin:[64] "Just as Moses lifted up the snake in the wilderness, so the Son of Man must be lifted up, that everyone who believes may have eternal life in him" (John 3:4–5).[65]

The symbolism of the snake as a healing symbol is not unique to the Hebrew Bible. Even today, the snake on a pole (staff) is a symbol of healing in medical health. This symbol traces itself back to Greek mythology as the Rod of Asclepius. Therefore, the symbol of the serpent in the Bible and Qur'an is understood not only as a symbol of evil but also of good. After all, Moses' rod turned into a serpent of good which devoured the falsehoods of the serpents of the sorcerers. Similarly, Moses' serpent in the wilderness is a symbol of goodness that heals those who were bitten by serpents. In general, those who were bitten by serpents in the wilderness, according to Numbers, symbolize those who were deluded by Satan, who is also described as a serpent in Genesis, and it was Moses' rod, symbolized as the serpent in the wilderness, that ate up their falsehoods and egos. In this regard, Jesus Christ is symbolized as the good serpent, doing away with the falsehoods of the deceiving serpents that cause sin. The dual nature of the symbol of the serpent is well represented in the Bible,[66] as well as the Book of Mor-

64. Thomas Erskine, *The Brazen Serpent or Life Coming Through Death* (Edinburgh: Waugh and Innes, no date), 1831. See also Jacob J. Enz, "The Book of Exodus as a Literary Type for the Gospel of John," *Journal of Biblical Literature* (1957), 76(3): 208–215; and Merrill C. Tenney, "The Old Testament and the Fourth Gospel," *Bibliotheca Sacra* (1963), 120: 300–308.

65. Interestingly, the bronze serpent that Moses made in the wilderness to heal the Israelites survived for many centuries until the reign of Hezekiah, son of Ahaz, king of Israel. 2 Kings commends him for ordering the bronze serpent to be smashed into pieces because the Israelites at the time had been burning incense to it, which he considered idolatrous (2 Kings 18:4). The Bible states that it was called *Nĕḥuštān*, meaning both bronze and snake.

66. For more on the dualistic nature of the serpent symbolism and its historical connection between Scriptures with Greek and Roman mythologies, see James H. Charlesworth, *The Good and Evil Serpent: How a Universal Symbol Became Christianized* (New Haven, CT: Yale University Press, 2010).

mon.[67] Manfred Lurker also shows that, just as in the Qur'an and the Bible, the serpent represents both death and life or resurrection, the understanding of the snake as the symbol of resurrection existed in ancient Egypt, where its periodic shedding of skin represented rebirth.[68]

*SA*c*Ī* FROM DEATH TO LIFE

As the "*sa*c*ī*" of the serpent symbolizes resurrection from death to life, perhaps "*sa*c*ī*" between Ṣafā and Marwah symbolizes the same. Although Ṣafā and Marwah are mentioned only once in the Qur'an as the signs of pilgrimage (Ḥajj and cUmrah), the word "*sa*c*ī*" occurs a great many times. In cUmrah, the dead soul wearing its funeral shroud (*iḥrām*) performs the "*sa*c*ī*" between Ṣafā and Marwah. Afterward, he shaves or cuts his hair and then removes the funeral shroud, symbolizing resurrection. The following Qur'anic verse alludes to how God brings the dead to life, perhaps similar to how the dead soul performing the cUmrah becomes resurrected.

> And when Abraham said, "My Lord, show me how Thou givest life to the dead," He said, "Dost thou not believe?" He said, "Yea, indeed, but so that my heart may be at peace." He said, "Take four birds and make them be drawn to thee. Then place a piece of them on every mountain. Then call them: they will come to thee in haste (*sa*c*yā*). And know that God is Mighty, Wise." [Qur'an 2:260]

As we see in this verse, when Abraham asks God to show him how He can resurrect the dead, He asks him to bring birds and put a portion on a different mountain. Then, when Abraham calls them, they will fly quickly (*sa*c*yā*) to life. Abraham is considered to be the person to have called people to the Ḥajj. The pilgrims called to the Ḥajj as dead souls perform the "*sa*c*ī*" between the hills and they are resurrected, just like the birds in the preceding verse. A reader may not appreciate an even

---

67. Andrew C. Skinner, "Serpent Symbols and Salvation in the Ancient Near East and the Book of Mormon," *Journal of Book of Mormon Studies* (2001), 10(2): 42–55.

68. Manfred Lurker, *The Gods and Symbols of Ancient Egypt* (New York, NY: Thames and Hudson, 1980), 108.

more astonishing mystery immediately. The verse is talking about dead birds. Birds have wings. Therefore, they can be made alive and they can fly between the hills. The Qur'an, by contrast, describes how the pilgrim, which has no wings (*falā junāḥ*), needs to float (*yaṭṭawwaf*) between the hills (Qur'an 2:158).

The Qur'an also states that the true goal for which people need to strive is another world and not this one. It is God's kingdom and not Pharaoh's or an earthly kingdom that is being sought: "And whosoever desires the Hereafter, and endeavours (*sa*ᶜ*ā*) for it earnestly (*sa*ᶜ*yahā*), and is a believer, it is they whose efforts (*sa*ᶜ*yuhum*) shall be appreciated" [Qur'an 17:19]. Similarly, the Qur'an also warns against striving for this life:

> Say, "Shall I inform you who are the greatest losers in respect to their deeds? Those whose efforts (*sa*ᶜ*yahum*) go astray in the life of this world, while they reckon that they are virtuous in their works." They are those who disbelieve in the signs of their Lord, and in the meeting with Him. Thus their deeds have come to naught, and on the Day of Resurrection We shall assign them no weight. [Qur'an 18:103–105]

Furthermore, just as the performance of *ṭawāf* is related to the story of Dhūl-Qarnayn, so is the performance of the *sa*ᶜ*ī*:

> And whosoever performs righteous deeds and is a believer, there shall be no ingratitude for his endeavour (*li-sa*ᶜ*yih*), and surely We shall write [it] down for him. And it is forbidden unto any town We have destroyed that they should ever return, till the time when Gog and Magog are unleashed, and they rush down (*yansilūn*) from every hill. [Qur'an 21:94–96]

These verses describe how the endeavours of the righteous will not be in vain. The verses then speak of Gog and Magog, which relates to the story of Dhul-Qarnayn. Even in the few verses before Gog and Magog are mentioned, the Qur'an describes how God breathed into Mary, the mother of Jesus, from His Spirit (Qur'an 21:91). The phraseology has some resemblance to Dhul-Qarnayn asking for the blowing of the bellows between the mountains (Qur'an 18:96), which is just a few verses before the mention of those whose endeavours (*sa*ᶜī) are lost (Qur'an 18:104).

The two mountains or hills in which Gog and Magog are,

according to the Qur'an, sound similar to the hills of Ṣafā and Marwah, where the pilgrim also endeavours (*sa*^{c}ī) so that God may breathe into the pilgrim from His Spirit that he may live. This is similar to Dhul-Qarnayn asking for the blowing of the bellows between the hills to seal Gog and Magog. Also, the root for Zion (*ṣiyyôn*) which, as described earlier and could symbolize the dead pilgrim, is used in the Book of Ezekiel for the burial post of the ones buried in the Valley of the Multitude of Gog (Ezekiel 39:15).

SA^{c}Ī OF FRIDAY

The root of Friday (*al-jumu^{c}ah*) is *j-m-^{c}*, which means to gather in Arabic and to sink or immerse in Syriac Aramaic.[69] The Arabic derives from the notion that the Friday prayer is a gathering of Muslim worshippers, as described in the Qur'an.

> O you who believe! When you are called (*nūdiya*) to prayer on the day of congregation[70] (*al-Jumu^{c}ah*), hasten (*fa-s^{c}aw*) to the remembrance of God and leave off trade. That is better for you, if you but knew. [Qur'an 62:9]

The word for proclaiming prayer on Friday is *nūdiya*, which shares the root for God calling Moses in the sacred valley (Qur'an 20:11, 27:8, 28:30). It also shares the root used for the proclamation on the Day of Resurrection.

> And listen on the Day when the caller (*al-munādī*) calls (*yunādī*) from near at hand, on the Day when they hear the Cry of Truth; that is the Day of coming forth. [43] Truly We give life and We cause death, and unto Us is the journey's end. That Day the earth is split asunder from about them—as they hasten forth. That is a gathering easy for Us. We know best that which they say. Thine is not to compel them. So remind, by means of the Quran, those who fear My Threat (*wa^{c}īd*). [Qur'an 50:41–45]

The Qur'an also uses the same terms for proclamation, *nidā*ʾ and

---

69. *Lisān al-^{c}arab*, 8: 53 on *j-m-^{c}*. Also refer to *Targum Lexicon* for the Syriac definition.

70. This is slight rewording of the *TSQ*, which completely misses the translation for the term *yawm*.

adhān, which are used for the Ḥajj (Qur'an 22:27), in a single verse:

> Unto Him is knowledge of the Hour referred. No fruits come forth from their sheaths, nor does any female bear or bring forth, save by His Knowledge. And on the Day when He will call unto them (*yunādīhim*), "Where are My partners?" they will say, "We admit unto Thee (*ādhannāk*) that none among us bears witness." [Qur'an 41:47]

According to Islamic tradition, there is a weak *ḥadīth* that states that the Day of Resurrection will occur on a Friday (*al-jumu*ᶜ*ah*),[71] although it may simply mean a day of gathering (*jam*ᶜ).

> Our Lord, Thou art the Gatherer (*jāmi*ᶜ) of humankind unto a Day about which there is no doubt. Truly God will not fail the tryst (*al-mī*ᶜ*ād*). [Qur'an 3:9]

> And We shall leave them, on that Day, to surge against one another like waves. And the trumpet (*al-ṣūr*) shall be blown, and We shall gather them together (*fa-jama*ᶜ*nāhum jam*ᶜ*ā*). [Qur'an 18:99]

EMIGRATION TO GOD AND ABANDONING THE WORLD

As the dead pilgrim traverses from one heaven to another on the heavenly ladder (*sullam*), he abandons (*hajr*) everything and everyone, including himself, and seeks only God. The *sa*ᶜ*ī*, which according to tradition is a re-enactment of Hagar's quest for water, symbolizes emigration (*hijrah*) to God and abandonment (*hajr*) of this world. This motif is essentially repeated in various parts of the Qur'an (Qur'an 2:218, 3:195, 4:89, 4:97, 4:100, 8:72–75, 9:20, 9:100, 9:117, 16:41, 16:110, 24:22, 29:26, 33:6, 59:8):

> And as for those who emigrate (*hājarū*) in the way (*sabīl*) of God and are then slain or die, God will surely provide them with a beautiful provision. And truly God is the best of providers. He will surely cause them to enter an entrance with which they shall

71. This is a weak *ḥadīth*, which states, "The grandest of days is Friday; on it Adam was created, on it he entered heaven, on it he left heaven, and on it will be the Day of Resurrection." See al-Ṭabarānī, *al-Mu*ᶜ*jam al-kabīr*, ed. Ḥamdī b. ᶜAbdulḥalīm Al-Salafī (Cairo: Ibn Taymiyyah, 1994), 13: 38 (#13656).

> be content (*yarḍawnah*). And truly God is Knowing, Clement. [Qur'an 22:58–59]

These verses from *Sūrat al-Ḥajj* show that while re-enacting Hagar's desert drama, the pilgrim is abandoning the world for the sake (*sabīl*) of God, where *sabīl* is also used to refer to broad mountain highways leading to the Ḥajj (Qur'an 21:31, 71:20). The Qur'an describes how God will admit pilgrims to a place that will please them (*yarḍawnah*):

> Whosoever migrates (*yuhājir*) in the way (*sabīl*) of God will find upon the earth many a refuge and abundance, and whosoever forsakes his home, emigrating (*muhājiran*) unto God and His Messenger, and death overtakes him, his reward will fall upon God, and God is Forgiving, Merciful. [Qur'an 4:100]

As the ego is slain, the earth quakes, the tomb is opened, and a new creation and birth come forth. With this rebirth, the pilgrim is resurrected with new eyes and new ears. As one prophetic tradition states:

> Abu Hurayrah (may Allah be pleased with him) said: "I heard the Prophet say: 'Whoever performs the Ḥajj for the sake of Allah and does not have sexual relations (with his wife), commit sin, or dispute unjustly (during the Ḥajj), will be restored to what he was on the day his mother bore him.' "[72]

72. *Ṣaḥīḥ al-Bukhārī*, 2: 133 (#1521), 3: 11 (#1819), (#1820).

6

HAIR: SHAVING OR CUTTING

After a pilgrim has concluded the rituals of the ᶜUmrah and traversed between the hills of Ṣafā and Marwah, the birth and resurrection are symbolized by removing the funeral shroud (*iḥrām*) after the shaving or cutting of the hair. However, in the rituals of the Ḥajj, after the pilgrim sacrifices himself for all the people's sins, only then can he shave his head, after which he is resurrected, symbolized by the removal of the funeral shroud (*iḥrām*). Immediately after the death of the ego, during this great sacrifice of the self, the pilgrim is dead in the earthly realm but is resurrected in the heavenly realm. According to Islamic tradition, a newborn male has his hair shaved.[1] Hence, shaving the hair signifies new birth.[2]

1. *Musnad Aḥmad*, 33: 271 (#20083); *Sunan Abī Dawūd*, 3: 106 (#2837).
2. This chapter is an expansion of a discussion found in Galadari, "The Role of Intertextual Polysemy."

A QUR'ANICALLY ORDAINED RITUAL

The Qur'an specifically requires pilgrims leaving the state of *iḥrām*, or ritual consecration, to either shave or cut the hair:

> Complete the *ḥajj* and *ᶜumrah* for God, and if you are hindered, then [make] such offering as is easy. And do not shave (*taḥliqū*) your heads until the offering reaches its place of sacrifice. But whosoever among you is ill or has an ailment of his head, then [let there be] a ransom (*fidyah*) by fasting, charity, or rite. When you are safe, let those who enjoy the *ᶜumrah* ahead of the *ḥajj* [make] such offering as is easy. Whosoever finds not [the means], let him fast three days during the *ḥajj*, and seven when you return. That is ten altogether. This is for those whose family dwells not near the Sacred Mosque. And reverence God, and know that God is severe in retribution (*al-ᶜiqāb*). [Qur'an 2:196]

The verse asserts that one cannot leave the state of *iḥrām* unless he shaves or cuts his hair short during the rituals of the Ḥajj or ᶜUmrah. However, if someone for any reason is not able to complete the rituals, he will remain in a state of *iḥrām* until a sacrificial offering is made. This rule may be a means of emphasizing that no one can be resurrected unless a sacrifice is performed, which symbolizes the sacrifice of the self, or ego. Another verse also refers to entering the Sacred Mosque, *al-Masjid al-Ḥarām*, after either shaving or cutting one's hair:

> Surely God has fulfilled for His Messenger the vision in truth: you shall enter the Sacred Mosque in security, if God wills, with the hair of your heads shaven (*muḥalliqīn*) or cut (*muqaṣṣirīn*), not fearing. For He knows what you know not, and He has given you therewithal a victory nigh. [Qur'an 48:27][3]

THE SIGNIFICANCE OF HAIR (*SHAᶜR*)

As noted, the rite of shaving or cutting the hair is the last ritual before a pilgrim can leave the state of ritual consecration, or

3. Classical exegetes such as al-Ṭabarī viewed this verse as describing the conquest (*fatḥ*) of Mecca and the Farewell Pilgrimage that occurred in the days of Muḥammad. See al-Ṭabarī, *Jāmiᶜ*, 22: 256–259 on Q. 48:27.

iḥrām, which symbolizes death. The root of the Arabic word for hair (*shaᶜr*) is *sh-ᶜ-r* (e.g., Qur'an 16:80), whose various semantic associations include feeling and perception (*shuᶜūr, mashāᶜir*), a slogan (*shiᶜār*), poetry (*shiᶜr*), rites and rituals (*shaᶜāʾir*).[4] The Qur'an frequently uses the same root to mean sense, feeling, understanding, and perception (e.g., Qur'an 2:9, 2:12, 16:21, 16:26, 16:45, 26:202), as well as poet (e.g., Qur'an 69:41). Since a poet (*shāᶜir*) speaks of feelings (*mashāᶜir*), the same root is used for both.[5]

The *sh-ᶜ-r* root is used by the Qur'an for the rituals of the Ḥajj, referred to as *shaᶜāʾir Allāh*, that is, the signs of God pointing to spiritual realities (Qur'an 5:2, 22:32), including the *saᶜī* between the hills of Ṣafā and Marwah (2:158) and the rite of sacrifice (22:36). The area of Muzdalifah, also part of the Ḥajj rituals, is called *al-Mashᶜar al-Ḥarām* (Qur'an 2:198).

Since it has been established that the Ḥajj and ᶜUmrah symbolize death and resurrection, the word for perception using the root *sh-ᶜ-r* in connection to death and resurrection is embedded in the Qur'an, as can be seen in the following verses:

> And say not of those who are slain in the way of God, "They are dead." Nay, they are alive, but you are unaware (*lā tashᶜurūn*). [Qur'an 2:154]

> Dead, not living, and they are not aware of (*lā yashᶜurūn*) when they will be resurrected. [Qur'an 16:21]

As seen in these verses, the Qur'an uses the root *sh-ᶜ-r* when discussing the difference between life and death. However, in this context, the word is usually understood to mean "perceive." The first of these two verses announces that martyrs, who appear to be dead, are actually alive, but people do not perceive it (*lā tashᶜurūn*). The second verse discusses how people who do not believe in the message, who appear to be alive, are actually dead and do not perceive (*lā yashᶜurūn*) when they will be resurrected.

The word for hair (*shaᶜr*) is derived from the same root as

4. *BDB*, 972–973; *Lisān al-ᶜarab*, 4: 409–417 on *sh-ᶜ-r*.

5. Ibid., 4: 409–417.

the word for perception (*shuᶜūr*). Hence, before pilgrims remove their funeral shrouds (*iḥrām*) symbolizing resurrection, they shave or cut their hair (*shaᶜr*). They do this because shaving or cutting the hair (*shaᶜr*) symbolizes the pilgrim's failure to perceive (*yashᶜurūn*) that they are being resurrected. Hence, we begin to see that what might otherwise appear to be an arbitrary act is actually infused with profound spiritual significance.

SHAVING (*ḤALQ*)

The Qur'an prescribes two ways by which a pilgrim can exit the state of *iḥrām*: shaving one's head and cutting one's hair short. Shaving is considered better for males, but not absolutely necessary.[6] The root of the word for shaving (*ḥ-l-q*) also yields words relating to going up, being suspended in the air, roundness, and throat.[7]

To understand the meanings of the act of shaving, however, the significance of the head must also be understood. The Arabic word for head, *raʾs*, can mean the uppermost part of anything, such as the beginning of a year, a capital fund, a chief or leader, etc.[8]

Deuteronomy 14:1 forbids shaving the head or trimming the hair for someone who has died. Accordingly, not performing the ritual of shaving for the dead may imply that it is to be done for the living. Leviticus, having laid down the priestly laws, uses the root *q-r-ḥ* (e.g., Leviticus 21:5), which refers in Hebrew and Aramaic to shaving and baldness.[9] In Arabic, the root *q-r-ḥ* means to cut or to wound,[10] perhaps because shaving tools can cut and wound.[11] The following Qur'anic passage uses the root *q-r-ḥ*.

6. This understanding is based on Muḥammad's saying, "God bless the shaved." When he was asked, "And those who cut their hair short?" he continued saying, "God bless the shaved" until at last he conceded and said, "And those who cut their hair short." See *Ṣaḥīḥ al-Bukhārī*, 2: 174 (#1727).

7. *Lisān al-ᶜarab*, 10: 58–67 on *ḥ-l-q*; see Qur'an 56:83.

8. *Ibid.*, 6: 91–94 on *r-ʾ-s*, and *BDB*, 910–912.

9. *BDB*, 901.

10. *Lisān al-ᶜarab*, 2: 557–558 on *q-r-ḥ*.

11. *Lisān al-ᶜarab* states that *qarḥ* could refer to the sharp part of a weapon that can cause a wound in the body.

> Many ways of life have passed before you; so journey upon the earth and behold how the deniers fared in the end (*ᶜāqibah*)! This is an exposition for humankind, and a guidance and exhortation for the reverent (*lil-muttaqīn*). Do not falter and do not grieve, for you will be ascendant if you are believers. If a wound (*qarḥ*) afflicts you, a like wound (*qarḥ*) has already afflicted that people. And such days We hand out in turns to humankind. And [this is] so that God may know those who believe, and take witnesses (*shuhadāʾ*) from among you—and God loves not the wrongdoers—[Qur'an 3:137–140].[12]

There are various intertextualities between this passage and the Ḥajj. This passage seems to describe the righteous as reverent (*muttaqīn*), which is the virtue that is required to enter the House of God (Qur'an 2:177, 2:189). It uses the word for those who have rejected the truth with a word rooted in "*ᶜ-q-b*," which shares the same root as *Jamrat al-ᶜAqabah* and Jacob's Ladder (*sullam Yaᶜqūb*), as described earlier. It also speaks of witnesses (*shuhadāʾ*). The passage later continues:

> And deem not those slain in the way of God to be dead. Rather, they are alive with their Lord, provided for, exulting in what God has given them from His Bounty, and rejoicing in those who have not yet joined them from among those who remain behind—that no fear shall come upon them, nor shall they grieve—rejoicing in Blessing and Bounty from God, and that God neglects not the reward of the believers, who responded to God and the Messenger after being afflicted by wounds (*al-qarḥ*); for those among them who have been virtuous and reverent there shall be a great reward, [Qur'an 3:169–172]

This passage speaks of wounds using the root *q-r-ḥ* concerning those who are slain in God's way as martyrs, or witnesses (*shuhadāʾ*). Significantly in this connection, one *ḥadīth* equates the Ḥajj to *jihād*, or the act of struggling for God's cause, and describes the *Ḥajj* as the best form of *jihād* for women:

> The Prophet was asked, "Which is the best deed?" He said, "To believe in God and His Apostle." He was then asked, "Which

12. See also Qur'an 3:169–172.

> is the next (in goodness)?" He said, "To participate in *jihād* in God's cause." He was then asked, "Which is the next?" He said, "To perform a *ḥajj* which is rewarded by God."[13]
>
> Similarly, when ᶜĀʾishah, the mother of the faithful believers, said, "O Messenger of God! We consider *jihād* is the best deed," the Prophet replied, "The best *jihād* is a *ḥajj* rewarded by God."[14]

The root of the word for shave (*ḥ-l-q*) also yields the word for throat (*ḥalq*) and is used as such by the Qur'an in connection with death (Qur'an 56:83).[15] As pilgrims die to their egos, they become martyrs (*shuhadāʾ*). In so doing, they achieve the greatest *jihād* of all, the struggle with one's self.[16] *Sūrat al-Ḥajj* ends on the theme of *jihād* and martyrdom, thereby drawing a link between the pilgrimage and *jihād*:

> And strive (*jāhidū*) for God as He should be striven (*ḥaqq jihādih*), for He has chosen [for] you—and has placed no hardship for you in the religion—the creed of your father Abraham. He named you muslims aforetime, and herein, that the Messenger may be a witness (*shahīdan*) for you, and that you may be witnesses (*shuhadāʾ*) for humankind. So perform the prayer and give the alms, and hold fast to God. He is your Master. How excellent a Master, and how excellent a Helper! [Qur'an 22:78]

---

13. *Ṣaḥīḥ al-Bukhārī*, 1: 14 (#26), 2: 133 (#1519).
14. *Ibid.*, 2: 133 (#1520), 3: 19 (#1861), 4:15 (#2784).
15. *Lisān al-ᶜarab*, 2: 557–558 on *ḥ-l-q*.
16. In this connection, see John Renard, "*Al-Jihad al-Akbar*: Notes on a Theme in Islamic Spirituality," *The Muslim World* (1988), 78(3–4): 225–242.

7

THE ḤAJJ IS ᶜARAFAH: *WUQŪF*

In the Greater Pilgrimage, the Ḥajj, the pilgrim travels to ᶜArafah wearing the funeral shroud, *iḥrām*. Most pilgrims flock there from Minā after sunrise and must arrive at ᶜArafah before the *ẓuhr* prayer, since they will need to devote themselves to supplication to God from noon until sunset.

ᶜArafah is the most important of all the rituals of the Ḥajj. Indeed, one *ḥadīth* tells us that, "The Ḥajj is ᶜArafah."[1] The pilgrim travels to ᶜArafah reciting the *talbiyah*, which is an acceptance of the call of God to the Ḥajj. As discussed earlier, the *talbiyah* is related to the term *labbayk*, which may, in turn, be related to *lubb*, meaning heart, in which case it can be understood to mean that the pilgrim gives his heart to God, allowing it to become God's House or Temple, that is, as the *qiblah*.

MEANING OF ᶜARAFAH

Going to ᶜArafah is spoken of as follows in the Qur'an:

> There is no blame (*junāḥ*) upon you in seeking a bounty from

1. *Musnad Aḥmad*, 31: 64 (#18774).

> your Lord. Then, when you pour out (*afaḍtum*) from Arafat, remember God at the sacred ground (*al-mashᶜar al-ḥarām*). And remember Him as He guided you, though formerly you were of those astray. [Qur'an 2:198]

Similar to the aforementioned interpretation of traversing between Ṣafā and Marwah using the word "*junāḥ*," which may mean wing, this Qur'anic verse also describes how those dead souls without a wing (*janāḥ*) to fly would pour down from ᶜArafah to *al-Mashᶜar al-Ḥarām*. To understand ᶜArafah, it is important to understand the meaning of its root, *ᶜ-r-f*, which means to know or confess.[2] The Qur'an speaks of the pilgrims pouring down (*afaḍtum*) from ᶜArafah, as though likening them to tears overflowing the eyes of people who know (*ᶜarafū*) the truth:

> And when they hear that which was sent down unto the Messenger, thou seest their eyes (*aᶜyunahum*) overflow (*tafīḍ*) with tears because of the truth they recognize (*ᶜarafū*). They say, "Our Lord, we believe, so inscribe us among the witnesses (*al-shāhidīn*)." [Qur'an 5:83]

This verse describes those who know the truth as having tears pouring from their eyes (*aᶜyunahum*), where the Arabic word for eye (*ᶜayn*) can also mean a spring.[3] According to Qur'an 5:83, not only do those who know (*ᶜarafū*) the truth have tears pouring from their eyes, but they also ask to be among the witnesses (*al-shāhidīn*), which is related to the term for martyr (*shahīd*). Perhaps they plan to engage in *jihād* against the self (ego) and sacrifice themselves to become martyrs (*shuhadāʾ*). Another verse in the Qur'an uses similar phraseology to describe those who want to spend in the path (*sabīl*) of God, but have nothing to offer. It speaks of "those who, when they came to thee [the Prophet] to give them a mount, and thou didst say to them, 'I find nothing upon which to mount you', turned back, their eyes flowing (*tafīḍ*) with tears, grieving that they found nothing to spend (*yunfiqūn*)" [Qur'an 9:92].

---

2. *Lisān al-ᶜarab*, 9: 236–243 on *ᶜ-r-f*.
3. See *Ibid.*, 13: 301–309 on *ᶜ-y-n*. Also see *BDB*, 744–746.

Recall that the root *n-f-q* can also mean death.[4] Similarly, the pilgrim at ᶜArafah finds nothing but himself to kill for the sake of God. Perhaps this symbolizes that they find nothing to kill but themselves as an offering to be carried on the Ark of salvation:

> So We opened the gates of the sky with pouring water, and We caused the earth to burst forth with springs (*ᶜuyūnan*), such that the waters met for a matter determined. Then We carried him upon a thing of planks and nails [Ark], coursing under Our Eyes (*bi-aᶜyuninā*) as a recompense for one who was rejected. [Qur'an 54:11–14]

As the pilgrim travels to ᶜArafah, it could possibly mean that the pilgrim is trying to know God, for he is seeking God. Additionally, it could mean that he is seeking to have God know him. Thus, the pilgrim is seeking to be known. During the *saᶜī* of the ᶜUmrah, a pilgrim abandons himself to seek God, although God was never lost; it is the pilgrim who is lost. Similarly, in ᶜArafah, the pilgrim seeks to know (*yaᶜrif*) God, when in reality, God is known (*maᶜrūf*), but the pilgrim is lost and needs to be known (*yuᶜraf*). Perhaps, whenever the Qur'an commands people to do what is good (*al-maᶜrūf* – literally, "the known"), it may be a commandment to know God or to be known by Him.

WUQŪF ON MT. ᶜARAFAH

SEEKING GOD

The pilgrim at ᶜArafah consecrates himself to God from noon to sunset in what is known as *wuqūf*, the root of which means variously to consecrate, to stand up, or to stop.[5] At ᶜArafah, the pilgrim abandons the world and seeks only God, surrendering to His Will as during the *saᶜī* between Ṣafā and Marwah.

The name ᶜArafah is derived from the same root as the title of the seventh *sūrah* of the Qur'an, *Sūrat al-Aᶜrāf*. Speaking of the realm that extends between Paradise and the Hellfire, the Qur'an reads:

---

4. *Lisān al-ᶜarab*, 10: 357 on *n-f-q*.
5. *Lisān al-ᶜarab*, 9: 359–362 on *w-q-f*.

> And there will be a veil between them. And upon the heights (*al-aᶜrāf*) are men (*rijāl*) who know (*yaᶜrifūn*) all by their marks. They will call out to the inhabitants of the Garden, "Peace be upon you!" They will not have entered it, though they hope. And when their eyes turn toward the inhabitants of the Fire, they will say, "Our Lord! Place us not among the wrongdoing people!" And the inhabitants of the heights (*al-aᶜrāf*) will call out to men whom they know (*yaᶜrifūnahum*) by their marks, "Your accumulating has not availed you, nor has your waxing arrogant. Are these the ones concerning whom you swore that God would not extend any mercy?" "Enter the Garden! No fear shall come upon you, nor shall you grieve." The inhabitants of the Fire will call out to the inhabitants of the Garden, "Pour some water down upon us, or some of that which God has provided you." They will respond, "Truly God has forbidden them both to the disbelievers, who took their religion to be diversion and play, and were deluded by the life of this world." [And God will say,] "So this Day We forget them, as they forgot the meeting with this Day of theirs, and as they used to reject Our signs. We have indeed brought them a Book, which We have expounded with knowledge, as a guidance (*hudā*) and a mercy for a people who believe." [Qur'an 7:46–52]

Within the greater context of the above passage (Qur'an 7:40–58), there are various keywords and motifs shared with the Ḥajj rituals. The Ḥajj has been described as providing sacrifice (*hadī*), which is derived from the same root as the word used for guidance in these verses (*hudā*), as the dead pilgrim comes to the Ḥajj to be sacrificed unto God (Qur'an 7:43, 7:52). As the Ḥajj is proclaimed using the word *adhdhin,* asking people to enter the *mīqāt,* and as the call to prayer (*adhān*) notes when prayer also enters its *mīqāt*, so is the root of the word used in these verses (Qur'an 7:44, 7:58, 22:27). With a similar meaning, the root of the word *nūdiya* applied to the call to prayer on Friday (*al-jumuᶜah*) (Qur'an 7:43–42, 7:46, 7:48, 7:50, 62:9) is also used in many of the aforementioned verses. This is to say that the Day of ᶜArafah shares similarities with *yawm al-jumuᶜah* (Friday), which means the day of gathering. According to Muslim tradition, the Day of ᶜArafah in the year in which the Prophet performed his Farewell

Ḥajj fell on a Friday.[6] Additionally, the *wuqūf* in ᶜArafah starts at noon (*ẓuhr*) and includes a sermon, similar to the Friday prayer. Consequently, many Muslims believe it is a great Ḥajj if these days coincide.[7]

The link between Friday and the Day of ᶜArafah is also found in the exoteric exegesis of the Qur'an. The witness and the witnessed described in Qur'an 85:3 are described to be Friday (*al-jumuᶜah*) and the Day of ᶜArafah, respectively, according to al-Ṭabarī.[8] Accordingly, as the dead pilgrim is seeking to see and witness (*shahad*) God, he sacrifices himself and becomes a martyr (*shahīd*), a witness to the glory of God. The verse that precedes it speaks of the Promised Day (*al-yawm al-mawᶜūd*) (Qur'an 85:2). The Promised Day heralds the Promised Land (*al-mīᶜād*). It is the day of the gathering (*al-jumuᶜah*). The pilgrim has traversed from the land of *al-Mīqāt* to the land of *al-Mīᶜād*.

The verses from Qur'an 7:40–58 describe "*al-Aᶜrāf*," from which the name of the *sūrah* is derived. *Al-Aᶜrāf* are described as people who know (*yaᶜrifūn*) men (*rijāl*) from their facial marks. As stated previously, the root of the word "*r-j-l*" is the same as the Hebrew word used for Ḥajj (*rĕgālîm*), as it was traditionally done walking.

> And proclaim the *ḥajj* among humankind: they shall come to thee on foot (*rijālan*) and upon all [manner of] lean beast (*ḍāmir*), coming from all deep and distant mountain highways, [Qur'an 22:27]

The proclamation of the Ḥajj in the Qur'an uses the word *rijālan*, meaning on foot, to describe pilgrimage, as it is also used in Exodus 23:14 (*rĕgālîm*). The Qur'anic verse describes people coming to Mecca on foot or mounted on every kind of camel, all of

6. *Ṣaḥīḥ al-Bukhārī*, 1: 18 (#45), 6: 50 (#4606).

7. The day is known as the great Ḥajj (see al-Qārī, *Mirqāt al-mafātīḥ sharḥ mishkāt al-maṣābīḥ* (Beirut: al-Fikr, 2002), 3: 1022). However, some scholars, such as al-Albānī (d. 1420/1999), reject the notion that there is anything distinctive about a Ḥajj in which the Day of ᶜArafah falls on a Friday. See al-Mubarakfūrī, *Mirᶜāt al-mafātīḥ sharḥ mishkāt al-maṣābīḥ* (India: Idārah al-Buḥūth al-ᶜIlmiyyah wal-Daᶜwah wal-Iftāᵓ, 1984), 9: 391.

8. Al-Ṭabarī, *Jāmiᶜ*, 24: 333–334 on Q. 85:3.

which are lean because of their journey through deep and distant mountain highways. Perhaps those camels are so lean that they, actually, can go through the eye of a needle! When comparing the passage of the camel passing through the eye of the needle in *Sūrat al-Aᶜrāf* (Qur'an 7:40) with its counterparts in the Synoptic Gospels, the main message the Qur'an attempts to deliver is its relationship with the ego. It might suggest that it is easier for a camel to pass through the eye of a needle than for a person with an inflated ego to enter the Kingdom of Heaven.[9]

THE GREAT DISPUTE (*AL-ḤAJJ*)

During the *wuqūf* at ᶜArafah, the dead pilgrim abandons all her selfish desires for the sake of God. The pilgrim prays fervently to God as an advocate against the suffering of all creation. To advocate is to argue for a cause; the root of the word *ḥajj* and the root of the word to dispute *jidāl* have the same meanings and are often used as such in the Qur'an (e.g., Qur'an 2:76, 2:139, 2:258,).

The root *j-d-l* means to twist, to bend, to build, or to wrestle.[10] It also means to dispute, to advocate, and to debate.[11] In Hebrew, it means to grow up or to be great.[12] The root of the word *ḥajj* means to go to a destination, or to dispute or debate. Additionally, it means pilgrimage, celebration, festival, or evidence.[13] However, although the root *ḥ-j-j* may mean to dispute and debate, pilgrims are commanded not to dispute at all during the pilgrimage using the term *j-d-l* (Qur'an 22:3, 22:8, 22:68).

> The *ḥajj* is to be performed during months well known. Whosoever undertakes the *ḥajj* therein, let there be neither lewdness, nor iniquity, nor quarrelling (*jidāl*) in the *ḥajj*. Whatsoever good you do, God knows it. And make provision, for indeed the best provision is reverence. And reverence Me, O possessors of intellect. [Qur'an 2:197]

---

9. Abdulla Galadari, "The Camel Passing through the Eye of the Needle: A Qur'anic Interpretation of the Gospels," *Ancient Near Eastern Studies* (2018), 55: 77–89.

10. *Lisān al-ᶜarab*, 11: 103–105 on *j-d-l*.

11. *Ibid.*, 11: 105–106 on *j-d-l*.

12. *BDB*, 152–154.

13. *Lisān al-ᶜarab*, 2: 226–230 on *ḥ-j-j*.

Perhaps the significance of Ḥajj is that it is not just any dispute, but a dispute between the pilgrim and God. The root *j-d-l* is used in Qur'an 11:74, where Abraham debates with God about the people of Lot after his guests inform him of what is to become of them (Qur'an 11:75; Genesis 18:22-33). Like Abraham in his debate with God, the dead pilgrim debates with God during the *wuqūf* of ᶜArafah over the suffering of creation. Here, the dead pilgrim who has abandoned all selfish desires becomes ready to offer herself as the lamb is offered to God for the sins of all creation. When God demands that people suffer for their sins, the pilgrim, who has abandoned her ego, willingly offers herself up to God so that others can enjoy His mercy.

As the root of *ᶜ-r-f* also means confession, the dead pilgrim confesses to God her sins and the sins of all creation. However, the confession here is without an intermediary. The dead pilgrim, be it the man who is not covering his head or the woman who is not concealing her face, is covered by nothing but the shadow of God's Throne and encounters God alone.

In *Sūrat al-Aᶜrāf*, the people on the heights (*al-aᶜrāf*) speak to men (*rijālan*)—or pilgrims, as stated earlier (Qur'an 7:48)[14]—asking to what avail they gather for something such as the Ḥajj. They are asked if these are the people they swore would never obtain the mercy of God, but who are told to enter heaven without fear (Qur'an 7:49). The inhabitants of Hell then ask the inhabitants of Heaven to pour out some of God's mercy for them (Qur'an 7:50).[15] The word used for pouring (*afīḍū*) is the same root used by the Qur'an to describe pilgrims pouring down from Mount ᶜArafah (Qur'an 2:198). The root of the word *fayḍ*, meaning to pour water, also means death.[16]

The interpretation (*taʾwīl*) of Scriptures as spoken of in *Sūrat al-Aᶜrāf* might be an allusion to the Day of Resurrection (Qur'an

14. As in the passage of the proclamation of the Ḥajj, where pilgrims "come to you on foot" (*yaᶜtūka rijālan*).

15. This may be compared to the passage in Luke 16:23–24 in which a rich man languishing in Hell who asks Abraham to allow Lazarus, now in Paradise, to bring water to cool his tongue.

16. *Lisān al-ᶜarab*, 7: 110 and 212 on *f-y-ḍ*.

7:53).[17] The word used for 'interpretation' is *taʾwīl*, which might also mean the exegesis of esoteric and inner meanings of the Qur'an. This might suggest that understanding of the Scriptures is not obtained through observable exoteric signs but, rather, through a grasp of their deeper meanings.

In *Sūrat Yūnus*, the root of the word *taʾwīl* and the root *ᶜ-q-b* are used together. This is explained even further on the Day of Sacrifice, the day after ᶜArafah, when pilgrims stone the pillar of *ᶜAqabah* to fulfill the Scriptures and reach resurrection (Qur'an 10:39). The next verse of *Sūrat al-Aᶜrāf* discusses the creation of the heavens and the earth in six days and God's establishment (*istawā*) on His Throne (Qur'an 7:54). The verses continue to ask people to pray fervently to God, which is necessary during the *wuqūf* at *ᶜArafah*, within themselves and in fear (Qur'an 7:55–56). It also states how the mercy of God is near the righteous, by using a root of the word *qarīb*. It is the same root of the word as *qurbān*, meaning sacrifice, which will be detailed further in the sacrificial rituals of Ḥajj.

Later, the verses state how wind (*riyāḥ*) is sent. The word for wind shares the same root as spirit (*rūḥ*). The root of the word used for sending (*yursil*) is the same as the root for messenger (*rasūl*). Hence, the Spirit is sent as a messenger to bring glad tidings (*bushrā*), using the same word for flesh, or human (*bashar*) (Qur'an 7:57).

Perhaps Qur'an 7:57 is describing how, after the Day of ᶜArafah, the Spirit of God is sent to resurrect the dead pilgrim, which occurs on the Day of Sacrifice, when the pilgrim removes his funeral shroud. The verse states that the wind drives clouds to a dead land. In ᶜArafah, as the pilgrim is coming to God thirsty, hungry, and naked, the Spirit of God brings forth the Water of Life for resurrection. It does not occur on the Day of ᶜArafah, which is symbolized as the sixth day,[18] the Day of Gathering (*al-jumuᶜah*), Friday, but rather on the following day, which is

17. Al-Ṭabarī, *Jāmiᶜ*, 12: 479 on Q. 7:53.

18. Note the earlier discussion of the relationship between the Day of ᶜArafah and Friday.

the Day of Sacrifice, Saturday (the seventh day), when the pilgrim is resurrected and God breathes into him from His Spirit, dwelling in his heart and flesh, making him His Throne.

Qur'an 7:57 may appear to be addressing the physical realm, but at the end of the verse, it perhaps implies that as it is in the physical realm, so is it in the spiritual; this is the same principle by which the dead are resurrected. The following verse addresses how good land brings forth good fruit by God's permission, using the root of the word *idhn*, which shares the same root as the proclamation of the Ḥajj (*adhdhin*) and call to prayers (*adhān*) when pilgrims enter the *mīqāt*. However, bad land brings forth very little, because it has not yet entered its *mīqāt*, and its Day of Resurrection (*yawm al-waqt al-maᶜlūm*) is therefore delayed.

THE PILGRIM AT ᶜARAFAH

The 'dead' pilgrim seeking to know (*yaᶜrif*) God does so by distancing himself from selfish desires (Qur'an 79:40): "As for one who fears standing (*maqām*) before his Lord and forbids (*nahā*) the soul from caprice (*al-hawā*), his end shall be Paradise." Thus, the pilgrim's only desire is God, and he abandons (*yuhājir*) the world, as was described in the *saᶜī* of the dead pilgrim. This perhaps might be compared with the Eastern Orthodox concept of *kenōsis*, which is self-emptying oneself to make way for God and the union with God (*theōsis*).[19]

During the *wuqūf*, the dead pilgrim consecrates himself, confessing his sins and those of all humankind. He brings the case of all people before God pleading and praying fervently for them. Having abandoned his own self (ego) for God, the pilgrim is ready to offer himself to God for the sins of all. In so doing, he carries his cross and could be seen to follow in the footsteps of Jesus leading to his crucifixion:

Qur'an 79:40 describes how the *maqām* of God is attained by restraining the soul from base desires (*hawā*), as one's only desire needs to be for God. It is noteworthy that the Arabic word

19. For more on this concept, see Sigurd Lefsrud, *Kenosis in Theosis: An Exploration of Balthasar's Theology of Deification* (Eugene, OR: Pickwick, 2020).

used to describe base desires, *hawā*, shares the same root as the word for air (*hawāʾ*),[20] while the word for wind, *riyāḥ*, shares the same root as the word for spirit (*rūḥ*). When air stands still, it brings no good. However, when it moves, thus becoming wind, it brings forth goodness. Hence, the dead pilgrim rejects his lower desires (*hawā*),and instead desires the Spirit (*rūḥ*) of God, the ultimate *kenōsis*.

20. *Lisān al-ᶜarab*, 15: 370–372 on *h-w-y*.

8

MUZDALIFAH

After pilgrims have completed the *wuqūf* by Mount ᶜArafah, they "pour" down to Muzdalifah where, from noon until sunset, they consecrate themselves in fervent prayers. After sunset, pilgrims "pour" out of ᶜArafah. As described earlier, the Western Corner symbolizes death and judgment represented by the setting of the sun. Thus, the 'dead' pilgrim leaves ᶜArafah at sunset to be judged (see Qur'an 2:198: "And when you surge downward in multitudes from ᶜArafat, remember God at the holy place (*al-Mashᶜar al-Ḥarām*), and remember Him as the One who guided you after you had indeed been lost on your way").

WHAT IS IN THE NAME?

MEANING OF *MUZDALIFAH*

The root of the name Muzdalifah is *z-l-f*, the meaning of which is to bring down, to bring forth, to bring near, or to offer.[1] It also means a garden, the beginning of the night, and anything filled

1. *Lisān al-ᶜarab*, 9: 138–140 on *z-l-f*.

with water, such as a pond, lake, or river.[2] In Aramaic, it means to sprinkle, to drop, or to pour.[3]

The Qur'an uses the related word *zuluf* to mean the beginning of the night (Qur'an 11:114). Just as the Qur'an uses the word *dhikr* to describe pilgrims' remembrance of God as they pour down from ᶜArafah to *al-Mashᶜar al-Ḥarām* (Qur'an 2:198), so does the Qur'an ask people to remember and celebrate God's praises, using that same word, when it discusses the beginning of the night, or *zuluf*.

> Surely for each, thy Lord shall pay them in full (*la-yuwaffiyannahum*) for their deeds. Truly He is Aware of what they do. So be steadfast (*f-astaqim*), as thou hast been commanded—and those who turn in repentance along with you—and be not rebellious. Truly He sees whatsoever you do. And incline (*tarkanū*) not toward the wrongdoers, lest the Fire should touch you—and you will have no protector (*awliyāʾ*) apart from God. Thereafter you will not be helped. And perform the prayer at the two ends of the day and in the early hours of the night (*zulufan min al-layl*). Truly good deeds remove those that are evil. This is a reminder for those who remember (*dhikrā lil-dhākirīn*). [Qur'an 11:111–114]

In these verses, the Qur'an describes how God shall fulfill (*yatawaffawn*) the deeds of all (Qur'an 11:111). Hence, a commandment is given to stand firm (*f-astaqim*), which is derived from the same root (*q-w-m*) from which we derive the word *qiyāmah*, meaning resurrection (Qur'an 11:112). Additionally, the Qur'an uses the negative command *lā tarkanū* ('do not rely upon'), which is derived from the same root as the word *rukn*, meaning corner (Qur'an 11:113). It should be remembered that the dead pilgrim leaves ᶜArafah at sunset, which is symbolized by the Western Corner (*al-rukn al-gharbī*). It is also noted that Dhul-Qarnayn judged people at the setting of the sun—those who were good and those who were evil (Qur'an 18:86–87). The word *ᶜarafa* is opposed to the word *nakar*; the Qur'an uses *nakar*

2. *Ibid.*, 9: 140 on *z-l-f*.
3. *BDB*, 273.

to describe the punishment of the evildoers by Dhul-Qarnayn (Qur'an 18:87).

The Qur'an reminds people to establish prayers in the early hours of the night (*zulufan min al-layl*), immediately after which it says that this is a remembrance using a root of the word *dhikr* (Qur'an 11:114). *Al-Mashᶜar al-Ḥarām* in Muzdalifah is described as a remembrance (*dhikr*) done at the early hours of the night (after sunset) (Qur'an 2:198). The Qur'an goes on to describe cities and generations using the word *qurūn*, which shares the same root as Dhul-Qarnayn (Qur'an 11:116).

Further, the Qur'an relates that there are no protectors (*awliyāʾ*) like God (Qur'an 11:113). The root of the word *awliyāʾ* resembles that of *taʾwīl,* and the Qur'an describes how God, who knows the *taʾwīl* of the Qur'an, is the only true protector (*walī*) (Qur'an 3:7). The Qur'an also uses the root *z-l-f* for heaven to draw near on the Day of Resurrection (Qur'an 50:31, 81:13).

> And disgrace me not on the Day they are resurrected, the Day when neither wealth nor children (*banūn*) avail, save for him who comes to God with a sound (*salīm*) heart. And the Garden will be brought nigh (*uzlifat*) unto the reverent, and Hellfire (*al-jaḥīm*) will become apparent to the errant. [Qur'an 26:87–91]

These verses describe the Day of Resurrection when nothing will help, except to come to God with a sound heart. To those who do so, heaven draws near (*uzlifat*). It should be noted that a sound heart is described by the Qur'an with the word *salīm*, which shares the same root as the word *aslama*, meaning to surrender to the Will of God. The Qur'an uses the root *s-l-m* to speak of the faith of Abraham, who "came to God with a sound heart" (*jāʾ rabbah bi-qalb salīm*) (Qur'an 37:84). These passages tell the story of Abraham's sacrifice of his son, and its relationship with *maqām Ibrāhīm* and *saᶜī* (Qur'an 37:102), further details of which will be discussed later. As described in the Qur'an, Abraham's faith is not typically understood as blind faith, but as an experiential one.[4] Elsewhere we read:

4. Abdulla Galadari, "Qur'anic Faith and Reason: An Epistemic Comparison with the Kālāma Sutta," *Studies in Interreligious Dialogue* (2020), 30(1): 45–67.

> It is not your wealth or your children that bring you nigh (*zulfā*) in nearness (*tuqarribukum*) unto Us, save those who believe and work righteousness—theirs is a manifold reward for what they did, and they will be secure in lofty chambers. And those who endeavour (*yasᶜawn*) to thwart Our signs, they will be arraigned unto the punishment. [Qur'an 34:37–38]

Here, the real sacrifice (*qurbān*) that brings people nearer (*tuqarrib*) to God in nearness (*zulfā*) is further explained. This verse also clarifies the relationship with Muzdalifah, where pilgrims go on the eve of sacrifice, and connects this with *saᶜī*, as Abraham also took his son for sacrifice when his son reached the age where he could share in his endeavours (*saᶜā*) (Qur'an 37:102). The Qur'an also uses the root *z-l-f* to describe David:

> Thus did We forgive him that. Truly nearness (*zulfā*) unto Us shall be his, and a beautiful return (*maᵓāb*). O David! Truly We have appointed thee as a vicegerent (*khalīfah*) upon the earth; so judge among the people with truth and follow not caprice (*al-hawā*), lest it lead thee astray from the way (*sabīl*) of God. Truly those who stray from the way (*sabīl*) of God, theirs shall be a severe punishment for having forgotten the Day of Reckoning. [Qur'an 38:25–26]

These verses describe how David was made a vicegerent (*khalīfah*) of God on earth just as God had informed the angels that he would have a vicegerent (*khalīfah*) on earth (Qur'an 2:30). According to the Qur'an, when God created Adam as a vicegerent (*khalīfah*) on earth, He asked the angels to bow before him once God had breathed into him from His Spirit (*rūḥ*). Perhaps, in the verse, David is asked not to follow his selfish desire (air / *hawā*), but instead to follow the spirit (wind / *rūḥ*). David is also asked to stay on the path (*sabīl*) of God, where the word *sabīl* is the same term as used for those who are capable (*sabīl*) of going to Ḥajj.

Another part of the Qur'an draws a connection between the desire to return to God, the root *z-l-f*, coming to God with a clear heart, and the surrender to God in peace (*salām*).

> And the Garden will be brought nigh (*uzlifat*) unto the reverent, not distant: "This is what is promised for every oft turn-

> ing (*awwāb*) keeper, who fears the Compassionate unseen and comes with a penitent (*munīb*) heart. Enter it in peace (*bi-salām*). This is the day of abiding." Therein they shall have whatsoever they will; and with Us there is more (*mazīd*). [Qur'an 50:31–35]

These verses describe those whose hearts turn to God in desire and devotion with the word *munīb*, which is also used to describe Abraham (Qur'an 11:75): "Abraham was ... most intent upon turning to God again and again (*munīb*)."

AL-MASH^cAR AL-ḤARĀM

After departing from ^cArafah, the pilgrim who is still dead and wearing a funeral shroud (*iḥrām*) arrives at *al-Mash^car al-Ḥarām* in Muzdalifah. The meaning of *al-Mash^car al-Ḥarām* may be described as a forbidden or consecrated perception. Another possibility from the meaning of gate, *al-Mash^car al-Ḥarām* could mean the forbidden or consecrated gate or portal, which the pilgrim passes through into sacrifice.

The pilgrim surrenders (*aslam*) to the divine will, presenting herself as an offering (*qurbān*) to God. In so doing, she ascends the heavenly ladder, 'Jacob's Ladder'. Naked and waiting to be clothed in God's garment, the pilgrim is led through the *sa^cī* in a way similar to how Abraham's son was led to his sacrifice (Qur'an 37:102). Abandoning all desires other than God, the pilgrim brings herself near (*zalaf*) to God for the sake of all others that they may be near (*qurb*) God as well.

THE WILL OF GOD

As the dead pilgrim abandons the world of his own selfish desires to seek the Will of God alone, all perceptions (*sh-^c-r*) are abandoned at *al-Mash^car al-Ḥarām*. The pilgrim willingly drives himself to the gallows, to the sacred portal of sacrifice. He prepares himself as an offering to God in complete surrender (*aslam*) and passes through the valley of the shadow of death.

> The LORD is my shepherd, I shall not be in want (*^ʾeḥsār*). He makes me lie down in green pastures, He leads me beside quiet

> waters, He restores my soul (*napšiy*). He guides me in paths of righteousness for His name's sake. Even though I walk through the valley of the shadow of death (*ṣalmāwet*), I will fear no evil, for You are with me (*ᶜimmādiy*); Your rod and your staff, they comfort me. You prepare a table before me in the presence of my enemies. You anoint my head (*rōᵓšiy*) with oil; my cup (*kôsiy*) overflows. Surely goodness and love will follow me all the days of my life, and I will dwell in the house of the LORD forever. [Psalm 23:1–6]

In this passage, the shadow of death is called *ṣal māwet* in Hebrew, which appears similar to the word *ẓulumāt* in Arabic, meaning darkness. The Qur'an may allude to this similarity in the following passage.

> Not equal (*yastawī*) are the blind and the seeing, nor the darkness (*al-ẓulumāt*) and the light, nor the shade (*al-ẓill*) and the scorching heat. Not equal (*yastawī*) are the living (*al-aḥyāᵓ*) and the dead (*al-amwāt*). Truly God causes whomsoever He will to hear, but thou canst not cause those in graves to hear. [Qur'an 35:19–22]

The word *ẓulumāt* has been used by the Qur'an many times to mean darkness, which can also be understood as the shadow of death. The dead pilgrim, clad in a funeral shroud, represents himself as a dead person in the coffin waiting for God to resurrect him from darkness (the shadow of death) into the light.[5]

The Qur'an describes how God brings people from the shadow of death (darkness) into light in the verse immediately after the description of the Throne of God (*āyat al-kursī*). This verse is immediately before the verses of Abraham disputing (*ḥajj*) over how God can bring life to the dead, and summoning dead birds that come to him quickly (*saᶜya*). Hence, it connects the Throne of God, Ḥajj, resurrection from death to life, and release from darkness into light (Qur'an 2:255–260).

---

5. See, for example, Qur'an 2:17, 2:19, 2:257, 5:16, 6:1, 6:39, 6:59, 6:63, 6:97, 6:122, 13:16, 14:1, 14:5, 21:87, 24:40, 27:63, 33:43, 35:20, 39:6, 57:9, 65:11.

> God is the Protector (*walī*) of those who believe. He brings them out (*yukhrijuhum*) of darkness (*ẓulumāt*) into light. As for those who disbelieve, their protectors (*awliyāʾuhum*) are the idols, bringing them out of the light into the darkness (*ẓulumāt*). They are the inhabitants of the Fire, abiding therein. [Qur'an 2:257]

In the Gospel of John, light points to life, while darkness points to death:

> In him was life, and that life was the light of men. The light shines in the darkness, but the darkness has not understood it. [John 1:4–5]
>
> This is the verdict: Light has come into the world, but men loved darkness instead of light because their deeds were evil. Everyone who does evil hates the light, and will not come into the light for fear that his deeds will be exposed. But whoever lives by the truth comes into the light, so that it may be seen plainly that what he has done has been done through God. [John 3:19–21]

Similarly, the Qur'an likens people who were dead and then brought to life to those who were in darkness (the shadow of death / *ẓulumāt*) and brought into the light:

> Is he who was dead (*maytah*), and to whom We give life (*fa-aḥyaynāh*), making for him a light by which to walk among humankind, like unto one who is in darkness (*ẓulumāt*) from which he does not emerge (*khārij*)? Thus for the disbelievers, what they used to do was made to seem fair unto them. [Qur'an 6:122]

Interestingly, Psalm 23 talks of walking through the valley of the shadow of death and speaks of God anointing. In it, the cup overflowing may be compared with the Synoptic Gospels, when Matthew, Mark, and Luke state that Jesus, who is the Messiah, meaning the anointed one, asks God to take the cup from his hand (Matthew 26:39, Mark 14:36, Luke 22:42), and alluding to it in John 18:11.

POURING DOWN TO *AL-MASHᶜAR AL-ḤARĀM*

As the pilgrims pour down from ᶜArafah and into *al-Mashᶜar al-Ḥarām*, their lifeless souls are coming to the portal of death and judgment, symbolized by the setting of the sun, and offering (*qurbān*) themselves to God. The pilgrims' hour of resurrection is now near (*qarīb*). The dead pilgrim walks closely (*yazdalif*) to it, in complete surrender to the Will of God. The dead pilgrim arrives at *al-Mashᶜar al-Ḥarām* on the eve of sacrifice, leaving it by sunrise for his own sacrifice and resurrection.

9

THE FINAL RITUALS

At sunset, which traditionally symbolizes death and judgment, the pilgrims pour down from ᶜArafah into Muzdalifah and walk through the valley of the shadow of death (*ẓulumāt*). However, at sunrise, which is a symbol for resurrection, the pilgrims leave Muzdalifah and start walking toward Minā. This is the Day of Sacrifice.

Before the sacrifice, the pilgrim needs to stone the pillar, which represents Satan's temptation. According to Islamic tradition, as well as in the medieval Jewish Book of Jasher (*sēper ha-yāšār*),[1] Satan tempted Abraham three times not to sacrifice his son. Although the three pillars that represent the temptations of Abraham by Satan are stoned every day during the days of Minā, on the Day of Sacrifice only one of them, *Jamrat al-ᶜAqabah*—which is the greatest pillar—is stoned. After the stoning of *Jamrat al-ᶜAqabah*, the 'dead' pilgrim sacrifices an offering to God. Then, he shaves or cuts his hair short and removes his funeral shroud (*iḥrām*), representing his resurrection.

1. Book of Jasher 23:25–39

STONING THE PILLAR

MEANING OF *MINĀ* AND *ᶜAQABAH*

The root of the word *minā* (*m-n-y*) means to appoint, to account, to measure (*al-qadar*), to reckon, to ordain, to designate, to count, to hope, to want, and to desire.[2] It also refers to death. It can mean destination, reason, or cause. *Lisān al-ᶜarab* suggests that the meaning of death comes from the notion that death is measured (*qadar*).[3] *Minā* is also a unit of weight or currency, equivalent to sixty shekels (e.g., Ezekiel 25:12).[4] The term is also perhaps related to the god of fate (*qadar*), such as Manāt.[5]

If the root of the word *minā* is considered an adjective of the root *n-w-y*, then it means that which is seeded [6]. It means purpose and aim, as in *niyyah.*[7] In Aramaic, it also means the place where sheep are kept or a dwelling place.[8] This meaning is also important, as the sacrifice during Ḥajj takes place in Minā.

There is a reference to the trumpets blowing twice in the esoteric exegesis of *saᶜī* during *iḥrām*. The first trumpet is blown to declare death, and the second to declare resurrection. The parallelism between the trumpets blowing is likened to the act of procreation. The father blowing into the mother's womb is death (*minā* or *maniyyah*), while the mother blowing out of her womb is life. Perhaps, for this reason, that, which is blown from the father, is called *manī*, because it resembles death that is entering its *mīqāt* waiting to be resurrected once it is born.

The Qur'an uses a word derived from the root *m-n-y* to refer to this in several verses (e.g., Qur'an 56:58, 75:37). Surprisingly, the Qur'an also uses a derivative of the root that means hope, and specifically hope for death, since the root means both hope and death (Qur'an 62:6–8). In the following verses, the Qur'an uses words rooted in *minā* and *ᶜaqabah.*

---

2. *Lisān al-ᶜarab*, 15: 292–297 on *m-n-y*; *BDB,* 584.
3. *Lisān al-ᶜarab*, 15: 292-293 on *m-n-y*.
4. *BDB,* 584.
5. *Ibid.*
6. *Lisān al-ᶜarab*, 15: 347–350 on *n-w-y*.
7. *Ibid., BDB,* 627.
8. *BDB,* 627.

> You did indeed long (*tamannawn*) for death before you met it (*talqūh*). Now you have seen it, looking on. Muhammad is naught but a messenger; messengers have passed before him. So if he dies or is slain, will you turn back on your heels (*aʿqābikum*)? Whosoever turns back on his heels (*ʿaqibayh*) will not harm God in the least, and God will reward the thankful. It is not for any soul to die save by God's Leave—an enjoined term). Yet whosoever desires the reward of this world, We shall give him of it; and whosoever desires the reward of the Hereafter, We shall give him of it. And We shall reward the thankful. [Qur'an 3:143–145]

These verses speak about people 'wishing,' using the word *tamannawn*, also derived from the root *m-n-y*. As Minā is the location of sacrifice in the rituals of Ḥajj, this verse perhaps shows the relationship between death and the word *minā*. It then talks about what appears to be the death of Muḥammad ﷺ. As mentioned previously, another Qur'anic verse that talks about eternal life states that Muḥammad ﷺ (or the Qur'an's audience) will not be granted eternal life in this world, as no other human (flesh) was ever granted the same (Qur'an 21:34).

When the Qur'an talks about the death of Muḥammad ﷺ in the preceding verses, it warns of people who will turn on their heels, using the same words as those who do not understand the changing of the *qiblah* (Qur'an 2:143). The word for turning (*yanqalib*) is derived from the same root as the word for heart (*qalb*). Thus, perhaps the true *qiblah* is in the heart once God breathes in it from His Spirit. As such, the Qur'an may be alluding to people needing to turn to their hearts to understand the mysteries of death and life, and not to turn on their heels. The word for heel is *ʿaqab*, which is etymologically related to the name Jacob (*Yaʿqūb*), as well as the name of the pillar that is stoned on the Day of Sacrifice (*Jamrat al-ʿAqabah*).

This passage also mentions words that share the same root as *minā* and *talqūh*. As mentioned earlier, the root of the word *alqi*, meaning to throw or cast, is used by the Qur'an in various verses, especially when God casts His Word into Mary (Qur'an 4:171), or when Moses casts his rod and it comes to life (Qur'an 20:19). Whether God's casting of His Word into Mary, or Moses' casting of the rod, the Qur'an is pointing out that the Spirit of God is being cast into them, using the root *l-q-y*. This casting of the Spirit is explicit in the verse below:

> The Raiser of degrees, the Possessor of the Throne, He casts (*yulqī*) the Spirit from His Command (*min amrih*) upon whomsoever He will among His servants to warn of the Day of the Meeting, [Qur'an 40:15]

The Qur'an tells us that God casts (*yulqī*) His Spirit by His Command. When Moses and the mysterious man meet a boy, who is killed, the Qur'an uses the word *yulqī*, and the man later says that he has done it not by his own command (*ᶜan amrī*), implying that he has done it by the Command of God (*min amrih*) (Qur'an 18:74, 18:82). The words *minā*, *yulqī*, and *shayṭān* (Satan) are conjoined elsewhere in *Sūrat al-Ḥajj*:

> And no messenger or prophet did We send before thee, but that when he had a longing (*tamannā*), Satan would cast (*alqā*) into his longing (*umniyyatih*), whereupon God effaces what Satan cast (*yulqī*). Then God makes firm His signs—and God is Knowing, Wise—that He might make what Satan casts (*yulqī*) to be a trial for those in whose hearts is a disease, and those whose hearts are hard—and truly the wrongdoers are in extreme schism. [Qur'an 22:52–53]

These verses are important for understanding what pilgrims do in Minā, which is stoning the pillar resembling Satan. Since *minā* means desire, the pilgrims are stoning their lowly, selfish desires, bearing in mind that it was *minā* that led to Satan's banishment from God's abode. As Minā is the location of sacrifice, the Qur'an uses the terms of sacrifice and *minā* in tandem:

> They are naught but names that you have named—you and your fathers—for which God has sent down no authority. They follow naught but conjecture and that which their souls desire (*tahwāh*), though guidance (*hudā*) has surely come to them from their Lord. Or shall man have whatsoever he longs for (*tamannā*)? Yet unto God belong the Hereafter and this world [the beginning] (*al-ūlā*). [Qur'an 53:23–25]

As just described, the pilgrim in Minā stones away that which symbolizes Satan, which is the lowly selfish desire that caused Satan's curse. The Qur'an warns against such selfish desires (*hawā*, similar to the word for air, *hawāʾ*), since the pilgrim should instead seek the spirit (*rūḥ*) or wind (*rīḥ*). We are then told that God has already sent down guidance (*hudā*, which shares the same root as the word for sacrifice, or *hadī*). While in Minā, the pilgrim must kill his selfish, base desire (*hawā*) and sacrifice (*yahdī*) his ego to allow the Spirit of God to be breathed into him.

In the Book of Daniel, we are told that Daniel interprets the word *minā* for King Belshazzar, son of Nebuchadnezzar, saying:

> This is the inscription that was written: MENE, MENE, TEKEL, PARSIN. "Here is what these words mean: Mene: God has numbered the days of your reign and brought it to an end. Tekel: You have been weighed on the scales and found wanting. Peres: Your kingdom is divided and given to the Medes and Persians." Then at Belshazzar's command, Daniel was clothed in purple, a gold chain was placed around his neck, and he was proclaimed the third highest ruler in the kingdom. That very night Belshazzar, king of the Babylonians, was slain, and Darius the Mede took over the kingdom at the age of sixty-two. [Daniel 5:25–30]

Meaning 'numbered," the word *minā* is interpreted by Daniel to mean that the kingdom has been brought to an end. Similarly, *minā* refers to the death that will come to Belshazzar. Thus, the pilgrim goes to Minā as the place where the soul is fulfilled and the ego is put to death through sacrifice. The word *pĕrēs* meant that the kingdom is divided between the Medes and the Persians. *Peres* (meaning to divide or break) and Persia share the same root; Medes were also Persians.[9]

JAMRAH

The root of the word *jamar* (*j-m-r*) has various meanings, including fire, a tribe not joined to any other, stone, excessive darkness, and grave; as well as to burn incense or combine things.[10] In

9. *BDB*, 828; *Lisān al-ʿarab*, 6: 160–161 on *f-r-s*.
10. *Lisān al-ʿarab*, 4: 144–148 on *j-m-r*.

Hebrew, it means to complete, to fulfill, or to come to an end.[11] In Aramaic, it also means to perfect, to destroy, to absolve, to eliminate, to delete, to extinguish, to be no more, to teach a tradition, to study, to learn, to burn coal, or to burn incense.[12] It is derived from the same root as that of the name Gomorrah, one of the towns in which the people of Lot lived and which was destroyed by God.

THROWING (*RAMĪ*) AND STONING (*RAJM*)

The act of throwing is referred to as *ramī*, derived from the root *r-m-y* meaning to throw or to cast out.[13] In Hebrew, the root also means to cheat, to defraud, to mislead, to deceive, to trick, to betray, or to loosen.[14] The root *r-m-y* is occasionally used in the Qur'an to refer to casting blame for sin on someone who did not commit it (Qur'an 4:112).

During the Ḥajj, pilgrims stone the pillars (an act referred to variously as throwing (*ramī*) and stoning (*rajm*). There exists an interesting correlation between throwing (*ramī*) and stoning (*rajm*). Although the Qur'an does not differentiate between fornication and adultery, different schools of jurisprudence do draw such a distinction. In the Qur'an, the only punishment for fornication or adultery is one hundred lashes (Qur'an 24:2). However, in some schools of jurisprudence, fornication (*zinā*) carries with it a punishment of one hundred lashes, while adultery (*zinā al-muḥṣan*) is punished with stoning (*rajm*).

Although the term for stoning (*rajm*) can also be used to mean throwing (*ramī*), as stoning is the act of throwing stones, the Qur'an seems to use the term throwing (*ramī*) exclusively concerning those who are unmarried and sexually undefiled (*muḥṣan*). However, just as the term *muḥṣan* is not used to mean married, the term *ramī* does not mean stoning in the following verses:

And as for those who accuse (*yarmūn*) chaste women (*al-muḥṣanāt*),

---

11. *BDB,* 170.
12. *Targum Lexicon.*
13. *Lisān al-ᶜarab*, 14: 335–338 on *r-m-y*. *BDB,* 941.
14. *BDB,* 941.

> but then do not bring four witnesses, flog them eighty lashes, and never accept any testimony from them. And it is they who are the iniquitous, [Qur'an 24:4]

> Truly those who accuse (*yarmūn*) chaste (*al-muḥṣanāt*) and heedless believing women are cursed in this world and the Hereafter, and theirs shall be a great punishment. [Qur'an 24:23]

STONES (*ḤAṢĀ* OR *ḤAJAR*)

The term *ḥaṣā* (meaning stones or pebbles) has various meanings. In Arabic, it means stones or the mind.[15] In Hebrew, it means to be plucked out or to divide.[16] From the same root, the term also means accounting or numbering.[17] The Qur'an uses these definitions numerous times.

The other term for stone rooted in *ḥ-j-r* also means cavity or room.[18] In Aramaic, it means to be crippled, to be immobile, or to gird.[19] The Qur'an uses the same term to refer to the stone Moses was asked to strike with his rod to provide water for the Children of Israel (Qur'an 2:60, 7:160).

STONING AND SACRIFICE

THE PILLAR AND SACRIFICE

The 'dead' pilgrim arrives in Minā from Muzdalifah after sunrise on the Day of Sacrifice (*ᶜĪd al-Aḍḥa*) with pebbles in his hands. After stoning the pillar referred to as *Jamrat al-ᶜAqabah* with seven pebbles, the pilgrim makes the sacrifice per Islamic principles, which is by slitting the throat (*fakk raqabah*) of the sacrificial animal, also known as *qurbān*. This sequence of tasks provides an interesting comparison to verses in the Qur'an describing the so-called "steep pass" (*ᶜaqabah*):

> Yet he has not assailed the steep pass (*al-ᶜaqabah*). And what will apprise thee of the steep pass (*al-ᶜaqabah*)? [It is] the free-

15. *Lisān al-ᶜarab*, 14: 183–184 on *ḥ-ṣ-y*.
16. *BDB*, 345.
17. *Lisān al-ᶜarab*, 14: 184 on *ḥ-ṣ-y*.
18. *Ibid.*
19. *BDB*, 291–292.

> ing of a slave (*fakk raqabah*), or giving food at a time of famine to an orphan near of kin (*maqrabah*), or an indigent, clinging to the dust (*matrabah*), while being one of those who believe and exhort one another to patience, and exhort one another to compassion. [Qur'an 90:11–17]

In these verses, it can be seen that the term *ᶜaqabah*, which is also the name of the pillar that is stoned by the pilgrim on the Day of Sacrifice, is defined by the Qur'an as the freeing of a slave. The pilgrim, who is dead, has been a slave to his ego. Additionally, the term for freeing a slave used by these verses is *fakk raqabah*, which literally means cutting a throat. As such, the pilgrim slaughters the sacrificial animal to draw near to God (*qurbān*). The sacrificial animal may be of different animal species per Islamic jurisprudence. However, the sacrifice is the re-enactment of Abraham sacrificing his son, who was ransomed by God with a great sacrifice (*dhabḥ*) (Qur'an 37:107). According to Genesis 22:13, the sacrificial animal with which Abraham's son was ransomed was a ram (*ayyil*). One of the words for ram in Arabic is *kharūf*, which shares the same root as *kharaf*, meaning the time for harvest, or autumn (*kharīf*).[20] The term also means the loss of mental ability.[21] The pilgrim's soul has long been dead inside the darkness of the cave or grave. As such, when the call for the Ḥajj is made, the Qur'an says that the pilgrims will come from deep and distant mountain valleys, as they are leaving the darkness for the light (Qur'an 22:27). The idea of coming out of darkness is significant. When in total darkness, you cannot see your hand if you place it in front of your eyes. If the pitch darkness continues, the brain attempts to make up for the lack of visual stimuli through hallucinations.[22] After a very long time, the eyes undergo

---

20. *Lisān al-ᶜarab*, 9: 62–65 on *kh-r-f*; *BDB*, 358.

21. *Ibid.*, 9: 62 on *kh-r-f*.

22. J. David Lewis-Williams, *The Mind in the Cave* (London: Thames and Hudson, 2008), 208–209; J. David Lewis-Williams, *A Cosmos in Stone: Interpreting Religion and Society through Rock* (Walnut Creek, CA: AltaMira, 2002), 271; Ruxandra Sireteanu, Viola Oertel, Harold Mohr, David Linden and Wolf Singer, "Graphical Illustration and Functional Neuroimaging of Visual Hallucinations during Prolonged Blindfolding: A Comparison to Visual Imagery," *Perception* (2008), 37(12): 1805–1821.

atrophy, becoming permanently blind, while the hallucinations continue. In the same way, the dead soul is in darkness, hallucinating. It thinks it sees things that are real when, in reality, they are nothing but an illusion. The sacrifice of the ram (*kharūf*) symbolizes the pilgrim who, having emerged from deep and distant mountain valleys, has slain the hallucinating self.

The sacrificial lamb provided for Abraham is also sometimes described with the term *kabsh*. The term for sacrifice is also *uḍḥiyah*, which is why the day is called ᶜ*Īd al-Aḍḥa*. The root of this term, *ḍ-ḥ-y*, means not only sacrifice, but also the morning hours between sunrise and noon.[23] It is used by the Qur'an when talking about Adam staying in the Garden of Eden and about feeling neither thirst nor the heat of the sun while in the Garden: "and that thou shalt neither thirst therein, nor suffer from the heat of the sun (*taḍḥā*)" [Qur'an 20:119]. Similarly, Qur'an 93 is called *Sūrat al-Ḍuḥā* and emphasizes God's guidance (*hudā*) (Qur'an 93:7).

From this verse, it may also be understood that there was no sacrifice (*uḍḥiyah*) in the Garden because there was no ego to be sacrificed. The story of Pharaoh and Moses was related earlier to show the relationship between the *mīqāt* of the sorcerers of Moses and the *mīqāt* of Ḥajj, as the sorcerers entered the *mīqāt* and were then resurrected. Additionally, the story reveals the relationship between *sa*ᶜ*ī* and life, as related earlier. In the same way, the story perhaps also allows us to understand that it is through sacrifice that resurrection occurs.

Elsewhere, the Qur'an uses the term *yuḥshar* to mean assemble, that is, assembly at the resurrection:

> He said, "Your tryst shall be on the Day of Adornment; let the people be gathered when the sun has risen high (*w-an yuḥshar al-nās ḍuḥā*)." [Qur'an 20:59]

The next verses show a relationship between the terms assembly and guidance (*hadī*). The term for guidance (*hadī*) is also used by the Qur'an to denote the sacrifice of Ḥajj.

23. *Lisān al-*ᶜ*arab*, 14: 474–479 on *ḍ-ḥ-y*.

> Whomsoever God guides (*yahdī*), he is rightly guided (*al-muhtadī*); and whomsoever He leads astray, thou wilt find no protectors for them apart from Him. And We shall gather them (*naḥshuruhum*) on the Day of Resurrection upon their faces—blind, dumb, and deaf—their refuge shall be Hell. Every time it abates, We shall increase for them a blazing flame. That is their recompense for having disbelieved in Our signs. And they say, "What! When we are bones and dust, shall we indeed be resurrected as a new creation?" [Qur'an 17:97–98]

Stoning the pillar before the sacrifice, which symbolizes the casting away of Satan, is perhaps parallel with the crucifixion of Jesus in the Gospel of Matthew, where Jesus is portrayed as casting away Satan for attempting to prevent Jesus from being sacrificed:

> From that time on Jesus began to explain to his disciples that he must go to Jerusalem and suffer many things at the hands of the elders, the chief priests and the teachers of the law, and that he must be killed and on the third day be raised to life. Peter took him aside and began to rebuke him. "Never, Lord!" he said. "This shall never happen to you!" Jesus turned and said to Peter, "Get behind me, Satan! You are a stumbling block to me; you do not have in mind the concerns of God, but merely human concerns." Then Jesus said to his disciples, "Whoever wants to be my disciple must deny themselves and take up their cross and follow me. For whoever wants to save their life will lose it, but whoever loses their life for me will find it. What good will it be for someone to gain the whole world, yet forfeit their soul? Or what can anyone give in exchange for their soul? For the Son of Man is going to come in his Father's glory with his angels, and then he will reward each person according to what they have done." [Matthew 16:21–27]

In these verses, it is shown that Jesus rebukes Peter, who says that Jesus should never suffer, and therefore, never be sacrificed. Jesus rebukes him and calls him Satan. In the same way, the pilgrim in Ḥajj stones the pillar before the sacrifice by rebuking Satan to ensure that the sacrifice of his soul takes place. As the Gospels show Jesus saying that those who want to become his disciples should renounce themselves and carry their crosses and follow him (Matthew 16:24, Luke 9:23), the pilgrim during the Ḥajj is perhaps following in the footsteps of Jesus by rebuking Satan to make way for sacrifice.

THE BREAD AND WINE OF SACRIFICE

The dead pilgrim makes an offering to God with a sacrificial animal, which the Qur'an calls *hadī*, which derives from the same root as the word for guidance (*hudā*):

> Complete the *ḥajj* and *ᶜumrah* for God, and if you are hindered, then [make] such offering as is easy. And do not shave your heads until the offering (*al-hadī*) reaches its place of sacrifice (*al-hadī*). But whosoever among you is ill or has an ailment of his head, then [let there be] a ransom (*fa-fidyah*) by fasting, charity, or rite. When you are safe, let those who enjoy the *ᶜumrah* ahead of the *ḥajj* [make] such offering (*al-hadī*) as is easy. Whosoever finds not [the means], let him fast three days during the *ḥajj*, and seven when you return. That is ten altogether. This is for those whose family dwells not near the Sacred Mosque. And reverence God, and know that God is severe in retribution. The *ḥajj* is during months well known. Whosoever undertakes the *ḥajj* therein, let there be neither lewdness, nor iniquity, nor quarreling in the *ḥajj*. Whatsoever good you do, God knows it. And make provision (*tazawwadū*), for indeed the best provision (*al-zād*) is reverence (*al-taqwā*). And reverence Me, O possessors of intellect. [Qur'an 2:196–197]

These verses emphasize the need to take provisions on the Ḥajj journey, stating that the best provisions are right conduct and reverence for God, known as *taqwā*.[24] The root of the word for provisions, *al-zād*, is *z-w-d*,[25] which in Hebrew means to boil or to cook.[26] As such, the term for meal provisions for a journey would be derived from the meaning of boiling or cooking.[27] In Hebrew, it also means to act proudly or presumptuously.[28] This meaning

24. *Lisān al-ᶜarab*, 14: 102 on *t-q-y*.
25. *Ibid*, 3: 198 on *z-w-d*.
26. *BDB*, 267.
27. *Gesenius' Hebrew-Chaldee Lexicon to the Old Testament Scriptures*, 240–241.
28. *BDB*, 267.

is perhaps interesting since the pilgrim needs to be God-fearing rather than arrogant. In Aramaic, *z-w-d* also means garments or funeral shrouds, which may also be understood as provisions.[29] This is interesting because, as noted earlier, the Qur'an refers to the garment of piety and righteousness (*libās al-taqwā*) as the best garment of all (Qur'an 7:26). The pilgrim removes all garments because God alone is his garment.

A different verse in the Qur'an states that it is neither the flesh (meat) nor the blood of the offering that reaches God but, rather, the piety (*taqwā*) of those who present it. The term for meat shares the same root as bread (*laḥm*). Bread is sometimes used to symbolize flesh or meat as the authors of the four Gospels use them interchangeably (e.g., Matthew 26:26, Mark 14:22, Luke 22:19, John 6:51, John 6:55). This symbolism is very prominent in the Bible, but also in the Qur'an's story of those imprisoned with Joseph, where eating bread is a symbol of crucifixion and of consuming human flesh (Qur'an 12:36, 12:41). In the Bible, wine is used to symbolize blood, especially at the Last Supper, where both bread and wine were offered as symbols of Jesus' flesh and blood:

> And We have placed the sacrificial animals[30] (*al-budn*) for you among God's rituals (*shaʿāʾir*). There is good for you in them. So mention the Name of God over them as they line up. Then when they have fallen upon their flanks, eat of them, and feed the needy who solicit and those who do not. Thus have We made them subservient unto you, that haply you may give thanks. Neither their flesh (*luḥūmuhā*) nor their blood will reach God, but the reverence from you reaches Him. Thus has He made them subservient unto you, that you might magnify God for having guided you (*hadākum*). And give glad tidings (*bashshir*) to the virtuous. [Qur'an 22:36–37]

These verses emphasize that the Ḥajj rituals are all symbols (*shaʿāʾir*), including the sacrificial animal. They stress that neither the meat (bread) nor the blood (wine) reaches God, but,

29. *Targum Lexicon.*

30. The *TSQ* renders *budn* specifically as "camels", whereas I have rendered it more generically as "animals."

rather, people's piety. The use of the term *bashshir* for proclaiming the good news is rooted in the term *bashar*, which means flesh or human being, as well as the meaning for Gospel (*bishārah*).

THE ULTIMATE SACRIFICE

Once the 'dead' soul has removed its funeral garment, the restrictions associated with the state of *iḥrām* are lifted, with only one exception: the living soul is still not allowed conjugal relations. This might symbolize that the act of sacrifice and dying in this world for the sake of God has resurrected the soul into the heavenly realm.

We read in the Gospel of Matthew that when Jesus was questioned by the Sadducees about resurrection, they asked him about marriage. According to Deuteronomy 25:5–6, if a man dies without having children, then his brother must marry his widow to raise seed for his dead brother. As the Sadducees did not believe in a resurrection, they asked ingenuously: if seven brothers die, each one taking his turn in marrying the widow, then whose wife will she be in the afterlife? (According to the Sadducees, this custom was proof that there is no resurrection, since a woman could not be married to all seven men when resurrected.) However, Jesus told them that resurrected people become like angels, who do not marry, and thus refuted their argument against resurrection.

> That same day the Sadducees, who say there is no resurrection, came to him with a question. "Teacher," they said, "Moses told us that if a man dies without having children, his brother must marry the widow and raise up offspring for him. Now there were seven brothers among us. The first one married and died, and since he had no children, he left his wife to his brother. The same thing happened to the second and third brother, right on down to the seventh. Finally, the woman died. Now then, at the resurrection, whose wife will she be of the seven, since all of them were married to her?" Jesus replied, "You are in error because you do not know the Scriptures or the power of God. At the resurrection people will neither marry nor be given in marriage; they will be like the angels in heaven. But about the resurrection of the dead—have you not read what God said to you, 'I am the God of

> Abraham, the God of Isaac, and the God of Jacob'? He is not the God of the dead but of the living." When the crowds heard this, they were astonished at his teaching. [Matthew 22:28–33]

Consequently, as the pilgrim sacrifices his hallucinating ego and surrenders to God, he removes his funeral shroud and, being instantly transported above the seven heavens, is resurrected in the heavenly realm. As Jesus describes it in the Gospel, he is not given into marriage because he becomes like the angels in heaven. When relating this story, perhaps the Gospel of Matthew uses the number seven to signify the seven heavens to which the dead soul is transported.

For pilgrims performing *Ḥajj al-Ifrād*, which is the Ḥajj without the ᶜUmrah, a sacrificial animal is not obligatory. Since those performing this type of Ḥajj have traversed between the hills of Ṣafā and Marwah (*saᶜī*) before going to ᶜArafah without counting it toward ᶜUmrah, they have already gone up the heavenly ladder. Therefore, they do not need to perform the sacrifice, as they already are in the heavenly realm for the Ḥajj and not for the ᶜUmrah.

ṬAWĀF AL-IFĀḌAH

Once the pilgrim's dead soul has been resurrected, he travels to Mecca to perform the circumambulation of the Kaᶜbah. *Ṭawāf al-ifāḍah* is similar to *ṭawāf al-qudūm* or the *ṭawāf* of the ᶜUmrah, and the symbolism is similar, but there is one major difference between them. During *ṭawāf al-qudūm* or the *ṭawāf* of ᶜUmrah, the pilgrim was wearing the funeral shroud. It signified that at the time, the pilgrim was dead while floating under the Throne of God. However, in *ṭawāf al-ifāḍah*, the pilgrim has been resurrected and is already alive in the heavenly realm.

When the pilgrim performed the circumambulation earlier while wearing a funeral shroud, the Kaᶜbah denoted the earthly temple. However, now that the pilgrim has been resurrected, it denotes the heavenly temple. When praying behind *maqām Ibrāhīm*, the same symbolism applies. The pilgrim has already sacrificed himself for the sake of God and everyone else, and he has surrendered his soul to God's will. It means that though the living soul is in heaven, it would still be willing to repeat the whole cycle of suffering again for the sake of God, if God thus willed. This would be similar to the Buddhist concept of the *bodhisattva*, an enlightened soul that postpones *nirvāṇa* in order to continue to reincarnate and help other wandering dead beings to reach *nirvāṇa* as well.

THE *SAᶜĪ* OF THE ḤAJJ

The *saᶜī* of the ᶜUmrah, which has already been described in detail, is very similar to the *saᶜī* performed during the Ḥajj, with one major difference. During the *saᶜī* of the ᶜUmrah, the pilgrim is portrayed as a dead soul, since he is wearing the funeral shroud and seeking the Water of Life from above the seven heavens. When the dead pilgrim reaches the seventh heaven, he is given the Water of Life that resurrects his soul. However, during the *saᶜī* of the Ḥajj, the pilgrim is not wearing a funeral shroud, as he has already been resurrected after the sacrifice.

As described earlier, the *saᶜī* could be a symbol for Jacob's Ladder, which is portrayed in Genesis as a stairway on which the angels of God go up and come down from heaven: "He [Jacob] had a dream in which he saw a stairway resting on the earth, with its top reaching to heaven, and the angels of God were ascending and descending on it." [Genesis 28:12]. During the *saᶜī* of ᶜUmrah, it shows dead souls going up the ladder to heaven. During the *saᶜī* of the Ḥajj, by contrast, the pilgrim is already in heaven and, hence, is coming back down the ladder. Jesus appeared to be likening himself to Jacob's Ladder when he said, "Very truly I tell you, you will see heaven open, and the angels of God ascending and descending on the Son of Man" [John 1:51].

While in heaven, though not subject to the restrictions of *iḥrām*, the pilgrim is still forbidden to engage in conjugal relations. However, upon his return from the seven heavens and descent into the earthly realm, conjugal relations are allowed once again.[31]

---

31. The Sunnī and Shīᶜī schools of thought differ slightly on this matter. According to the Shīᶜīs, conjugal relations are allowed only after *ṭawāf al-nisāʾ*, the

THE DAYS OF MINĀ

THE NIGHTS OF MINĀ

After the pilgrim has completed the *saᶜī* of Ḥajj, he stays in Minā for two or three days. On each day, he throws seven pebbles at each of the three pillars symbolizing the temptation of Satan:

> Remember God in days numbered, but whosoever hastens on (*taᶜajjal*) after two days, no sin shall be upon him, and whosoever delays (*taᵓakhkhar*), no sin shall be upon him—for the reverent (*ittaqā*). So revere[32] (*ittaqū*) God, and know that unto Him shall you be gathered (*tuḥsharūn*). [Qur'an 2:203]

There are two options given to the pilgrim. The pilgrim can do it quickly in two days, where the Qur'an uses the term *taᶜajjal*, which shares the same root as *ᶜijl,* meaning lamb, or the suffering wheel of Samsara (*ᶜajal*). Alternately, the pilgrim may delay until the third day, to which the Qur'an applies the term *taᵓakhkhar*. The root of the verb *taᵓakhkhar* is *a-kh-r*, which is related to the words meaning last, end, delay, back part, posterity, behind, late, future, and other.[33]

Just as there could possibly be a resemblance between the sacrifice of the pilgrim and the crucifixion of Jesus, there is also a resemblance between Jesus' crucifixion and the three days into his resurrection, and the pilgrim's stay in Minā. The Gospels narrate that the Jews asked Jesus for a sign, and he gave them "the sign of Jonah" (Matthew 16:1–4, Luke 11:29–30), which has been understood to refer to Jesus' crucifixion, his remaining in the heart of the earth for three days, and then his resurrection:

> Then some of the Pharisees and teachers of the law said to him, "Teacher, we want to see a sign from you." He answered, "A wicked and adulterous generation asks for a sign! But none will be given it except the sign of the prophet Jonah. For as Jonah was three days and three nights in the belly of a huge fish, so the Son of Man will be three days and three nights in the heart of the earth." [Matthew 12:38–39]

---

women's circumambulation. The probable reason behind this difference will be discussed later.

32. The *TSQ* translates this as a noun, but it is a verb.

33. *Lisān al-ᶜarab*, 4: 11–15 on *ᵓ-kh-r*; *BDB,* 29–31.

Peter implied in his first epistle that, in the three days between his crucifixion and resurrection, Jesus descended into Hell to preach to those who had been imprisoned there since the time of Noah:

> For Christ also suffered once for sins, the righteous for the unrighteous, to bring you to God. He was put to death in the body but made alive in the Spirit. After being made alive, he went and made proclamation to the imprisoned spirits—to those who were disobedient long ago when God waited patiently in the days of Noah while the ark was being built. In it only a few people, eight in all, were saved through water, and this water symbolizes baptism that now saves you also—not the removal of dirt from the body but the pledge of a clear conscience toward God. It saves you by the resurrection of Jesus Christ, who has gone into heaven and is at God's right hand—with angels, authorities and powers in submission to him. [1 Peter 3:18–22]

After having walked in the footsteps of Jesus, as it were, the pilgrim 'crucifies' his ego in order to be made alive in the spirit and to enter the heavenly realm. Once in the heavenly realm, he comes down the ladder from the seven heavens and back to the earth. He enters "the heart of the earth," as Jesus described the period between his crucifixion and bodily resurrection. The pilgrim has undertaken the Ḥajj because he is capable of taking on the burden of the journey (*sabīl*). As he sacrifices his self, the ego, he is now described as one of those who were killed in the path (*sabīl*) of God. Now that he has become a martyr in the path (*sabīl*) of God, he is not dead, but alive in the heavenly realm, and has become a witness (*shahīd*) to the glory of God:

> And say not of those who are slain in the way (*sabīl*) of God, "They are dead." Nay, they are alive, but you are unaware. [Qur'an 2:154]
> And deem not those slain in the way (*sabīl*) of God to be dead. Rather, they are alive with their Lord, provided for, [Qur'an 3:169]

After walking in the footsteps of Jesus Christ during the days of Minā, the pilgrim must return to earth alive to preach and bear witness to those who are still dead. Some of those who are alive may choose to hasten back (*ta^cajjal*) from earth for two "days" (ages), becoming *bodhisattvas* to help others defeat Satan, the ego, and the Wheel of Samsara, while others may choose to prolong their existence on earth. Although the days of Minā are understood to be either two or three, similar to the time Jesus Christ spent in the heart of the earth. For those who prolong their stay, however, the Qur'an does not specify a number. Perhaps there are bodhisattvas who choose to stay to the End of Days (*ta^ʾakhkhar*), helping others to break the chains of the prisons of this Hell.

THE SIGN OF JONAH

For the next two or three nights (depending on the pilgrim's choice), the pilgrim remains in Minā. These days are called *Ayyām al-Tashrīq*, meaning the Days of the East or the Days of Shining. The root *sh-r-q* also means to whisper,[34] or a type of noble vine. Although etymologically, the name for Easter does not seem to have come from a Semitic translation, the days of shining could also be interpreted as the days of resurrection.

The nights of Minā could be likened to the three days and nights that Jonah spent in the belly of the whale, and during which time he prayed earnestly to God, just as a pilgrim does during the nights of Minā:

> From inside the fish Jonah prayed to the LORD his God. He said: "In my distress I called to the LORD, and he answered me. From the depths of the grave (*šĕʾôl*) I called for help, and you listened to my cry." [Jonah 2:1–2]

The word used for grave here is *sheol* (*šĕʾôl*): an obscure term unique to Hebrew. Some scholars have suggested that its etymology is related to the root *š-ʾ-l*, meaning to ask, since it may be related to judgment.[35] Hence, it could refer to the netherworld. The Epistle of Peter tells us that during the three days between his crucifixion and resurrection, Jesus was in *sheol* preaching among the prisoners from the time of Noah (1 Peter 3:19–22). During these days in *sheol*, to which the pilgrims have returned

34. *TDOT*, 15: 480.
35. *TDOT*, 14: 239–240.

from the seven heavens, they pray fervently to God. Each day, the pilgrims stone the three pillars seven times, as they resemble the locations where Satan is said to have tempted Abraham away from sacrificing his son.

In his prayer, Jonah pledged that regardless of the punishment, he would continue to pray toward God's holy temple (Jonah 2:4, 2:7). Similarly, the pilgrims' prayers are toward the Kaᶜbah, which symbolizes the holy temple beneath the Throne of God. As in the story of Jesus, where God's salvation was through an act of sacrifice, so also did God's salvation come through sacrifice in the story of Jonah.

> But I, with a song of thanksgiving, will sacrifice to you. What I have vowed I will make good. Salvation comes from the LORD.' And the LORD commanded the fish, and it vomited Jonah onto dry land. [Jonah 2:9–10]

The Qur'an states that if Jonah had not praised God while in the belly of the whale, he would have remained there until the Day of Resurrection (Qur'an 37:143–144). Interestingly, Jonah went back to Nineveh and informed its people that in forty days—the number of days Jesus ministered to his disciples between his resurrection and his ascension (Acts 1:3)—the wrath of God would descend upon them. In Nineveh, Jonah's visit also lasted for three days (Jonah 3:3). All the people of Nineveh, including their king, believed in God, consecrated a fast and, humbling themselves in repentance, put on sackcloth and ashes.

ṬAWĀF AL-WADĀᶜ

After the pilgrim, now alive, has remained in the heart of the earth for two or three days, he journeys again to the Sacred Mosque for the circumambulation of farewell (*ṭawāf al-wadāᶜ*), the final rite of the Ḥajj journey. To understand this *ṭawāf*, it is important to understand the meaning of *wadāᶜ*. The root of the term *w-d-ᶜ* or *y-d-ᶜ* in Arabic is typically understood to mean to leave, to depart, or to be quiet.[36] It is sometimes understood to be related to

36. *Lisān al-ᶜarab*, 8: 380–388, on *w-d-ᶜ*.

d-^{c}*-*^{c}, which means to expel or to push.[37] Other relevant meanings include: to give, to know, to cohabit, or to deposit.[38] The Hebrew Bible uses the term to refer to knowledge, including the knowledge of good and evil when Adam ate from the forbidden fruit (e.g., Genesis 3:5, 3:7, 3:22),[39] as well as to a sexual relationship that is expected to lead to conception, such as Adam's relationship with Eve (e.g., Genesis 4:1), whereby a seed is deposited (*y-d-*^{c}) in the womb so that, later, it can be withdrawn in the form of a newborn.

After the pilgrim has been in the heart of the earth for two or three days, he is nudged back out into the earthly realm, then 'deposited' alive around the Temple of God during the farewell circumambulation (*ṭawāf al-wadā*^{c}). As in all circumambulations, the pilgrim again sees the journey of the soul from death to life. After being emitted as water that pours down from heaven to bring life to the dead earth, he floats into the earthly temple to deposit the heavenly seed in people's hearts, hoping that his testament and knowledge will remain on earth and with the prisoners of Hell, so that they may benefit from it and take the same journey from death to life that he has.

37. *Ibid.*, 8: 85, on *d-*^{c}*-*^{c}.

38. *BDB*, 393–396.

39. Although the Arabic root seems somewhat distinct from other Semitic roots, some links among them are apparent. See D. Winton Thomas, "The Root *yd*^{c} in Hebrew," *The Journal of Theological Studies* (1934), 35(139): 398–306. In other Semitic languages as well, including Ethiopic and even modern South Arabic dialects, the root *y-d-*^{c} means to know (*TDOT*, 5: 448–452, on *y-d-*^{c}).

10

CONCLUSION: ESOTERIC EXEGESIS OF THE ḤAJJ RITUALS

The Ḥajj is not a simple performance of rituals. It contains meanings that go beyond the rites. Hence, they are called signs (*sha*ᶜāᵓ*ir*). Those rituals cannot be completely arbitrary, because that would defeat the purpose of the message of the Qur'an, which requires people to try to understand, to contemplate, to think, to meditate, and to ponder its meanings. Some Muslim scholars might state that the purpose of the Ḥajj is to show that all people from all backgrounds of life are equal before God. They may even state that Ḥajj teaches people patience and so forth. Though there are ethical and moral lessons that could be derived from the performance of the ritual, and these are not without interest, this could also be viewed as a superficial understanding. What could be the specific moral lesson of a pilgrim needing to shave or cut his hair short before leaving the state of *iḥrām*? If rituals are arbitrary, then they defeat the purpose of their existence.

The Ḥajj rituals have deeper lessons to offer us than simply the morals that can be deduced from them. They describe the journey of a soul and the secret of its existence. As such, they provide us with a glimpse into the meaning of life. If words alone were capable of describing life's meaning, then perhaps the Scriptures would have given a plain answer to the question. However, words are but symbols of life's meaning and not the reality. The Ḥajj portrays the meaning of life in the form of a ritualistic performance, which goes beyond verbal description to rituals that embody deeper symbolic messages. We might liken this performance to that of watching a historical film rather than reading a history book, as the visual and sensory aspects of the film may be more powerful and engaging than words on a page.

Similarly, with the Ḥajj rituals, their performance may help us comprehend the archetypal journey of the soul in a manner that cannot be conveyed by a textual description. The physical journey mirrors and clarifies the spiritual journey undertaken by the soul.

Many potential lessons and meanings that might be drawn from the Ḥajj rituals have not been explored here. It should be remembered, however, that no single understanding of these rituals is necessarily the only "true" one. Personally, every time I contemplate a verse or a ritual relating to the Ḥajj, I find myself understanding things even deeper, and the deeper I understand things, the more I see that I do not understand. There is no such thing as a single authoritative interpretation, but rather, a plurality of multi-level interpretations. What makes sense to me may not necessarily make sense to everyone.

The situation might be likened to map projections of the earth. When people view airplanes traveling on a two-dimensional map, they may not grasp why airplanes travel in a curve and not in a straight line. However, if you understand that the Earth is spherical, then it makes perfect sense for airplanes to travel along a curve, and that it would be foolish for them to travel along a straight path as though they were on a two-dimensional map. The definition of "straight" is different for a three-dimensional reality than it is for a two-dimensional one. Similarly, people may misunderstand some Scriptures and rituals because they do not fully comprehend their multi-dimensional reality.

The rituals of the Ḥajj re-enact the soul's journey from death to resurrection, from darkness to light, and convey a way for a dead soul to abandon both itself and the world to seek life in God. The pilgrimage offers a way of support for the soul's enlightenment. It also seems to parallel the message embedded in other major religions. Many religious traditions preach the same spiritual message using different forms and rituals. If we remove the symbol, then the core of the Ḥajj is simply to seek the Truth, sacrificing the self (ego) for the sake of all others, and the surrendering of oneself to the will of God.

Abdulla Galadari is an Associate Professor of Islamic Studies at Khalifa University. His area of interest is in Qur'anic hermeneutics, the philology of the Qur'an, and its possible engagement with Near Eastern traditions in Late Antiquity. He also works in comparative theology and religion. Galadari is the author of Qur'anic Hermeneutics: Between Science, History, and the Bible (2018) and Metaphors of Death and Resurrection in the Qur'an: An Intertextual Approach with Biblical and Rabbinic Literature (2021).

After completing the Ḥajj twice, he felt compelled to pursue studies which would help lead to a more profound understanding of the inner and spiritual meanings of the pilgrimage. Because Galadari felt he lacked the expertise to do research in the humanities, he pursued a master's degree, which led to a Ph.D. in Arabic and Islamic Studies from the University of Aberdeen. He also studied Biblical languages at the Hebrew University of Jerusalem.

While searching for a position in the humanities, he audited classes at Harvard and was especially engaged with the Center for the Study of World Religions. Galadari became a research fellow at al-Maktoum College in Dundee, and was later appointed to his current faculty position.

Prior to his career in the humanities, he completed a B.Sc. in Civil Engineering with minors in Astrophysics, Computer Science, and Mathematics from the University of Colorado, a second B.Sc. in Applied Mathematics, a M.Sc. in Civil Engineering, a M.Eng. in Geographic Information Systems, and a Ph.D. in Civil Engineering. Galadari's work is often interdisciplinary, combining religion and science. He is invited to give lectures at various universities, institutions, and academic societies around the world, including Harvard University, University of Notre Dame, University of Toronto, and New York University. He is active in interfaith dialogue both locally and internationally, regularly presenting at the Parliament of the World's Religions.

BIBLIOGRAPHY

A

Abu ᶜUbayd al-Qāsim ibn Salām. *Gharīb al-ḥadīth*. Ed. Muḥammad ᶜAbdul-Muᶜīd Khān. Hyderabad: Dāʾirat al-Maᶜārif al-ᶜUthmāniyyah, 1964.

Abu-Rahma, Khalil. "A Reading in Talbiyat of the Jahili Arabs." *Arab Journal for the Humanities*. 1987, 7(27).

Ahmad, Wahaj D. "An Islamic View of Death and Dying." *Journal of the Islamic Medical Association of North America*. 1986. 28(4): 175–177.

Ahmed, Aziz. *Change, Time and Causality, with Special Reference to Muslim Thought*. Lahore: Pakistan Philosophical Congress, 1974.

Akhtar, Mohsin. *Oracle of the Last and Final Message: History and the Philosophical Deductions of the Life of Prophet Muhammad*. Bloomington, IN: Xlibris Corporation, 2008.

Al-Azraqī. *Akhbār Mecca wa mā jāʾ fīhā min al-āthār*. Ed. Rushdī Mulḥis. Beirut: al-Andalus, no date.

Al-ᶜAynī, Badr al-Dīn. *ᶜUmdat al-qārī sharḥ ṣaḥīḥ al-Bukhārī*, Beirut: Iḥyāʾ al-Turāth al-ᶜArabī, no date.

Al-Bukhārī. *Ṣaḥīḥ al-Bukhārī*. Ed. Muḥammad Zuhayr bin Nāṣir al-Nāṣir. Beirut: Ṭawq al-Najāh, 2002.

Al-Buṣayrī, ᶜAbdullah ibn Muḥammad. *al-Ḥajj wal-ᶜumrah wal-ziyārah*. Riyadh: Maktabah al-Malik Fahad al-Waṭaniyyah, 2003.

Al-Ghazālī. *Asrār al-ḥajj*. Ed. Mūsā Muḥammad ᶜAlī. Sidon: Al-Maktabah al-ᶜAṣriyyah, no date.

———. *Iḥyāʾ ᶜulūm al-dīn*. Beirut: al-Maᶜrifah, no date.

Al-Khawlānī. *Tārīkh dāryā*. Ed. S. al-Afghānī. Damascus: al-Birqī, 1950.

Al-Lehaibi, Majed S. "The Islamic Ritual of Hajj: Ancient Cosmology and Spirituality." *Journal of Inter-Religious Dialogue*. 2012. 10: 31–32.

Al-Maqdisī. *al-Muntaqā min masmūᶜāt marū* [manuscript].

Al-Majlisī. *Biḥār al-anwār*. Beirut: al-Wafāʾ – Iḥyāʾ al-Turāth al-ᶜArabī, 1983.

Al-Mubarakfūrī. *Mirᶜāt al-mafātīḥ sharḥ mishkāt al-maṣābīḥ*. India: Idārat al-Buḥūth al-ᶜIlmiyyah wal-Daᶜwah wal-Iftāʾ, 1984.

Al-Nawawī. *al-Minhāj sharḥ ṣaḥīḥ Muslim bin al-Ḥajjāj*. Beirut: Iḥyāʾ al-Turāth al-ᶜArabī, 1972.

———. *al-Īḍāḥ fī manāsik al-ḥajj wal-ᶜumrah*. Beirut: al-Bashāʾir al-Islāmiyyah, 1994.

Al-Naysābūrī. *Gharāʾib al-Qurʾān wa-raghāʾib al-Furqān*. Ed. Zakariyyā ᶜUmayrāt. Beirut: al-Kutub al-ᶜIlmiyyah, 1996.

Al-Nuᶜmānī, Sirāj al-Dīn. *al-Lubāb fī ᶜulūm al-kitāb*, Ed. ᶜĀdil Muᶜawwaḍ. Beirut: al-Kutub al-ᶜIlmiyyah, 1998.

Al-Qaḥṭānī, Saᶜīd. *Manāsik al-Ḥajj wal-ᶜUmrah fil-Islām fī ḍawʾ al-kitāb wal-sunnah*. al-Qasab: Markaz al-Daᶜwah wal-Irshād, 2010.

Al-Qārī. *Mirqāt al-mafātīḥ sharḥ mishkāt al-maṣābīḥ*. Beirut: al-Fikr, 2002.

Al-Qinnawjī, Ṣiddīq Ḥasan Khān. *Abjad al-ᶜulūm*. Beirut: Ibn Ḥazm, 2002.

Al-Qushayrī. *al-Risālah al-Qushayriyyah*. Eds. ᶜAbdul-Ḥalīm Maḥmūd and Maḥmūd b. al-Sharīf. Cairo: al-Maᶜārif, no date.

———. *Laṭāʾif al-ishārāt*. Ed. Ibrāhīm al-Basyūnī. Cairo: al-Hayʾah al-Miṣriyyah al-ᶜĀmmah lil-Kitāb, no date.

Al-Rāzī. *Mafātīḥ al-ghayb*. Beirut: Iḥyāʾ al-Turāth al-ᶜArabī, 2002.

Al-Sarkhasī. *al-Mabsūṭ*. Beirut: al-Ma[c]rifah, 1993.

Al-Suyūṭī. *al-Ḥabā[ʾ]ik fī akhbār al-malā[ʾ]ik*. Ed. Muḥammad Zaghlūl. Beirut: al-Kutub al-[c]Ilmiyyah, 1985.

Al-Ṭabarānī. *Faḍl [c]ashr Dhil-Ḥijjah*. Ed. Abū [c]Abdullāh al-Jazā[ʾ]irī. Sharjah: Al-[c]Umarayn al-[c]Ilmiyyah, no date.

Al-Ṭabarānī. *al-Mu[c]jam al-kabīr*. Ed. Ḥamdī b. [c]Abdulḥalīm Al-Salafī. Cairo: Ibn Taymiyyah, 1994.

Al-Ṭabarī. *Tarīkh al-rusul wal-mulūk*. Beirut: al-Turāth, 1967.

———. *Jāmi[c] al-bayān fī ta[ʾ]wīl al-Qur[ʾ]ān*. Ed. Aḥmad M. Shākir. Damascus: al-Risālah, 2000.

Al-Tirmidhī. *Sunan al-Tirmidhī*. Eds. Aḥmad M. Shākir. Muḥammad F. [c]Abdulbāqī, Ibrāhīm A. [c]Awaḍ. Cairo: Muṣṭafā al-Bābī al-Ḥalabī, 1975.

Al-[c]Utbī, Muḥammad ibn Aḥmad. *Kitāb al-ḥajj*. Ed. Miklūsh Mūrānī. Beirut: Ibn Ḥazm, 2007.

Al-[c]Uthaymīn. *Majmū[c] fatāwā wa-rasā[ʾ]il faḍīlah al-shaykh Muḥammad ibn Ṣāliḥ al-[c]Uthaymīn*. Ed. Fahad al-Sulaymān. Riyadh: al-Waṭan, 2001, 1993.

Al-Zabīdī, Murtaḍā. *Tāj al-[c]arūs min jawāhir al-qāmūs*. al-Hidāyah, no date.

[c]Alī, Jawād. *al-Mufaṣṣil fī tarīkh al-[c]arab qabl al-Islām*. Beirut: al-Sāqī, 2001.

Allen, James P. *The Ancient Egyptian Pyramid Texts*. Leiden: Brill, 2005.

Amos, Clare. "Incomplete without the Other: Isaac, Ishmael and a Hermeneutic Diversity." *Islam and Christian-Muslim Relations*. 2009. 20(3): 247–256.

Asad, Talal. *The Idea of an Anthropology of Islam*. Washington, DC: Georgetown University Center for Contemporary Arab Studies, 1986.

B

Baruti, L. T. W. *The Practice of Easter Morning Service and Its Theological Implication into Christian Faith: In North-Eastern Diocese of Lutheran Church of Tanzania*. Master's Thesis, Norwegian School of Theology, 2011.

Beit-Hallahmi, Benjamin and Michael Argyle. *The Psychology of Religious Behaviour, Belief, and Experience*, London: Routledge, 1997.

Bell, Richard. "The Origin of the Eid al-Adha." *Muslim World* (1933) 23(2): 117–120.

Botterweck, G. J., H. Ringgren and H-J. Fabry, eds. Trans. J. T. Willis. *The Theological Dictionary of the Old Testament (Revised Edition) (TDOT)*. Grand Rapids, MI: William B. Eerdmans Publishing Company, 2011.

Bowen, John R. "On Scriptural Essentialism and Ritual Variation: Muslim Sacrifice in Sumatra and Morocco." *American Ethnologist*. 1992. 19: 656–657.

Böwering, Gerhard. "Ideas of Time in Persian Sufism," *Iran*. 1992. 30: 77–89.

———. "The Concept of Time in Islam." *Proceedings of the American Philosophical Society*. 1997. 141(1): 55–66.

Brown, Francis, Samuel R. Driver, and Charles A. Briggs. *Enhanced Brown-Driver-Briggs Hebrew and English Lexicon (BDB)*. Oak Harbor, WA: Logos Research Systems, 2000.

Burhān al-Dīn. *al-Mubdi[c] fī sharḥ al-muqni[c]*. Beirut: al-Kutub al-[c]Ilmiyyah, 1997.

C

Campbell, Joseph and Bill Moyers. *The Power of Myth*. Ed. Betty Sue Flowers. New York, NY: Anchor Books, 1991.

Charlesworth, James H. *The Good and Evil Serpent: How a Universal Symbol Became Christianized*. New Haven, CT: Yale University Press, 2010.

D

Darnell, John C. *The Enigmatic Netherworlds Books of the Solar-Osirian Unity: Cryptographic Compositions in the Tombs of Tutankhamun, Ramesses VI and Ramesses IX*. Fribourg: Academic Press, 2004.

Daum, Werner. "A Pre-Islamic Rite in South Arabia." *Journal of the Royal Asiatic Society*. 1987. 119: 5–14.

De Vries, Arthur. *Dictionary of Symbols and Imagery*. Amsterdam: North-Holland, 1974.

Denny, Frederick M. "Islamic Ritual: Perspectives and Theories." In *Approaches to Islam in Religious Studies*. Ed. Richard C. Martin. Tucson, AZ: University of Arizona Press, 1985.

Doniger, Wendy. "God's Body, or, the Lingam Made Flesh: Conflicts over the Representation of the Sexual Body of the Hindu God Shiva." *Social Research: An International Quarterly*. 2011. 78(2): 485–508.

Donner, Fred. *Muhammad and the Believers: At the Origins of Islam*. Cambridge: Harvard University Press, 2010.

D'Orazio, Massimo. "Meteorite Records in the Ancient Greek and Latin Literature: Between History and Myth." In *Myth and Geology*. Eds. L. Piccardi and W. B. Masse. London: Special Publications, The Geological Society of London, 2007.

E

Eaton, John H. "Dancing in the Old Testament." *The Expository Times*. 1975. 86(5): 136–140.

El-Zein, Abdul Hamid. "Beyond Ideology and Theology: The Search for the Anthropology of Islam." *Annual Review of Anthropology*. 1977. 6: 241–252.

Enz, Jacob J. "The Book of Exodus as a Literary Type for the Gospel of John." *Journal of Biblical Literature*. 1957. 76(3): 208–215.

Erskine, Thomas. *The Brazen Serpent or Life Coming Through Death*. Edinburgh: Waugh and Innes, 1831.

Eskola, Timo. *Messiah and the Throne: Jewish Merkabah Mysticism and Early Christian Exaltation Discourse*. Philadelphia, PA: Coronet Books, 2001.

F

Fernie, Eric. "The Use of Varied Nave Supports in Romanesque and Early Gothic Churches." *Gesta*. 1984. 23(2): 107–117.

Finnestad, Ragnhild B. "Ptah, Creator of the Gods: Reconsideration of the Ptah Section of the Denkmal." *Numen*. 1976. 23(2): 81–113.

Fishbane, Michael. *Biblical Interpretation in Ancient Israel*. Oxford: Oxford University Press, 1985.

Fortes, Meyer. "Ritual Festivals and the Social Cohesion in the Hinterland of the Gold Coast." *American Anthropologist*. 1936. 38(4): 590–604.

G

Galadari, Abdulla. "Joseph and Jesus: Unearthing Symbolisms within the Bible and the Qur'an." *The International Journal of Religion and Spirituality in Society*. 2011. 1(1): 117–128.

———. "Behind the Veil: Inner Meanings of Women's Islamic Dress Code." *The International Journal of Interdisciplinary Social Sciences*. 2012. 6(11): 115–125.

———. "The Role of Intertextual Polysemy in Qur'anic Exegesis." *Quranica: International Journal on Quranic Research*. 2013. 3(4): 35–56.

———. "The *Qibla*: An Allusion to the *Shema*ᶜ," *Comparative Islamic Studies*. 2013. 9(2): 165–194.

———. "*Creatio ex Nihilo* and the Literal Qur'an." *Intellectual Discourse*. 2017. 25(2): 381–408.

———. *Qur'anic Hermeneutics: Between Science, History, and the Bible*. London: Bloomsbury Academic, 2018.

———. "The Camel Passing through the Eye of the Needle: A Qur'anic Interpretation of the Gospels." *Ancient Near Eastern Studies*. 2018. 55: 77–89.

———. "Psychology of Mystical Experience: Muḥammad and Siddhartha." *Anthropology of Consciousness*. 2019. 30(2): 152–178.

———. "Qur'anic Faith and Reason: An Epistemic Comparison with the Kālāma Sutta." *Studies in Interreligious Dialogue*. (2020). 30(1): 45–67.

———. *Metaphors of Death and Resurrection in the Qur'an: An Intertextual Approach with Biblical and Rabbinic Literature*. London: Bloomsbury Academic, 2021.

Galloway, Dalton. "The Resurrection and Judgement in the Koran." *The Muslim World*. 2019. 12(4): 348–372.

Gesenius, Wilhelm. *Gesenius' Hebrew and Chaldee Lexicon to the Old Testament Scriptures*. Trans. Samuel P. Tregelles. Bellingham, WA: Logos Bible Software, 2003.

Gordon, B. L. "Sacred Directions, Orientation, and the Top of the Map." *History of Religions*. 1971. 10(3): 211–227.

Graham, William A. "Islam in the Mirror of Ritual." In *Islam's Understanding of Itself*. Eds. Richard G. Hovannisian and Speros Vryonis, Jr. Malibu, CA: Undena, 1983.

H

Hart, George L. *The Routledge Dictionary of Egyptian Gods and Goddesses*. Oxford: Routledge, 2005.

Hawting, Gerald R. "'We Were Not Ordered with Entering It but Only with Circumambulating It': Ḥadīth and Fiqh on Entering the Kaᶜba." *Bulletin of the School of Oriental and African Studies*. 1984. 47(2): 228–242.

Hornung, Erik. *The Ancient Egyptian Books of the Afterlife*. Trans. David Lorton. Ithaca, NY: Cornell University Press, 1999.

I

Ibn ᶜAbdulwahhāb, Muḥammad. *Mansak al-ḥajj*. Ed. Bandar ibn Nāfiᶜ al-ᶜAbdalī. Riyadh: al-Waṭan, 2002.

Ibn Abī ᶜĀṣim. *al-Sunnah li-Ibn Abī ᶜĀṣim*. Ed. Muḥammad Nāṣir al-Dīn al-Albānī. Beirut: al-Maktab al-Islāmī, 1980.

Ibn al-Jawzī. *Muthīr al-ᶜazm al-sākin ila ashraf al-amākin*. Ed. Marzūq ᶜAlī Ibrāhīm. al-Rāyah, 1995.

Ibn ᶜArabī. *al-Futūḥāt al-Makkiyyah*. Ed. A. Shams-ul-Dīn. Beirut: al-Kutub al-ᶜIlmiyyah, no date.

———. *Fuṣūṣ al-ḥikam*. Ed. Abul-ᶜAlā ᶜAfīfī. Beirut: al-Kutub al-ᶜArabiyyah, no date.

Ibn ᶜĀshūr, Muḥammad al-Ṭāhir. *al-Taḥrīr wal-tanwīr*. Tunis: Al-al-Tūnisiyyah, no date.

Ibn Baṭṭūṭa. *Tuḥfah al-nuẓẓār fī gharāʾib al-amṣār wa-ᶜajāʾib al-asfār*. Rabat: Akādīmiyyat al-Mamlakah al-Maghribiyyah, 1997.

Ibn Ḥanbal. *Musnad*. Ed. Aḥmad Muḥammad Shākir. Cairo: al-Ḥadīth, 1995.

———. *Musnad Aḥmad*. Damascus: al-Risālah, 2001.

Ibn Isḥāq. *Sīrah*. Ed. Suhayl Zakkār. Beirut: al-Fikr, 1978.

Ibn Jubayr. *Riḥlat Ibn Jubayr*. Beirut: al-Hilāl, no date.

Ibn Kathīr. *Tafsīr al-Qurʾān al-ᶜaẓīm*. Ed. Sāmī M. Salāmeh. Riyadh: Ṭaybah, no date.

Ibn Manẓūr. *Lisān al-ᶜarab*. Beirut: Ṣādir, 1994.

Ibn Rajab al-Ḥanbalī. *Laṭāʾif al-maᶜārif fīmā li-mawāsim al-ᶜām min al-waẓāʾif*. Beirut: Ibn Ḥazm, 2004.

J

Jacobs, Martin. "An Ex-Sabbatean's Remorse: Sambari's Polemics against Islam." *Jewish Quarterly Review*. 2007. 97(3): 347–378.

Jaᶜfar al-Ṣādiq. *Miṣbāḥ al-sharīᶜah*. Beirut: al-Aᶜlamī, 1980.

Janin, Hunt. *Four Paths to Jerusalem: Jewish, Christian, Muslim, and Secular Pilgrimages, 1000 BCE to 2001 CE*. Jefferson, NC: McFarland, 2006.

K

Kaufman, Stephen A., ed. *Targum Lexicon: A Lexicon to the Aramaic Versions of the Hebrew Scriptures from the Files of the Comprehensive Aramaic Lexicon Project*. Cincinnati, OH: Hebrew Union College, no date.

Kielstra, Niko. "Law and Reality in Modern Islam." In *Islamic Dilemmas: Reformers, Nationalists and Industrialization*. Ed. Ernest Gellner. New York, NY: Mouton Publishers, 1985.

Kister, M. J. "*Maqām Ibrāhīm*: A Stone with an Inscription." *Le Muséon*. 1971. 84: 477–491.

Koehler, Ludwig and Walter Baumgartner. *The Hebrew and Aramaic Lexicon of the Old Testament*. Leiden: Brill, 2000.

L

Lachmann, Renate. "Mnemonic and Intertextual Aspects of Literature." In *Cultural Memory Studies: An International and Interdisciplinary Handbook*. Eds. Astrid Erll and Ansgar Nünning. Berlin: De Gruyter, 2008.

Lazarus-Yafeh, Hava. *Some Religious Aspects of Islam*. Leiden: Brill, 1981.

Laᶜzūzī, Muṣṭafa. *Thaqāfat al-ḥajj*. Beirut: al-Kutub al-ᶜIlmiyyah, 2006.

Lefsrud, Sigurd. *Kenosis in Theosis: An Exploration of Balthasar's Theology of Deification*. Eugene, OR: Pickwick, 2020.

Leslau, Wolf. *Comparative Dictionary of Geᶜez*. Wiesbaden: Harrassowitz, 2006.

Lewis-Williams, J. David. *The Mind in the Cave*. London: Thames and Hudson, 2002.

———. *A Cosmos in Stone: Interpreting Religion and Society through Rock*. Walnut Creek, CA: AltaMira, 2002.

Lurker, Manfred. *The Gods and Symbols of Ancient Egypt*. New York, NY: Thames and Hudson, 1980.

Lutfi, Huda. "The Feminine Elements in Ibn 'Arabi's Mystical Philosophy." *Alif: Journal of Comparative Poetics*. 1985. 5: 7–19.

M

Maghniyyah, Muhammad J. *The Hajj according to Five Schools of Islamic Law* (vol. iv). Tehran: Islamic Culture and Relations Organization, 1997.

Masud, Muhammad Khalid. "Sufi Views of Pilgrimage in Islam." In *Sacredscapes and Pilgrimage Systems*. New Delhi: Shubhi Publications, 2011.

Moore, George F. "Baetylia." *American Journal of Archaeology*. 1903. 7(2): 198–208.

Morenz, Siegfried. *Egyptian Religion*. York: Methuen, 1973.

Muqātil bin Sulaymān. *Tafsīr Muqātil*. Beirut: Iḥyāᵓ al-Turāth, 2003.

Muslim. *Ṣaḥīḥ Muslim*. Ed. Muḥammad Fuᵓād ᶜAbdul-Bāqī. Beirut: Iḥyāᵓ al-Turāth al-ᶜArabī, no date.

Myerhoff, Barbara. *Peyote Hunt: The Sacred Journey of the Huichol Indians*. Ithaca, NY: Cornell University Press, 1974.

N

Nasr, Seyyed Hossein, ed. *The Study Quran*. New York, NY: HarperOne, 2015.

Netton, Ian R. *Ṣūfī Ritual: The Parallel Universe*. Abingdon: Routledge, 2003.

Nordin, Andreas. "Ritual Agency: Substance Transfer and the Making of Supernatural Immediacy in Pilgrim Journeys." *Journal of Cognition and Culture*. 2009. 9(3): 195–223.

Norenzayan, Ara and Azim F. Shariff. "The Origin and Evolution of Religious Prosociality." *Science*. 2008. 322(5898): 58–62.

O

Oglu, Kerimov G. M. "Basic Principles Distinguishing Orthodox Islam from Sufism." *Journal of Muslim Minority Affairs*. 1988. 9(2): 245–250.

Olick, Jeffrey K. "From Collective Memory to the Sociology of Mnemonic Practices and Products." In *Cultural Memory Studies: An International and Interdisciplinary Handbook*. Es. Astrid Erll and Ansgar Nünning. Berlin: De Gruyter, 2008.

Olyan, Saul M. "What Do Shaving Rites Accomplish and What Do They Signal in Biblical Ritual Contexts?" *Journal of Biblical Literature*. 1998. 117(4): 611–622.

P

Petrushevsky, Ilya P. *Islam in Iran*. Albany, NY: State University of New York Press, 1985.

Powers, Paul R. "Interiors, Intentions, and the 'Spirituality' of Islamic Ritual Practice." *Journal of the American Academy of Religion*. 2004. 72(2): 425–459.

Q

Quasem, Muhammad A. "Understanding the Qur'an and its Explanation by Personal Opinion Which Has Not Come Down by Tradition." *The Recitation and Interpretation of the Qur'an: Al Ghazali's Theory*. Kuala Lumpur, Malaysia: University of Malaya Press, 1979.

R

Renard, John. "*Al-Jihad al-Akbar*: Notes on a Theme in Islamic Spirituality." *The Muslim World* 1988. 78(3–4): 225–242.

Reynolds, Gabriel S. *The Qur'ān and Its Biblical Subtext*. Abingdon: Routledge, 2010.

Rezae, Muhammad J., Muhammad Najafi, Abdul-Majid Mahyger, and S. Masud Keshavarz. "The Role of Pilgrimage to Mecca (Hajj) in Gaining Moral Virtues and Avoiding Moral Vices." *Scientific Journal of Pure and Applied Sciences*. 2014. 3(5): 313–317.

Rippin, Andrew, ed. *Approaches to the History of the Interpretation of the Qur'ān*. Oxford: Clarendon Press, 1988.

Robinson, A. "Zion and Saphon in Psalm XLVIII 3." *Vetus Testamentum*. 1974. 24(1): 118–123.

Rossini, K. Conti, ed. *Chrestomathia Arabica Meridionalis Epigraphica*. Rome: Istituto per L'Oriente, 1931.

Rubin, Uri. "The Great Pilgrimage of Muhammad: Some Notes on Sura IX." *Journal of Semitic Studies* 1982. 27(2): 241–260.

S

Sabiq, As-Sayyid. *Fiqh us-Sunnah: Hajj and Umrah*. Indianapolis: American Trust Publications, 1985.

Sarna, N. M. *The JPS Torah Commentary: Exodus*. Philadelphia, PA: The Jewish Publication Society, 1991.

Scagliarini, Florella. "The Word ṣlm/ṣnm and Some Words for 'Statue, Idol' in Arabian and Other Semitic Languages." *Proceedings of the Seminar for Arabian Studies*. 2007. 37: 253–262, 27–29 July 2006, London, UK.

Schaff, Philip and Henry Wace, eds. *A Select Library of the Nicene and Post-Nicene Fathers of the Christian Church*. New York, NY: The Christian Literature, 1898.

Seidel, Matthias and Regine Schulz. *Egypt Art and Architecture*. New York, NY: Barnes and Noble Books. 1995.

Schept, Susan. "Jacob's Dream of a Ladder: Freudian and Jungian Perspectives." *Psychological Perspectives: A Quarterly Journal of Jungian Thought*. 2007. 50(1): 113–121.

Shariati, Ali. *Hajj: The Pilgrimage*. Trans. Ali A. Behzadnia, and Najla Denny. Costa Mesa, CA: Evecina Cultural and Education Foundation (Jubilee Press), no date.

Shariff, Azim F. and Ara Norenzayan. "God is Watching You: Priming God Concepts Increases Prosocial Behavior in an Anonymous Economic Game." *Psychological Science*. 2007. 18(9): 803–809.

Shariff, Azim F., Ara Norenzayan, and Joseph Henrich. "The Birth of High Gods:

How the Cultural Evolution of Supernatural Policing Influenced the Emergence of Complex, Cooperative Human Societies, Paving the Way for Civilization." In *Evolution, Culture and the Human Mind*, eds. Mark Shaller, Ara Norenzayan, Steven J. Heine, Toshio Yamagishi, and Tatsuya Kameda. New York, NY: Psychology Press, 2010.

Shaykh ᶜAlwān. *al-Fawātiḥ al-ilāhiyyah wal-mafātiḥ al-ghaybiyyah al-muwaḍḍiḥah lil-kalim al-Qurʾāniyyah wal-ḥikam al-furqāniyyah*. Cairo: Rikābī, 1999.

Sireteanu, Ruxandra, Vioa Oertel, Harald Mohr, David Linden, and Wolf Singer. "Graphical Illustration and Functional Neuroimaging of Visual Hallucinations during Prolonged Blindfolding: A Comparison to Visual Imagery." *Perception*. 2008. 37(12): 1805–1821.

Skinner, Andrew C. "Serpent Symbols and Salvation in the Ancient Near East and the Book of Mormon." *Journal of Book of Mormon Studies*. 2001. 10(2): 42–55.

Smith, Mark S. "The Near Eastern Background of Solar Language for Yahweh." *Journal of Biblical Literature*. 1990. 109(1): 29–39.

Sosis, Richard and Candace Alcorta. "Signaling, Solidarity, and the Sacred: The Evolution of Religious Behavior." *Evolutionary Anthropology*. 2003. 12(6): 264–274.

Sosis, Richard and Eric R. Bressler. "Cooperation and Commune Longevity: A Test of the Costly Signaling Theory." *Cross-Cultural Research*. 2003. 37(2): 211–239.

Sousa, Ana P., Alexandra Amaral, Marta Baptista, Renata Tavares, Pedro C. Campo, Pedro Peregrín, Albertina Freitas, Artur Paiva, Teresa Almeida-Santos, and João Ramalho-Santos. "Not All Sperm Are Equal: Functional Mitochondria Characterize a Subpopulation of Human Sperm with Better Fertilization Potential." *PLoS ONE*. 2011. 6(3): e18112.

Sperling, S. David. "Joshua 24 Re-examined." *Hebrew Union College Annual*. 1987. 58: 119–136.

Spero, Shubert. "Turning to Jerusalem in Prayer." *Jewish Bible Quarterly*. 2003. 31(2): 97–100.

Storl, Wolf-Dieter. *Shiva: The Wild God of Power and Ecstasy*. Rochester, VT: Inner Traditions, 2004.

T

Tarrant, Harold. "Orality and Plato's Narrative Dialogues." In *Voice into Text: Orality and Literacy in Ancient Greece*, ed. Ian Worthington. Leiden: Brill, 1996.

Taylor, H. M. "The Position of the Altar in Early Anglo-Saxon Churches." *The Antiquaries Journal*. 1973. 53(1): 52–58.

Tenney, Merrill C. "The Old Testament and the Fourth Gospel." *Bibliotheca Sacra*. 1963. 120: 300–308.

Thomas, D. Winton. "The Root *ydᶜ* in Hebrew." *The Journal of Theological Studies*. 1934. 35(139): 398–306.

Tourage, Mahdi. "The Hermeneutics of Eroticism in the Poetry of Rumi." *Comparative Studies of South Asia, Africa and the Middle East*. 2005. 25(3): 600–616.

———. "Phallocentric Eroticism in a Tale from Jalal al-Din Rumi's *Masnavi-yi Maᶜnavi*." *Iranian Studies*. 2006. 30(1): 47–70.

———. *Rūmī and the Hermeneutics of Eroticis*. Leiden: Brill, 2007.

———. "The Erotics of Sacrifice in the Qur'anic Tale of Abel and Cain." *The International Journal of Žižek Studies*. 2011. 5(2).

Ṭurad, Ḥassan. *Falsafat al-ḥajj fil-Islām*. Beirut: al-Zahrāʾ, 2011.

Turner, David I. "The Structure and Sequence of Matthew 24:1–41: Interaction with Evangelical Treatments." *Grace Theological Journal*. 1989. 10(1): 3–27.

U

Uddin, Asma T. "The Hajj and Pluralism."

The Review of Faith and International Affairs. 2008. 6(4): 43–47.

W

Ward, William A. "Some Egypto-Semitic Roots." *Orientalia*. 1962. 31(4): 397–412.

Weintritt, Otfried. "Interpretations of Time in Islam." In *Time and History: The Variety of Cultures*, ed. Jörn Rüsen. New York, NY: Berghahn Books, 2007.

Wells, Ronald A. "The Mythology of Nut and the Birth of Ra." *Studien zur Altagyptischen Kultur*. 1992. 19: 305–321.

Werbner, R. *Ritual Passage, Sacred Journey: The Process and Organization of Religious Movement*. Washington, DC: Smithsonian Institution Press, 1989.

Witt, Reginald E. *Isis in the Graeco-Roman World*. London: Thames and Hudson, 1971.

Wolfe, Michael, ed. *One Thousand Roads to Mecca: Ten Centuries of Travelers Writing about the Muslim Pilgrimage*. New York, NY: Grove, 1997.

Wolfson, Elliot R. "Images of God's Feet: Some Observations on the Divine Body in Judaism." In *People of the Body: Jews and Judaism from an Embodied Perspective*, ed. Howard Eilberg-Schwartz. Albany, NY: State University of New York Press, 1992.